CRIMES
OF THE
CENTURY

First published in 2009. A catalogue record for this book is available from the British Library

ISBN: 978-1-844258-51-2

Published by Haynes Publishing, Sparkford, Yeovil, Somerset BA22 7JJ, UK

Tel: 01963 442030 Fax: 01963 440001 Int. tel: +44 1963 442030 Int. fax: +44 1963 440001

E-mail: sales@haynes.co.uk Website: www.haynes.co.uk

Haynes North America Inc., 861 Lawrence Drive, Newbury Park, California 91320, USA

All images © Mirrorpix

Creative Director: Kevin Gardner

Packaged for Haynes by Green Umbrella Publishing

Printed and bound in Great Britain by J F Print Ltd., Sparkford, Somerset

CRIMES
OF THE
CENTURY

AN ILLUSTRATED HISTORY OF BRITISH FELONY & MISDEMEANOUR

WRITTEN BY JIM CRAWLEY

CONTENTS

LEFT: Newcastle police detectives June, 1900.

"... MOST PEOPLE OBSERVE LEGAL, MORAL, AND ETHICAL BOUNDARIES FOR IMMEDIATE PERSONAL COMFORT OR FROM TIMIDITY. THE CRIMINAL IS MORE ATTRACTED AND STIMULATED BY THE EXCITEMENT OF CHALLENGING THE NORM, OF STEPPING INTO FORBIDDEN TERRITORY LIKE A SOLITARY EXPLORER, CONSCIOUSLY THIRSTING TO EXPERIENCE THAT WHICH THE MAJORITY HAVE NOT AND DARE NOT ..."

IAN BRADY, THE GATES JANUS

LEFT: 21st century murder scene.

INTRODUCTION

"WHAT I FEEL IS THE EMPTINESS OF MY SOUL."

GRAHAM YOUNG, THE POISONER WHEN ASKED ABOUT
WHAT HE FELT ABOUT HIS VICTIMS

"ANY MAN DOING A KILLING ENJOYS IT. IT IS AN ANIMAL EXPERIENCE."

PATRICK MACKAY, SERIAL MURDERER

Any selection which claims to cover the most important examples of any activity will always be partial and dependent on the taste of the compiler. This collection of the most infamous British crimes of the 20th century is no exception. Most of the crimes have been included because they have achieved lasting fame, are classical examples of a certain type, demonstrate the development of police technique and forensic science or form an important part of the history of capital punishment. I have not included the politically motivated crimes such as the Birmingham pub bombing or the attempted assassination of the prime minister.

Despite the horror that these crimes involved the political motivation differentiates them from the individual obsessions and greed that

motivated the other crimes in the book. The vast majority of the crimes featured here are of murder. Robberies very rarely have the epic qualities of murder. The two that are featured, the Great Train Robbery and the Brinks-Mat Bullion Heist both netted great financial rewards but brought disaster and tragedy in their wake, which reverberate through to the modern day.

Any reader will quite rightly ask about the victims when a writer examines memorable crimes. No book should be allowed to ignore the misery and suffering that the offenders have caused. However, to gain insight into the most heinous crimes of the century one cannot focus on the victims. It is the criminals themselves, be they murderers or thieves, whom we must examine.

Our sympathy is with the victim and our fascination with the criminal. Most of the criminals who feature prominently in *Crimes of the Century* are male. Women are most likely to be involved with crimes of passion such as the murders carried out by Ruth Ellis and Edith Thompson. When women do commit crimes of extreme brutality, as in the cases of Myra Hindley and Rose West, it would seem that men are the main instigators. It is doubtful whether Hindley and West would have become infamous criminals without the trigger of a male. Why some men commit murder and major crimes is still a mystery. Psychiatrists provide us with insights into some criminals but fail to answer why anybody would believe that murder is the answer to any situation. I suspect such an understanding will for ever remain illusive.

LEFT: Donald Neilson leaves court, with a blanket on his head.

PAPER FOR DAILY MIRROR

GREAT CENTRAL RAILWAY

"LOVE AND DEATH, POSSESSING AND KILLING ARE THE DARK FOUNDATIONS OF THE HUMAN SOUL."

EMILE ZOLA

1900-1909

1905 THE STRATTON BROTHERS: The ill-conceived and poorly executed raid on a chandler's store in London's East End.

1905 ARTHUR DEVEREUX: The murder of his wife and twins sons. A pioneer of the trunk form of body disposal.

1907 GEORGE RAYNER: The murder of department store owner William Whiteley by a deluded young man.

1908 OSCAR SLATER: The murder of Marion Gilchrist. The wrongful conviction of Oscar Slater and the attempts to overturn it became a cause célèbre.

1909 THE TOTTENHAM OUTRAGE: Two East European anarchists cause chaos in north London.

LEFT: Large rolls of paper being delivered to the *Daily Mirror* offices on Bouverie Street in London for printing the newspaper in 1905.

ALBERT & ALFRED STRATTON

MURDER OF THOMAS AND ANN FARROW 27TH MARCH 1905

TRIAL BEGAN FRIDAY 5TH MAY

HANGED 23RD MAY 1905

Alfred and Albert Stratton are typical of many of the characters we will meet in this book: young, violent, petty criminals, who were poor, male and with little education. Their crime of murdering the elderly couple Thomas and Ann Farrow was unnecessary and ill-conceived. They achieved undeserved fame by being the first criminals to be convicted of a capital offence based largely on fingerprint evidence.

Thomas and Ann Farrow ran Chapman's Oil and Colour Shop, a chandler's store in Deptford. At 8.30am on Monday 27th March 1905 the old couple were found bludgeoned to death and the week's takings, a miserable 13 pounds, stolen. The police found the empty cash box with a greasy smudged thumbprint on it. This would prove crucial in the trial. The police also found a pair of stockings that had been used as masks and deduced that there were probably two culprits. Two witnesses identified local Alfred Stratton as one of the men seen running away, and after checking with local villains the police discovered that the Stratton brothers had disappeared from their normal East End haunts. Unfortunately for the brothers, one of the investigating offices was Assistant Commissioner Melville MacNaghten, who had been on the Belper Committee assessing the viability of the new science of fingerprinting. The police took a copy of the thumbprint on the Farrows' cash box and eliminated other people in the vicinity.

A week later the brothers were apprehended and fingerprints taken and sent to Scotland Yard's recently created Fingerprint Department, headed by Detective Inspector Collins. Collins studied the prints and Alfred's was found to match the one on the cash box. The police and the prosecutor still had a major problem in finding a way to persuade a jury of the new science's validity. There was great professional rivalry between experts about this new technique and alternative methods of identification such as anthropometry. The prosecution counsel took great efforts to explain the new science to the jury and used powerful expert witness testimony. The defence contested the fingerprint evidence by calling

THE BROTHERS STRATTON TO BE HANGED TO-DAY FOR THE DEPTFORD MURDERS.

Alfred Stratton, who spoiled a promising career and killed Mr. and Mrs. Farrow for a few pounds.

Medals won by Alfred Stratton in the Deptford Football League, of which he was once an honoured member.

Albert Stratton, formerly in the Navy. Taken at Devonport. Made a confession in Wandsworth Prison.

on their own expert, but he was completely undermined when it was shown that he had also offered himself to the prosecution. When the fingerprint identification was combined with the testimony of eyewitnesses the prosecution won a historic conviction with a guilty verdict from the jury. The brothers hanged together on 23rd May 1905.

THE THUMB-PRINTS THAT CONVICTED THE MASKED MURDERERS.

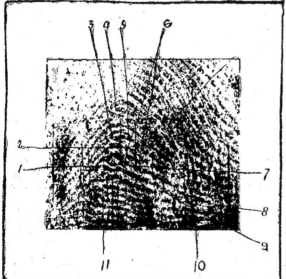

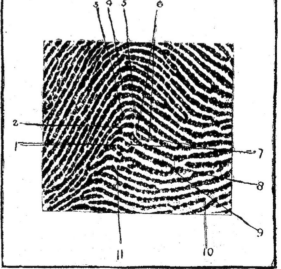

These photographs were made by the Scotland Yard authorities, and did much towards securing the conviction of the men guilty of the masked murder. The photograph on the left shows an enlargement of the thumb-mark left on the cash-box of the murdered man. That on the right is an enlarged imprint made by Alfred Stratton's thumb. The various points of resemblance are indicated by the numbered lines. This is a reproduction of the print handed to the jury.

ABOVE: The Farrow brothers and their medals.

LEFT: Fingerprint evidence.

ARTHUR DEVEREUX

ARTHUR DEVEREUX

MURDER OF WIFE AND TWIN CHILDREN JANUARY 1905

HANGED 15TH AUGUST 1905

Arthur Devereux committed the first of the great British trunk murders in the 20th century. Putting the body in a trunk seems a strategy close in effectiveness to the ostrich putting its head in the sand. "If I can't see the body nobody will notice the missing person or bother to look inside the trunk." Judges and juries frequently consider the gruesome disposal of the body to be the most heinous part of the crime and pass their sentence or verdict accordingly. Arthur Devereux would be the first of many to discover this to their cost.

Arthur Devereux met Beatrice Gregory in 1898 and soon they were married and raising a child, Stanley on very modest assistant chemist's wages. Things were tough financially and despite his love for his son Arthur became depressed. When his wife gave birth to twin sons his financial concerns and despair deepened. He decided to deal with the situation, not by finding a better paid job or simply leaving with his first son, but by murder. In January 1905 he applied for another job, describing himself as a widower with a young son. He bought a large tin trunk and from

TRUNK TRAGEDY—PRISONER BEHIND BARS.

Arthur Devereux was brought up at Harlesden Police Court yesterday charged with the murder of his wife and two children. Our photograph shows the accused, who is on the left of the picture, looking out through the bars of the Kensal Rise Police Station window just before he appeared in court.

TRUNK MYSTERY PHOTOGRAPHS.

The School Where Mrs. Devereux's Son Is Being Educated and a Portrait of Arthur Devereux.

The college, Kenilworth, where Stanley Devereux, the son of the dead woman, is being educated.

Arthur Devereux, the chemist's assistant who is charged with committing one of the most awful crimes of recent years.

work he brought home a bottle of morphine and somehow persuaded his wife and the twins to drink it. By the morning they were dead and placed in the trunk which was taken to a warehouse in Harrow.

Devereux then moved with his surviving son to another part of London and thought that he had put his previous life behind him. However, he had failed to take into consideration his wife's formidable mother who, on learning that a removal truck had taken a trunk to the Harrow depository, informed the police. The next day the story of the discovery of three bodies in a trunk filled the papers and Devereux realized he would be found if he didn't move on again, this time to Coventry. The police were helped by a piano hire company who were attempting to retrieve their piano for which Devereux had not been keeping up payments. When confronted by the police he blurted out: "You're making a mistake. I don't know anything about a tin trunk." However, the police had made no

mention of the tin trunk. Devereux's defence attempted to show that the family had a harmonious relationship and that his wife had killed the twins and then committed suicide.

The defence team suggested that his wife's family had suicidal tendencies. They claimed that when Devereux had found the bodies their client had merely disposed of them because he feared that the police investigation would be unfair and cause distress to his son. An unusual feature during the trial was the defendant regularly falling asleep. The trial was over quickly and the case was easily proved with damming evidence such as Devereux applying for a job and describing himself as a widower when his wife was still alive! An appeal was launched on the grounds of insanity but this had been undermined by his previous defence strategy. He went to the gallows still protesting his innocence.

KENSAL RISE TRUNK TRAGEDY.

Men Who Arrested Devereux, and Scenes in London and Coventry.

Mr. Charsley, the chief constable of Coventry, who supervised the shadowing of Devereux and his arrest.

The furniture warehouse at Buller-road, Kensal Rise, in which the trunk was stored.

Chief Inspector Imber, of Coventry, who shadowed Devereux for a week before arresting him.

Alderman Bird's chemist's shop in Spon-street, Coventry, where Devereux worked and was arrested. The smaller photograph is a portrait of Mr. Bird.

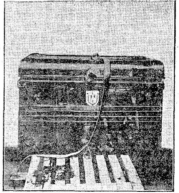

The tin trunk in which the three bodies were found. It is only three feet long, two feet broad, and one foot ten inches deep.

OPPOSITE LEFT: Devereux charged with murder.

LEFT: Devereux's son's school.

BELOW: The men behind Devereux's arrest.

HORACE GEORGE RAYNER

MURDER OF WILLIAM WHITELEY ON 25TH JANUARY 1907

TRIAL OPENED MARCH 1907

The murder of William Whiteley is one of the few crimes where the name of the victim is far better known than that of the perpetrator. William Whiteley was one of the great innovative retailers of the Victorian age and was one of the creators of the modern department store concept. Rayner was sentenced to hang but a huge mobilization of public opinion culminating in the presentation of an 800,000-name petition caused the home secretary to commute the sentence to penal servitude for life.

William Whitely was born in Yorkshire and completed an apprenticeship as a draper. During a visit to the Great Exhibition of 1851 he saw a huge range of goods produced by modern manufacture available in one hall but nothing for sale. He wanted to make all these goods available for purchase in one building. It took a while to save sufficient capital but in 1863 he opened his own store on Westbourne Grove. He employed two staff one of whom, Harriet Hall, was to become his wife. Later in the decade he bought up 17 shops in the same street and turned them into departments of his store, increasing the number of staff to over 600. The

THE TRAGEDY OF MR. WHITELEY'S LIFE—BLACKMAILED AND HARASSED FOR 25 YEARS AND THEN MURDERED. PORTRAITS OF THOSE ASSOCIATED WITH THE PITIFUL STORY NOW TOLD FOR THE FIRST TIME. —(See page 3.)

Mrs. Rayner, wife of the murderer.

Mrs. E. L. Turner, grandmother of the murderer.

H. G. Rayner, or Turner, Mr. Whiteley's murderer.

Mr. Whiteley's daughter Clara at age of 11.

Mr. William Whiteley, murdered January 24.

Mr. Whiteley's daughter Ada at age of 12.

Mr. W. Whiteley, elder son of the victim.

Mrs. Whiteley, widow of the murdered man.

Mr. Frank Whiteley, younger son of the murdered man.

Sensational developments accompany the clearing up of the Whiteley murder mystery. Blackmail figures largely amongst these disclosures. For twenty-five years Mr. Whiteley paid out thousands of pounds to people who professed to know one of the secrets of his middle age. The man Rayner, or Turner, who committed the murder, became a party to this secret, and on his last visit to Mr. Whiteley is said to have attempted to extort a large sum of money. It is said by the police that he was sent by someone else, who is being closely watched until they have completed their inquiries, when further sensational developments may be expected. (Photographs of Rayner's children appear on page 9.)

Yesterday Horace George Rayner was charged at the Marylebone-Police Court with the murder of Mr. William Whiteley in his shop at Westbourne-grove on January 24. The photograph shows the accused man (marked with a cross) in the dock. Inset are Mr. Whiteley and H. G. Rayner. It was noticed how terribly the latter had aged. Rayner has grown a short beard since he was admitted to St. Mary's Hospital suffering from self-inflicted wounds.—(*Daily Mirror* photographs.)

business continued to grow and by 1900 it employed 6,000 staff. He referred to himself as *The Universal Provider* and was one of the great celebrities and businessmen of his age.

Despite Whiteley's hugely successful business life the rest of his world caused him great pain. His marriage had not been a success and his wife had left him. He had many affairs and some illegitimate children. For the 25 years before his murder Whiteley had paid out thousands of pounds to blackmailers. He was very insecure about his respectability and feared that his legitimate family would suffer. One of his mistresses might well have been Emily Turner whose sister Louie had been employed as an assistant by Whiteley. Emily had given birth to a child named Horace, claiming George Rayner was the father. Despite his doubts Rayner had agreed to act as stepfather to Horace. Subsequently a rumour developed in the family that the real father was William Whiteley. Meanwhile Emily Turner had died in the 1890s.

Horace George Rayner had convinced himself that William Whiteley was his father. Horace Rayner, a married man with two children, had struggled to settle in life and suffered long periods of unemployment before the shooting. On 25th January 1907 Rayner went to Whiteley's store and won an audience with the owner. Rayner wanted money from the man whom he believed was his father. When Whiteley denied him and turned to leave Rayner drew a gun and shot Whiteley twice. He then turned the gun on himself but only succeeded in causing injury.

The trial revealed the complexities of Whiteley's family life and the sad, pathetic character of the murderer and his family. Rayner was found guilty, but a huge campaign inspired by the plight of his young, attractive, pregnant wife and the two children won a reprieve from the hangman.

Undoubtedly Rayner owes his life to the sympathy and pity aroused throughout the world for his young wife. This photograph of Mrs. Rayner was specially taken by the *Daily Mirror* after she had learned the glad news of her husband's reprieve.

OPPOSITE LEFT: Portraits of the people involved.

ABOVE: Rayner's trial.

LEFT: Mrs Rayner, after Rayner's reprieve.

OSCAR SLATER

MURDER OF MARION GILCHRIST ON 21ST DECEMBER 1908

TRIAL OPENED 3RD MAY 1909

RELEASED IN 1927 UNDER LICENCE

The murder of an 82-year-old widow became a cause célèbre when the conviction of Oscar Slater was investigated by Conan Doyle. Slater had been sentenced to hang but after the presentation of a large petition the sentence was commuted to life imprisonment. Doyle showed that there had been a major miscarriage of justice, which led to Slater's release in 1927 under licence. Eventually he was cleared of all charges.

The Slater case is one of many where the authorities preferred to see an innocent man hang or remain in jail and where convenience and vested interest were more important than justice. The parallels of the case associated with the Glasgow Ice Cream Wars 80 years later are clear and very uncomfortable.

In December 1908 a wealthy Glaswegian widow was murdered in her flat. She possessed a substantial collection of jewellery valued at £60,000 at today's prices. The flat had been ransacked but only one item had been stolen, a brooch. Witnesses spoke of seeing a well-dressed man leaving the flat. Strangely, the police didn't question the victim's well-to-do family. Instead the investigation focused on

Oscar Slater, an illegal gambling den operator, pimp and, in the words of the police, "a bad lot". He was also German and Jewish.

Four days after the murder Slater had tried to sell a pawn ticket for a brooch and a few days later had sailed with his girlfriend under false names to the United States. The police construed this as evidence of fleeing the crime and alerted the New York Police, who apprehended them on arrival. Slater didn't contest extradition and was duly extradited

LEFT: The murder victim, Marion Gilchrist.

BELOW: Oscar Slater on trial.

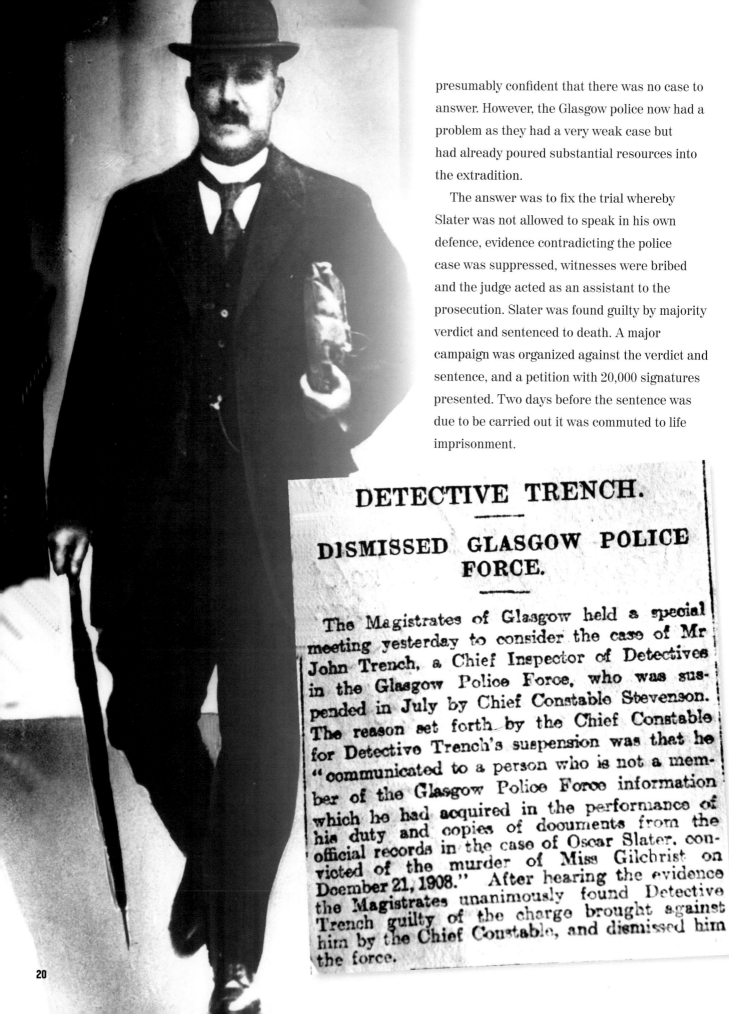

presumably confident that there was no case to answer. However, the Glasgow police now had a problem as they had a very weak case but had already poured substantial resources into the extradition.

The answer was to fix the trial whereby Slater was not allowed to speak in his own defence, evidence contradicting the police case was suppressed, witnesses were bribed and the judge acted as an assistant to the prosecution. Slater was found guilty by majority verdict and sentenced to death. A major campaign was organized against the verdict and sentence, and a petition with 20,000 signatures presented. Two days before the sentence was due to be carried out it was commuted to life imprisonment.

DETECTIVE TRENCH.

DISMISSED GLASGOW POLICE FORCE.

The Magistrates of Glasgow held a special meeting yesterday to consider the case of Mr John Trench, a Chief Inspector of Detectives in the Glasgow Police Force, who was suspended in July by Chief Constable Stevenson. The reason set forth by the Chief Constable for Detective Trench's suspension was that he "communicated to a person who is not a member of the Glasgow Police Force information which he had acquired in the performance of his duty and copies of documents from the official records in the case of Oscar Slater, convicted of the murder of Miss Gilchrist on Dcember 21, 1908." After hearing the evidence the Magistrates unanimously found Detective Trench guilty of the charge brought against him by the Chief Constable, and dismissed him the force.

The case was taken up by Conan Doyle in his book *The Case of Oscar Slater* published in 1912. The book was highly critical of the police and their case, and implied that the Gilchrist family had friends in high places in Glasgow society.Two years later a highly respected police detective, John Trench, accused witnesses of perjury and was hounded out of the force. Despite the book and further letters by Conan Doyle Slater continued in prison until the publication in 1927 of a further book, *The Truth About Oscar Slater* by Glasgow journalist

William Park. Like Conan Doyle, Park showed that Miss Gilchrist knew her killer and that she had been murdered with a chair leg.

Although it was not stated explicitly it was made clear that the chief suspect was her nephew. The furore caused the original witnesses to retract their statements and the story of police falsification was revealed. In 1927 the Secretary of State for Scotland conceded and authorized Slater's release on licence. Eventually the case was reopened and at the retrial Slater was acquitted and paid £6,000.

OPPOSITE LEFT: Detective Lieutenant John Trench.

MIDDLE: Trench's dismissal.

LEFT: Oscar Slater.

PAUL HEFELD AND JACOB LEPIDUS

MURDER OF RALPH JOSCELYN, PC TYLER ON 23RD JANUARY 1909

INQUEST HELD ON 26TH JANUARY 1909

BOTH THE MURDERERS COMMITTED SUICIDE

KNOWN AS THE TOTTENHAM OUTRAGES

Two Latvian anarchists named Hefeld and Lepidus set out to commit a simple wages heist and ended up becoming involved in a chase that would rival anything depicted in the Keystone Cops films. They killed two people and injured many more before being cornered and attempting suicide.

The Tottenham Outrages were the first of a series of violent incidents involving foreign anarchists that would shock Edwardian Britain and lead to a wave of hostility towards immigrants.

Hefeld and Lepidus were well-known Lithuanian anarchists and members of the Lettish League living in the large Russian colony in Tottenham. Their target was the weekly wages delivery of about £80 to Schnurrman's rubber factory on the corner of Tottenham High Road and Chestnut Road. Both robbers were armed with automatic pistols. The heist quickly went wrong when the chauffeur intervened and Hefeld responded by opening fire and injuring him. There followed a sequence of events which would shock Britain.

Twenty-one people were shot, two fatally. The chase went on for six miles, starting with the chauffeur's attempt to run over the robbers. The car was stopped by a shot hitting the radiator. However, the chase had been joined by police on bikes and horses. It was now that a 10-year-old boy, Ralph Joscelyn, was shot dead. Reinforcements were called from across North London. PC Tyler tried to persuade Hefeld and Lepidus to give up but was instead shot dead. The chase was joined by some wildfowlers and shots were exchanged. A tram was hijacked and the police followed on a commandeered tram that had been going the other way. Abandoning the tram as they approached a police station

THE TOTTENHAM TRAGEDY: SCENES AT YESTERDAY'S INQUEST.

There was a further development in the Tottenham outrage yesterday, a foreigner named Nideroest being taken to the police-station. The man called at the Prince of Wales' Hospital and asked to see Paul Hefeld, alleging that he was his brother. Being suspicious of his story, the police conveyed the man, who is seen in the picture with two police-officers, to the police-station. The small portrait is also of Nideroest.

The coroner's inquiry into the deaths of Police-constable Tyler and Ralph John Joscelyn was opened yesterday. Above is Mr. A. M. Forbes, the coroner.

The father and aunt of the boy victim of the man hunt, Ralph John Joscelyn, leaving the coroner's court at Tottenham yesterday at the conclusion of the proceedings.—(Daily Mirror photograph.)

POLICE CONSTABLE TYLER, WHO WAS MURDERED BY ALIEN TERRORISTS AT TOTTENHAM, GIVEN A HERO'S FUNERAL.

Ralph Joscelyn, the ten-year-old boy who was shot dead.

(A) Sir Edward Henry, Commissioner of Police, and (B) Mr. H. Samuel, Under-Secretary Home Department.

View of the procession, giving an idea of the large number of policemen present and the size of the crowd. The portrait is one of the murdered policeman.

The coffin containing Police-Constable Tyler's body being carried by brother-constables from his house in Arnold-street to the hearse.

Mrs. Tyler, widow of the heroic constable, for whom a fund is being raised.

the robbers now hijacked a milk van but soon turned it over and moved on to a grocery van. They could not release the brake and returned to escaping on foot. Eventually they were confronted by a high wire fence which Hefeld, after the six-mile chase, was too exhausted to climb and on the point of arrest he shot himself. Lepidus sought refuge in a house but when cornered committed suicide with his last bullet. About 400 bullets had been fired. There was outrage in the press and reports of "alien desperados" and "foreign riff-raff". Heroes such as George Harwood, an unemployed labourer who had borrowed a gun and rushed the anarchists, wounding one, were acclaimed. The police were outgunned by the anarchists and their poor equipment would become an even bigger issue two years later in the battle of Sidney Street.

It was estimated that half a million people, including 3,000 police, lined the route of the funeral cortège.

OPPOSITE LEFT: The inquest.

ABOVE: PC Tyler's funeral.

ABOVE INSET: Ralph Joscelyn.

"HAWLEY HARVEY CRIPPEN: AGE 50, 5FT. 3" OR 4",
COMPLEXION FRESH, HAIR LIGHT BROWN, INCLINED
SANDY, SCANTY, BALD ON TOP, RATHER LONG SCANTY
MOUSTACHE, SOMEWHAT STRAGGLY, EYES GREY,
BRIDGE OF NOSE RATHER FLAT, FALSE TEETH, MEDIUM
BUILD, THROWS HIS FEET OUTWARDS WHEN WALKING
... SOMEWHAT SLOVENLY APPEARANCE, WEARS HIS
HAT RATHER AT THE BACK OF HEAD. VERY PLAUSIBLE
AND QUIET SPOKEN, REMARKABLY COOL AND
COLLECTED DEMEANOUR."

POLICE DESCRIPTION OF CRIPPEN FOLLOWING THE ISSUING OF
THE WARRANT FOR HIS ARREST.

1910-1919

1910 DOCTOR CRIPPEN: The murder of his wife Cora. He was apprehended by the use of the telegraph system.

1910 HOUNDSDITCH MURDERS: Three policemen are gunned down in a politically motivated jewellery raid.

1911 STEINIE MORRISON: The murder of Leon Beron in what the authorities claimed was just a brutal robbery and murder.

1911 FREDERICK SEDDON: The murder of the lodger, Eliza Barrow. A traditional tale of remarkable greed.

1914 GEORGE SMITH: Best known as the *Brides In the Bath* case. Smith drowned three wives before a pattern was noticed.

1919 HAROLD GREENWOOD: The acquittal of solicitor Harold Greenwood would provide one of the great trials of the 20th century.

LEFT: The courtyard of the Old Bailey with horse and carriages bringing witnesses to the trial of Doctor Crippen.

DR CRIPPEN AND ETHEL LE NEVE

MURDER OF CORA CRIPPEN ON 31ST JANUARY 1910

ARRESTED 23RD JULY 1910 BY INSPECTOR DEW IN QUEBEC

TRIAL STARTED 18TH OCTOBER 1910

HANGED AT PENTONVILLE 23RD NOVEMBER 1910

Doctor Hawley Harvey Crippen's name has been seen as synonymous with murder and evil in the 20th century. Why is this when his crime was the relatively common one of murdering his wife? The murder of a close relative seldom causes much stir so what has made Doctor Crippen so different?

The Daily Mirror

THE MORNING JOURNAL WITH THE SECOND LARGEST NET SALE

No. 2,110.   MONDAY, AUGUST 1, 1910   One Halfpenny.

END OF THE ATLANTIC CHASE: "DR." CRIPPEN, WHO WAS ARRESTED AT FATHER POINT, CANADA, YESTERDAY.

Both Doctor Crippen and Cora were American. He was described as being 5ft 4in tall with bulging, permanently blinking eyes and thick glasses. Cora was described as dumpy and buxom with a voice somewhat lacking in "feminine charm". In 1898 they moved to London, where the doctor earnt £3 a week plus commission working as manager of Munyon's Remedies, a patent medicine company. Cora was earning little money and spending a lot as she sought to establish herself on the stage in music hall. However, her career was impaired by a shortage of talent. During this time the Crippens' relationship deteriorated, with the doctor commenting, "she no longer cares for me". Cora was taking lovers from the theatrical world in which she was becoming increasingly prominent as honorary treasurer of the Music-Hall Ladies Guild. Meanwhile the doctor had met Ethel Le Neve, a typist at his employer's and very different from Cora with

her more delicate boyish figure and genteel manner. Despite the gentility this was clearly a passionate relationship which they were consummating in London hotel rooms. Passions were heightened when Cora learned that Ethel

was pregnant and only abated after Ethel miscarried.

There were frequent rows between the Crippens and threats to leave, with Cora giving notice to the bank that she intended to withdraw her money from the joint account. What made Doctor Crippen purchase poison and plan such a grisly solution to his matrimonial problems, rather than consider a separation or divorce? Crime writer William Le Queux stated that in 1908 he corresponded with a man he later learned to be Doctor Crippen regarding poison and murder plots. Perhaps Crippen feared for his financial future if Cora was to take most of the couple's savings, or the scandal of divorce. Whatever the case, things came to a head after a dinner with Cora's friends, retired theatricals Paul and Clara Martinetti. It is possible that Cora's death was an accident but given the state of the doctor's

OPPOSITE LEFT: Crippen on the *Daily Mirror* cover.

LEFT: Cora Crippen dressed as her stage persona, Belle Amore.

BELOW: Crippen and Le Neve.

METROPOLITAN POLICE
MURDER
AND MUTILATION.

Portraits, Description and Specimen of Handwriting of HAWLEY HARVEY CRIPPEN, alias Peter Crippen, alias Franckel; and ETHEL CLARA LE NEVE, alias Mrs. Crippen, and Neave.

Wanted for the Murder of CORA CRIPPEN, otherwise Belle Elmore; Kunigunde Mackamotzki; Marsangar and Turner, on, or about, 2nd February last.

Description of Crippen. Age 50, height 5 ft. 3 or 4, complexion fresh, hair light brown, inclined sandy, scanty, bald on top, rather long scanty moustache, somewhat straggly, eyes grey, bridge of nose rather flat, false teeth, medium build, throws his feet outwards when walking. May be clean-shaven or wear beard and gold rimmed spectacles, and may possibly assume a wig.

Sometimes wears a jacket suit, and at other times frock coat and silk hat. May be dressed in a brown jacket suit, brown hat and stand up collar (size 15).

Somewhat slovenly appearance, wears his hat rather at back of head

Very plausible and quiet spoken, remarkably cool and collected demeanour.

Speaks French and probably German. Carries Firearms.

An American citizen, and by profession a Doctor.

Has lived in New York, Philadelphia, St. Louis, Detroit, Michigan, Coldwater, and other parts of America.

May obtain a position as assistant to a doctor or eye specialist, or may practise as an eye specialist, Dentist, or open a business for the treatment of deafness, advertising freely.

Has represented Munyon's Remedies, in various cities in America.

Description of Le Neve alias Neave.—A shorthand writer and typist, age 27, height 5 ft. 5, complexion pale, hair light brown (may dye same), large grey or blue eyes, good teeth, nice looking, rather long straight nose (good shape), medium build, pleasant, lady-like appearance. Quiet, subdued manner, talks quietly, looks intently when in conversation. A native of London.

Dresses well, but quietly, and may wear a blue serge costume (coat reaching to hips) trimmed heavy braid, about ¾ inch wide, round edge, over shoulders and pockets. Three large braid buttons down front, about size of a florin, three small ones on each pocket, two on each cuff, several rows off stitching round bottom of skirt; or a light grey shadow-stripe costume, same style as above, but trimmed grey moire silk instead of braid, and two rows of silk round bottom of skirt; or a white princess robe with gold sequins; or a mole coloured striped costume with black moire silk collar; or a dark vieuxrose cloth costume, trimmed black velvet collar; or a light heliotrope dress.

May have in her possession and endeavour to dispose of same:—a round gold brooch, with points radiating zig-zag from centre, each point about an inch long, diamond in centre, each point set brilliants, the brooch in all being slightly larger than a half-crown; and two single stone diamond rings, and ; a diamond and sapphire (or ruby) ring, stones rather large.

Absconded 9th inst. and may have left, or will endeavour to leave the country.

Please cause every enquiry at Shipping Offices, Hotels, . and other likely places, and cause ships to be watched.

Information to be given to the Metropolitan Police Office, New Scotland Yard, London. S.W., or at any Police Station.

E. R. HENRY, *The Commissioner of Police of the Metropolis.*

Metropolitan Police Office, New Scotland Yard. 15th July, 1910.

(17000c.–1.) Wt. P 1591—5866. 3,000. 7/10. D & S.

"right up in the wilds of the mountains of California". The story later changed to that of serious illness with double pneumonia. On Thursday 24th March Ethel and Crippen left for a trip to Dieppe, stopping at Victoria Station to send a telegram to Mrs Martinetti saying, "Belle died yesterday at 6 o'clock ..." It was strange behaviour and not what you would expect from a bereaved husband, even an estranged one.

It would seem that Cora's death would be accepted with only a few mutterings from her friends until the return from the States of Cora's friend Mrs Nash who had been touring as Lil Hawthorne. She didn't accept the explanations offered for Cora's disappearance and, unfortunately for Crippen, she was a friend of Detective Superintendent Froest of the newly created Serious Crimes Squad. On 8th

love life it would have been a very convenient one. According to evidence at the trial it was the poison hyoscine that killed Cora. Some people reported hearing shots. However she was killed, by the end of the night Cora's body had been decapitated, dismembered, filleted and probably stored away under the floor of the coal cellar. Over the next few weeks the doctor created the story of his wife's journey to the United States, while at the same time moving in Ethel Le Neve, pawning some of his wife's jewellery and giving other pieces to his lover. On 20th February they attended a dinner and ball for the Music-Hall Ladies Guild benevolent fund, with Ethel wearing one of Cora's brooches. When asked about Cora Crippen reported that she was

ABOVE: Wanted poster.

RIGHT: Ethel Le Neve not entirely convincingly dressed as a boy.

July an Inspector Dew arrived to investigate, and Crippen's world started to unravel. Crippen dictated a new statement in which he claimed his wife had left him for another man. After looking through the house Inspector Dew seemed satisfied and left. Yet Dew thought about the situation and returned to the house after the weekend to ask a few more questions. To his amazement the house was empty: the only explanation was an ominous letter written to Ryland, Crippen's business partner, which said: "In order to escape trouble I shall be obliged to absent myself for a time." After a thorough search the gory remains of body parts were discovered in the coal cellar. By now the Crippen and Le Neve were staying at the Hotel Des Ardennes in Belgium. A young Bernard Spilsbury, a pathologist who will stalk the pages of this book, examined the remains

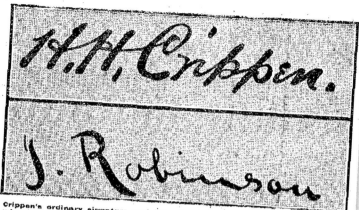

Crippen's ordinary signature and his entry in the visitors' book at the cafe where he stayed at Brussels. They are enlarged for purposes of comparison. It will be noticed that the "n's" in Crippen and Robinson are very similar. A reference to page one will show that the "e's" in Quebec and Crippen are also much alike.

and found traces of hyoscine sufficient to poison the victim, and remnants of a pyjama top that could be traced to the Crippins. On the 16th a warrant was issued for their arrest. On 20th July Ethel and the doctor boarded the SS *Montrose* in Antwerp as Mr John Robinson and his 16-year-old son, Master John Robinson. Boys' clothes had been bought in London before their departure although

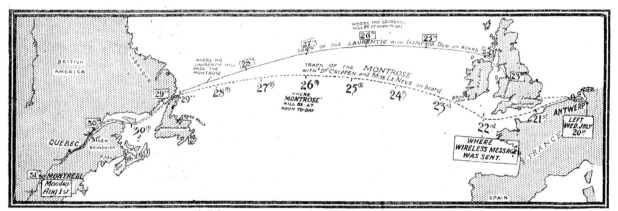

Chart of the Atlantic, showing the relative positions of the Montrose and the Laurentic day by day. The figures in brackets relate to the Laurentic.

The Montrose leaving the Thames for Montreal via Antwerp on Thursday, July 14.

The Laurentic, on which Inspector Dew is pursuing them.

The Montrose, on which Crippen and Ethel le Neve are attempting to reach safety in Canada, and the Laurentic, on which Inspector Dew is pursuing them. They are now in mid-ocean. Meanwhile, in New York, Mrs. Mills, step-sister of the murdered Belle Elmore, and Mrs. Ginnett, one of the victim's dearest friends, are still meeting every liner arriving in New York in the belief that it is still possible that Crippen is bound on one of the boats journeying to that port. Mrs. Ginnett will go to Canada to assist Inspector Dew in identifying Crippen, and Mrs. Mills may accompany her,

they didn't fit very well. Unknown to the lovers an alert had been put out for their arrest which was read by the captain of the *Montrose*, Captain Kendall. His ship was one of only 60 in the world equipped with radio telegraph. He noticed the over-affectionate father and son and alerted his superiors with the message: "Have reason to believe Dr. Crippen and Miss Le Neve are travelling as passengers on my ship. They are posing as father and son and should reach Quebec July 31st. Await instructions." Inspector Dew sailed from Liverpool on 23rd July on the faster ship SS *Laurentic* to arrive in Quebec ahead of the lovers. The doctor and Ethel were unaware that their plans had been discovered and sailed on oblivious while Captain Lawrence kept the rest of the world updated. Maps appearing in the press charted their progress across the Atlantic. The lovers' world collapsed on 31st July as the *Montrose* steamed up the St Lawrence and Inspector Dew, disguised as a pilot, boarded the ship and arrested the fugitives. Three weeks later they returned on the SS *Megantic* escorted by Dew and his assistants, to be greeted by vast crowds and the world's press when they docked in Liverpool. They were tried separately, with Crippen's trial opening on 18th October. His defence was that there was no proof that the remains found at 39 Hilldrop Crescent were those of Cora or even human and that they had been deposited there before the Crippens had moved in. However, the prosecution used the evidence of the pyjamas to prove that the material had been made after the Crippens had moved in and had been delivered to the address in January 1909. It took just 27 minutes for the jury to find the doctor guilty. Ethel's trial only lasted one day during which she was acquitted and freed. The doctor went to the gallows on 23rd November extolling the purity of the couple's love and his own innocence. His last granted request was that

he should be buried with Ethel's photograph and letters. Ethel remarried a few years later and had two children. She died in 1967 and was buried with a locket holding a picture of Doctor Crippen that she had worn since his death over 50 years earlier.

In many ways this was the first great murder of the mass media age. The public were able to follow and feel part of the chase. They could track the fugitives across the Atlantic and share the drama of Crippen's shock as Inspector Dew introduced himself on the deck of the *Montrose*. There was the vicarious thrill of a social superior, a doctor, the spice of the murder of an extrovert American theatrical who changed her name to the exotic Belle Elmore and the disgust at the brutal disposal of her body. The public wondered at the involvement of a young, pretty English girl who dressed as a young boy in poignant contrast with the rather more earthy American wife. All this was wrapped up

with the use of the latest technology in the form of radio telegraphy and the brilliant forensic work of Bernard Spilsbury. No wonder we still remember this as one of the great murders of the 20th century. However, when Crippen is compared to many other murderers and criminals in this book it is difficult to regard him as especially evil.

There has recently been some debate about whether Crippen was innocent after all. Some of the DNA on a slide kept after the trial has been analysed, compared with that from a relative of Cora and found to be different. An American scientist even argues that the remains found at Hilldrop Crescent were male. If Crippen was innocent a large number of the police and forensic team involved would have needed to lie and falsify evidence. This would be very brave if it were likely that the larger-than-life form of Cora might reappear at any minute. I think that we can be reasonably confident of Crippen's guilt.

OPPOSITE LEFT: The return to Liverpool.

BELOW LEFT: The Crippen's in the dock.

BELOW: Scene of the trial.

HOUNDSDITCH MURDERS

BURGLARY OF THE JEWELLER'S SHOP AT 119 HOUNDSDITCH ON THE 16TH DECEMBER 1910

ONE OF THE ROBBERS, GEORGE GARDSTEIN, AND THREE POLICEMAN, SERGEANTS, BENTLEY AND TUCKER AND CONSTABLE CHOATE, DIED IN THE INITIAL ROBBERY

FRITZ SVAARS AND WILLIAM SOKOLOW DIED IN THE SUBSEQUENT SIEGE OF SIDNEY STREET

The Houndsditch murders and the subsequent siege of Sidney Street made apparent the scale and activities of the anarchist émigré community in the East End of London. As in the Tottenham Outrage two years earlier, the willingness of the anarchists to use violence on such a massive scale was a shock to the poorly equipped British police who finally had their weaponry upgraded after the incident.

In December 1910 a group of Latvian anarchists rented a house in Houndsditch and were attempting to break through the wall into a

CITY OF LONDON POLICE.
MURDER OF POLICE OFFICERS.
£500 REWARD

WHEREAS Sergeants Charles Tucker and Robert Bentley, and Constable Walter Charles Choat, of the City of London Police, were murdered in Exchange Buildings, in the said City, at 11.30 p.m., on the 16th December, 1910, by a man who is now dead, and other persons now wanted, whose descriptions are given below, and who were also concerned with the deceased Murderer in attempting to feloniously break and enter a Jeweller's shop, and killed the Officers to prevent arrest.

PORTRAIT AND DESCRIPTION OF THE DEAD MURDERER.

Name said to be GEORGE GARDSTEIN, alias POOLKA MILOWITZ.

Both may be incorrect.

DESCRIPTION :—

Age about 24, height 5ft. 9 in., complexion pale, hair brown, slight dark moustache worn slightly up at ends, good physique.

DESCRIPTION OF THE PERSONS WANTED.

FIRST.—A man named FRITZ SVARRS, lately residing at 59, Grove Street, Commercial Road, London, E., age about 24 or 25, height 5 feet 8 or 9 inches, complexion sallow, hair fair, medium moustache—turned up at ends, lighter in colour than hair of head—eyes grey, nose rather small—slightly turned up—chin a little upraised, has a few small pimples on face; cheek-bones prominent, shoulders square, but bend slightly forward; dress brown tweed suit (thin light stripes), dark melton overcoat (velvet collar, nearly new), usually wears a grey Irish tweed cap (red stripes), but has been sometimes seen wearing a trilby hat; a Locksmith; native of Libau, Russia.

SECOND.—A man known as "PETER THE PAINTER," also lately residing at 59, Grove Street, Commercial Road, London, E., age 28 to 30, height 5 feet 9 or 10 inches, complexion sallow, hair and medium moustache black, clear skin, eyes dark, medium build, reserved manner; dress brown tweed suit (broad dark stripes), black overcoat (velvet collar, rather old), black hard felt hat, black lace boots, rather shabby, believed to be a native of Russia.

Both are Anarchists.

THIRD.—A woman, age 26 to 30, height 5 feet 4 inches, slim build, fairly full breasts, complexion medium, face somewhat drawn, eyes blue, hair brown ; dress dark three-quarter jacket and skirt, white blouse, large black hat (trimmed black silk), light-coloured shoes.

The above reward of £500 will be paid by the Commissioner of Police for the City of London to any person who shall give such information as shall lead to the arrest of these persons, or in proportion to the number of such persons who are arrested.

Information to be given to the City Police Office, 26, Old Jewry, London, E.C., or at any Police Station.

J. W. NOTT BOWER,
Commissioner of Police for the City of London.

City Police Office,
26, Old Jewry, London, E.C.
22nd December,

WERTHEIMER, LEA & CO., Printers, Worship Street, London, E.C.

jeweller's. The loud banging was heard by local residents who reported the noise to the police. On arrival the police, in the best British tradition, knocked on the door which was opened by the anarchists' leader George Gardstein. Feigning incomprehension Gardstein disappeared back into the house leaving the police at the door. Eventually losing patience they moved into the house to be met by gunshots and were either injured or killed. As the gang attempted to escape the leader Gardstein was grabbed by Constable Choate. Other gang members shot Choate and in the process injured Gardstein. They retreated into the East End,

leaving Gardstein at 59 Grove Street, where he died the next day. Three police officers had been killed in the incident, which led to a surge in anger towards immigrants. This was to be the highest number of police fatalities in an incident in English history and wasn't equalled until the Shepherd's Bush massacre in 1966. The police quickly rounded up most of the gang members and on a tip-off from an informer descended on 100 Sidney Street and surrounded the area. A gun battle developed in which the police were clearly outgunned.

The home secretary, Winston Churchill, was contacted and he authorized the deployment of troops. Controversially, he visited Sidney Street and viewed the battle at first hand, refusing to authorize the fire brigade to put out the fire that had developed. Many felt that the home

ABOVE: Police outside the jeweller's.

OPPOSITE LEFT: Murder of Police Officers wanted poster.

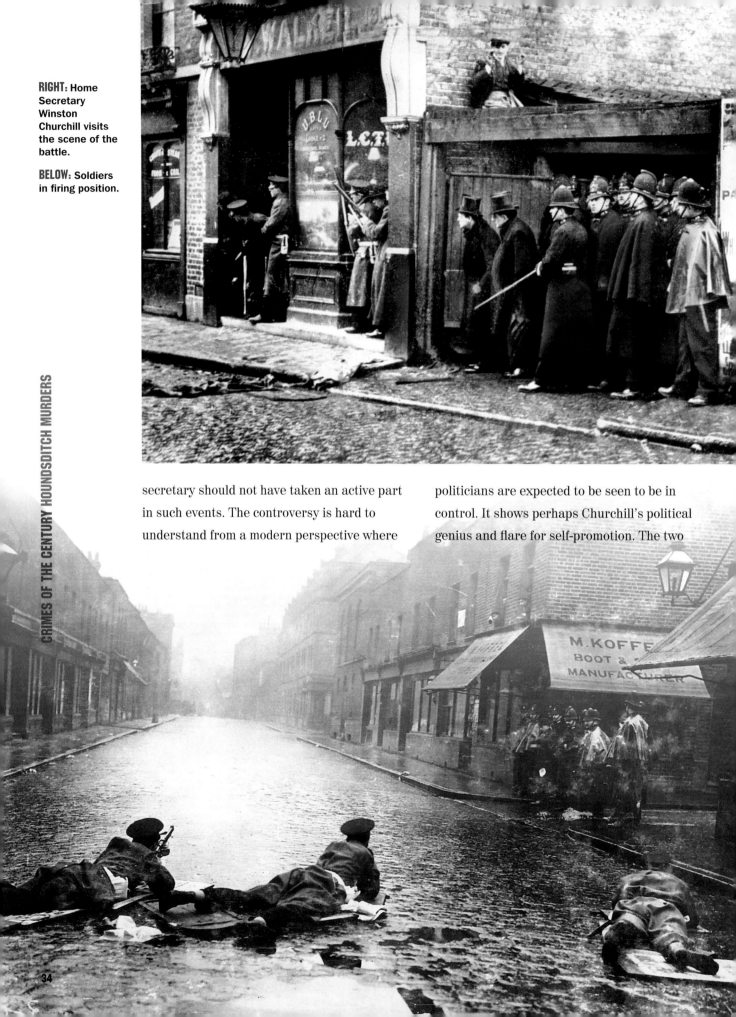

RIGHT: Home Secretary Winston Churchill visits the scene of the battle.

BELOW: Soldiers in firing position.

secretary should not have taken an active part in such events. The controversy is hard to understand from a modern perspective where politicians are expected to be seen to be in control. It shows perhaps Churchill's political genius and flare for self-promotion. The two

34

anarchists, Svaars and Sokolow, refused to surrender and died in the house. The rest of the gang were arrested in the following weeks but at the trial the seven suspects either had the charges dropped, were acquitted or had their convictions quashed. The defence successfully placed all responsibility with the dead members of the gang.

ABOVE: Peter the Painter, a leading member of the gang, later played a leading role in the Russian Revolution.

LEFT: People looking at the bullet holes after the siege.

STEINIE MORRISON

THE MURDER OF LEON BERON 1ST JANUARY 1911

ARRESTED 8TH JANUARY 1911

TRIAL STARTED 6TH MARCH 1911

SENTENCED TO DEATH BUT COMMUTED TO LIFE IMPRISONMENT BY HOME SECRETARY WINSTON CHURCHILL. HE DIED AFTER A HUNGER STRIKE IN 1921, PROCLAIMING HIS INNOCENCE

The murder of Leon Beron occurred soon after the Houndsditch murders and the ensuing siege of Sidney Street. Two years earlier the Tottenham Outrages had rocked London. The East End was a hotbed of revolutionary, anarchist and largely Jewish culture. Revolutionaries who had migrated to London from across Eastern Europe brought with them a culture where violence, murder and a determination to resist arrest at all costs were normal. The judge rejected all such connections and treated the death of Beron as a simple robbery. This now seems rather a simplification.

Steinie Morrison was a Russian Jew with a long history of burglary who had recently been released on parole after 12 years in prison. It was alleged that he murdered and robbed Leon Beron, another émigré Russian Jew, in the early morning of 1st January. They had met regularly at a Jewish restaurant and were seen to leave together at 11.30pm. The body of Beron was found on Clapham Common with its legs crossed and S-shaped scratch marks on the face. There was evidence that it had been dragged some distance. The case against Morrison was largely circumstantial and confused, and the identification from two hansom cab drivers was suspicious. The cab drivers came forward only after a reward had been offered. One of them referred to a man of 5ft 10in in height whereas Morrison was 6ft 3in. There was no adequate explanation of why Beron was taken six miles to Clapham Common or for the S-shaped marks that had been scratched on his face. The prosecution made much of a brown parcel returned to Morrison in the restaurant. Morrison said it was a flute, the prosecution an iron bar.

There was contradictory evidence from the waiter and a 10-year-old girl, Becky Snelwar. The victim's brother Solomon Beron provided eccentric testimony and would later be incarcerated in a lunatic asylum. The trial lasted nine days, an epic by the standards of the time. Richard Muir led for the prosecution

MORRISON'S UNCHANGING ATTITUDE IN THE DOCK.

EVA FLITTERMAN JUMPS ON AN OMNIBUS TO ESCAPE THE CROWD.

At the police-court.

In the dock at the Old Bailey.

At the police-court.

Solomon Beron.   Eva Flitterman escapes the crowd.   Mr. Abinger at the police-court.

Throughout his trial and during the police-court proceedings Stinie Morrison has always stood in the same attitude, and at the Old Bailey he declined the proffered chair. Yesterday's proceedings were marked by a sensational scene, Solomon Beron, the brother of the murdered man, waving his fist and shouting, "When are you going to stop," to Mr. Abinger, who is defending the prisoner.

and presented the case as a simple violent robbery. He ignored all the evidence of a link to the Houndsditch murders and the gang being linked to Peter the Painter. The defence focused on an anarchist conspiracy, depicting the murder of Beron as revenge on a spy. Why was he taken to Clapham Common and why were the S-shaped marks left on his face? Where were the proceeds of the crime? The jury believed the prosecution and Morrison was found guilty and sentenced to hang. After a petition for clemency his sentence was reduced to life imprisonment by Home Secretary Winston Churchill. It is thought that Churchill felt that the jury may have been overenthusiastic in giving their verdict in the wake of the siege of Sidney Street and the murder of policemen. Morrison always protested his innocence and petitioned to be released or the sentence be carried out. He eventually died in prison in 1921 after a hunger strike.

THE MYSTIC SIGN ON A MURDERED MAN'S FACE.

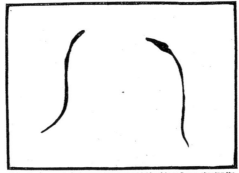

Lines drawn over a photograph of the dead body of Leon Beron, showing the exact shape of the lines, said to be "S's," which a German or Russian unused to English written characters cut with a knife on the murdered man's face. The rest of the photograph has been obliterated since the lines were drawn.

OPPOSITE LEFT:
The victim, Leon Beron.

ABOVE LEFT:
Steinie Morrison at his trial.

ABOVE RIGHT:
Becky Snelwar, who gave evidence in Morrison's defence.

LEFT: Mystic marks found on the body.

FREDERICK HENRY SEDDON AND MARGARET ANN SEDDON

MURDER OF ELIZA BARROW ON 14TH SEPTEMBER 1911

TRIAL OPENED 4TH MARCH 1912

HANGED 18TH APRIL 1912

This is the classic crime of greed where Mr Seddon was found guilty of murder and his wife not guilty despite greater evidence against her. It would seem that Mr Seddon, an insurance agent, was as much found guilty of avarice as of the murder of Mrs Barrow.

Mr Seddon was obsessed by money and renowned for his meanness. He would undertake almost any activity to turn a profit, and even charged his teenage sons six shillings a week for living at home. He enjoyed dealing in property and boasted of owning 17. In January 1910 he bought 63 Tollington Park, a house with three floors, and let the top floor to a Miss Eliza Barrow. Miss Barrow was not the most attractive character, with a reputation for meanness, bad temper and an excessive fondness for gin. These faults did not concern Seddon because she was also rather rich and this was to be her undoing. Over the next year much of Eliza Barrow's considerable wealth was transferred to Seddon in exchange for the purchase of annuities worth about £150 a year. In the late summer of 1911 Miss Barrow's health began to deteriorate and by September she had taken to her bed, laid low with diarrhoea and sickness. Despite instructions from her doctor to go to hospital she remained in the increasingly uncongenial bedroom. Flypaper impregnated with arsenic was ordered to control the flies. Shortly before her death Miss Barrow rewrote her will and made Seddon her sole executor.

On 14th September Miss Barrow died and, remarkably, the doctor wrote out a death certificate without visiting the corpse. Seddon quickly arranged a cheap funeral for the following afternoon with burial in a public grave. He excused the haste of the funeral saying that he had a slack business day. Not surprisingly, Miss Barrow's family, who had not been informed of her death, were suspicious and informed the police. Meanwhile the Seddons had been busy spending gold coin. On 15th November the body was exhumed and found to be in a remarkably well-preserved state. It was examined by Dr Spilsbury who had made his reputation the previous year with the case of Doctor Crippen. Arsenic poisoning was diagnosed. On 4th December Mr Seddon was arrested and said, memorably: "Absurd. What a terrible charge ... It is the first of our family that has ever been accused of such a crime." Mrs Seddon was arrested on 15th January 1912.

The police case was not strong and the evidence largely circumstantial. Any evidence that was offered against him was equally applicable to his wife. However, Frederick Seddon gave a terrible impression in the dock of arrogance, coldness and parsimony. The jury clearly believed that he could have committed the crime. However, it is hard to disagree with Seddon's own statement: "There was no motive for me to commit such a crime ... I would have to be a greedy inhuman monster ... as I was in good financial circumstances ..." Seddon made a final appeal to the judge, citing their shared Freemasonry, but to no avail. The judge sentenced him to hang and despite a 250,000-strong petition Seddon was hanged on 18th April 1912. Curiously, Mr Seddon never confessed, but his wife, who was found not guilty, did do so, blaming it all on her husband. She later retracted the confession, explaining that it had been made for money!

OPPOSITE LEFT: The house, 63 Tollington Park.

ABOVE: Seddon looking out of a window during a lunchbreak at court.

LEFT: Seddon arriving at court and during the court case.

GEORGE SMITH

CASE KNOWN AS THE BRIDES IN THE BATH

MURDER OF BESSIE MUNDY ON 11TH JULY 1912

ALICE BURNHAM ON 12TH DECEMBER 1913

MARGARET LOFTY ON 18TH DECEMBER 1914

TRIAL OPENED 22ND JUNE 1915

HANGED 13TH AUGUST 1915

George Smith combined extraordinary charisma with extreme callousness. For 20 years he charmed, swindled and eventually murdered his way across Britain, preying on lonely, vulnerable, middle-class women. His success gives an insight into the lives of quiet desperation that many women were living in Edwardian England.

Born in the East End in 1872, Smith engaged in petty crime from an early age with periods in a reformatory and eventually prison. His first wife, Caroline Thornhill, described him as having a strong aversion to work, and "extraordinary power … in his eyes … that seemed to rob you of your will". At the start of his career Smith persuaded women to steal from their employers. He later moved on to seducing, marrying and defrauding lonely women. He used a number of pseudonyms including George Love, George Rose and Henry Williams. His progression to murder began in 1910 when he met Bessie Mundy while walking in Clifton in Bristol. Bessie had inherited £2,500 from her bank manager father in a trust managed by her uncle. Her uncle regarded her as a fool with money and restricted her to an allowance of £8 a month. The couple soon absconded to Weymouth where they married. Because of the trust Smith could only access £135 of Bessie's fortune. When he had obtained this money he disappeared, leaving a note accusing Bessie of having passed on a social disease.

Bessie might have lived had it not been for a chance meeting between the two a year later on the Weston-super-Mare seafront. Bessie, clearly not one to learn from experience, agreed to go back to Smith. The second time around Smith took legal advice and discovered that if Bessie made a will and died he would inherit her fortune.

Bessie's fate was sealed. A zinc bath was purchased and Smith took Bessie to a doctor explaining that she had been suffering from fits. The next day Bessie was found drowned in her bath. There was no police investigation, no post-mortem, and Bessie was buried in a common grave. The family tried to contest the will but six months later Smith was £2,500 richer. He was now wealthy and should have been able to relax. Instead, he now believed that he had found a new source of easy money. The next victim was Alice Burnham. Her father was suspicious and wrote to Smith asking for details of his life. Smith replied with the vituperative: "Sir – In answer to your application concerning my parentage… my mother was a bus-horse, my father a cab-driver, my sister a rough rider …" Clearly he was not trying to charm the in-laws. Alice was insured for £500, her savings emptied, the will drawn up, the doctor called and the bath readied. Alice was drowned on the 12th and buried on the 15th with a verdict of accidental death. Smith's last victim was Margaret Lofty, daughter of a deceased clergyman. The same pattern of marriage, life insurance, bath and drowning followed. Margaret was married on 17th December and dead by the 21st. He was reported to have played "Nearer Thy God to Thee" as she drowned. Smith was undone by the simple report in the *News of the World*, "Bride's Tragic Fate on the Day After Wedding". Alice Burnham's father and landlady saw the similarities between the deaths and contacted the police who began inquiries across the country. Margaret Lofty's body was exhumed and examined by the already legendary Dr

Bernard Spilsbury. Shortly after, Smith was arrested on the holding charge of bigamy. On 23rd March 1915 Smith was charged with the murder of the three women.

Spilsbury had a problem. Although it could be shown that the women had not died because of fits or other natural causes, how was it possible for them to drown without any signs of a struggle? The answer was provided when Spilsbury surprised an unfortunate woman diver who had been helping with the experiments. He suddenly pulled her feet, causing her head to submerge. She lost consciousness and it took half an hour to revive the poor woman. The experiment was repeated to great effect at the trial. The jury took just 20 minutes to come to the guilty verdict, and George Smith was hanged, unrepentant, at Maidstone gaol on 13th August 1915.

OPPOSITE LEFT: George Smith in court.

ABOVE LEFT: George Smith and Bessie Mundy.

ABOVE RIGHT: Caroline Thornhill.

ABOVE RIGHT BOTTOM: Alice Burnham.

BELOW: Marriage certificate of Margaret Lofty and John Lloyd, the name that Smith had assumed.

14. Marriage solemnized at	The Register Office			in the County of	Bath and Somerset		
in the District of	Bath						
1 When Married.	2 Name and Surname.	3 Age.	4 Condition.	5 Rank or Profession.	6 Residence at the time of Marriage.	7 Father's Name and Surname.	8 Rank or Profession of Father.
Seventeenth December	John Lloyd	38 years	Bachelor	Land Agent	Balkeith House 4 Stanley Road Bath	John Arthur Lloyd (deceased)	Land Agent
	Margaret	38	Spinster		Balkeith House 4 Stanley Road	Fitzroy Fuller Lofty	Clerk in Holy Orders

HAROLD GREENWOOD

The murder of Mabel Greenwood involved a
great web of complexity and a fascinating cast of
characters including the solicitor, his daughter,
the maid, the nurse and the doctor. The case
turned on the lack of financial motive. Mabel
Greenwood's fortune went to the children. The
only person who might have had a financial
motive was the daughter Irene! Her evidence
would be vital in the acquittal of her father.

Harold Greenwood, a solicitor, moved to
Kidwelly in southwest Wales from Yorkshire in
1898 with his wife Mabel. She was well liked
but he always struggled to fit in. They had four
children, the eldest of whom was Irene who had
come of age by 1919. By this time Mabel was
47 and had been in poor health. On 15th June
the family settled down to Sunday lunch of a
roast followed by gooseberry tart washed down
with a bottle of burgundy. During the afternoon
Mabel complained of diarrhoea and sickness.
Her husband gave her some brandy but this
made her violently sick whereupon he went for
Doctor Griffiths who prescribed more brandy. At
no time did either of the men seem particularly
concerned and there was no sense of urgency
in the treatment. A nurse, Miss
Gladys Jones, was sent for but she
found Mabel collapsed and sent
again for Doctor Griffiths. Despite
his wife's worsening condition
he went to bed. During the night
the daughter Irene implored her
father to get the doctor again.
Unaccountably, he showed
no haste on his mission and
returned after an hour without
the doctor, whom he claimed he
could not raise. The nurse went
herself and successfully raised
the doctor who gave her some
pills. However, it was all too
late, and Mabel died at 3.30 in
the morning. Doctor Griffiths
certified the death to be due to heart disease,
something that made his casual treatment even
more curious.

Rumours filled the town and the sense
of concern and outrage only grew when

Greenwood remarried his deceased wife's nurse, Gladys Jones, just three months later. Despite the rumours it wasn't until April of the next year that the body was exhumed in a remarkably good condition and found to have no sign of heart failure. There were, however, signs of arsenic to which Greenwood commented: "Oh dear". The trial opened in June 1920 and focused on conflicting evidence from the staff and the daughter Irene Greenwood. The parlourmaid testified that Greenwood had spent 30 minutes alone in the china pantry, giving plenty of time to add the arsenic to the burgundy, and the housekeeper reported that only Mabel had drunk the wine. Irene was sure that her father was cleaning the car at the time and that she had also drunk the wine. There was also no motive for the murder. Greenwood lost all his wife's substantial fortune through her death and the inheritance went to the children. Enough confusion was evident to make a verdict of guilty impossible.

Greenwood's reputation never recovered and he had to move away to Herefordshire, where he died eight years later.

"... IT MEANS THAT THE LOVE
OF A HUSBAND FOR HIS WIFE IS
SOMETHING IMPROPER ... AND THAT
THE LOVE OF A WOMAN FOR HER
LOVER, ILLICIT AND CLANDESTINE, IS
SOMETHING GREAT AND NOBLE."

THE JUDGE COMMENTING ON THE RELATIONSHIP

BETWEEN THE MARRIED EDITH THOMPSON AND HER LOVER

FREDERICK BYWATEORS:

1920-1929

1920 PERCY TOPLIS: Best known as the "monocled mutineer", he survived by his remarkable ability to impersonate the upper classes.

1921 MAJOR HERBERT ARMSTRONG: The story of the murder of his wife, gaining him the dubious distinction of being the only solicitor to hang.

1922 RONALD TRUE: Sentenced to hang by the jury but reprieved by the home secretary due to True's insanity.

1922 FREDERICK BYWATERS AND EDITH THOMPSON: The murder of Percy Thompson by his wife and her lover.

1924 PATRICK MAHON: The brutal murder and dismemberment of Emily Kaye in an Eastbourne bungalow.

1924 NORMAN THORNE: Chicken farmer commits murder most foul.

1927 JOHN ROBINSON: The murder and dismemberment of Minnie Bonati.

1927 FREDERICK BROWN AND PATRICK KENNEDY: The cold-blooded shooting of PC Gutteridge when he stopped the gunmen on a quiet Essex country lane.

LEFT: Bywaters and Thomson, the lovers..

PERCY TOPLIS

MURDER OF TAXI DRIVER GEORGE SPICER ON 24TH APRIL 1920

SHOT RESISTING ARREST IN CUMBRIA JUNE 1920

Percy Toplis is one of the few fugitives of the last century who died "resisting arrest" and didn't face the courts for their major crimes. His impersonations of the upper classes caused him to become notorious and dangerous in what was a class-bound society undergoing massive upheaval. They helped earn him his nickname, the "monocled mutineer".

Born in 1896 to a mining family Toplis had been in trouble for most of his life. It took the First World War to move his misdemeanours onto a higher level when in 1915 he joined the Royal Army Medical Corps as a stretcher bearer. Toplis had a varied career punctuated by frequent desertions. He invented a dangerously sick pregnant wife and was sent on leave to Britain. He was given a hero's welcome back at the Miners Welfare in Nottingham and was even photographed for the *Nottingham Post*. Toplis decided not to return to the front and instead headed off to London where he impersonated the officer class with his trademark gold

MOTOR CRIME VICTIM BURIED: HUNT FOR 'WANTED' MAN

Private Toplis, the "wanted" man, in officer's uniform. The photograph was supplied to *The Daily Mirror* by the Andover police.

The body of the shot motor driver was brought to Salisbury Cemetery in a car, and thirty Salisbury taxi-drivers followed the remains of their late comrade to the grave.

Bearing the wreath-laden coffin into the cemetery, followed by the mourners.

Private Percy Toplis, who is believed to be in London.

A profile portrait of Toplis. His height is 5ft. 8½in.

The home of Mrs. Toplis, the "wanted" man's mother. At Alfreton, Derbyshire.

Members of the Royal Ancient Order of Buffaloes, to which Spicer belonged, attended, and accorded their dead brother the ceremonial rites of the Buffs.

Sidney George Spicer, the victim of the Hampshire motor tragedy, was buried with simple ceremony yesterday at Salisbury. A pathetic figure among the mourners was the dead man's wife, who had to be assisted from the graveside, weeping and almost swoon-ing. Interest now centres in the police hunt for Private Percy Toplis, who is wanted in connection with the tragedy. Remarkable stories are told of his extraordinary personality. He is the central figure of many adventures.—(*Daily Mirror* photographs.)

monocle. Part of the Toplis myth says that he took part in the Étaples mutiny. It seems unlikely that he was even in Europe at the time but his undermining of the class system by impersonating an officer was almost as damaging. After the war he re-enlisted in the Royal Army Service Corp and started running a petrol rationing scam with taxi drivers at his camp near Andover. In an argument Toplis shot one of the drivers, George Spicer, with a Webley revolver, which he had retained from the First World War, and again deserted. He was tried *in absentia* and found guilty of murder by the inquest.

He was tracked down to a bothy below the Lecht near Tomintoul in the Cairgorms in northeast Scotland. When challenged he shot a policeman and gamekeeper and cycled away to Aberdeen singing, "Good-byee, don't sigh-ee, wipe the tear, baby dear, from your eye-ee …". From Aberdeen he took a train to Carlisle where he stayed the night with the Border Regiment at Carlisle Castle. In the morning he walked away towards Penrith where he was spoken to by a local policeman who became suspicious and returned with armed reinforcements including the chief constable's civilian son, Norman de Courcy-Parry. Toplis was shot dead near Romanway in Cumbria. The exact circumstances are disputed but a jury later gave a verdict of justifiable homicide.

Toplis' whole life remains shrouded in mystery as well as his death. The legend is sure to continue. Paul McGann, who played Toplis in the BBC drama *The Monocled Mutineer*, said of him: "He became a figurehead … like Robin Hood. His story is a mixture of fact, fiction and folklore, which adds to the mystery around him. The context is still absolutely fascinating. World War I changed the British way of life. The officer class, the idea of elders and betters, died on the fields of the Somme. Toplis cocked a snook at all that because he played officers and took the piss out of officers."

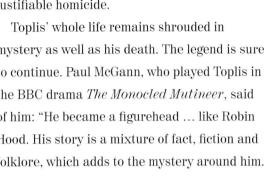

OPPOSITE
LEFT: Toplis as featured in the *Daily Mirror*.

BELOW LEFT: Norman de Courcy-Parry, who helped reconnoitre the route.

BELOW RIGHT: Toplis in civilian clothes.

MAJOR HERBERT ARMSTRONG

MURDER OF WIFE ON 21ST FEBRUARY 1921
TRIED 3RD APRIL 1922
HANGED GLOUCESTER 31ST MAY 1922

Major Herbert Armstrong has the distinction of being the only solicitor to hang in British legal history. He seems in part to have been inspired by the recent acquittal of Welsh country solicitor Harold Greenwood who was declared not guilty of murdering his wife by the use of arsenic. However, it is one thing to poison one's wife, it is quite another to poison a fellow solicitor as Armstrong would find to his cost.

The Armstrongs lived in Hay-on-Wye. The major's wife, although intelligent, had been suffering from severe mental problems and had spent the latter half of 1920 in an asylum. Mrs Armstrong had been an authoritarian figure in the household and while she was away her husband had enjoyed a less than puritan lifestyle including an affair with Mrs Gale, a widow in London, and the contraction of a social disease. In November that year, soon after he'd read of the acquittal of Harold Greenwood, the major started agitating for the return of his wife from the asylum, arguing that her health had improved. Although it seems that there had been little improvement, she arrived back home on 22nd January 1921 to a house that had been well stocked up with arsenic, strangely a long time ahead of the dandelion season. By 21st February Mrs Armstrong was dead and a mystified Doctor Hincks had diagnosed heart disease brought on by nephritis and gastritis. If the major had left things at that he might well have joined Harold Greenwood as a contented widower.

Instead, a large number of severe gastric complaints afflicted the professional classes of

FAR LEFT:
Armstrong
arrives at court.

LEFT: The
Chemist's shop
where the
arsenic was
purchased.

Hay-on-Wye, including rival solicitor Mr Martin. Martin was sent what he subsequently learned to be an arsenic-laced box of chocolates, and later a poisoned scone was passed to him by Major Armstrong. He not unnaturally became suspicious and spent the next six months avoiding numerous invitations to tea with his professional colleague. The partially consumed box of chocolates would be a leading exhibit at the later trial.

The poor gastric health of many people associated with the major started to arouse the suspicions of Mrs Armstrong's physician, Doctor Hincks. Hinks was spurred to contact the Home Office, who instigated a secret police investigation. The police found the chocolates to have traces of arsenic.

On 31st December Major Armstrong was arrested for the attempted murder of Mr Martin, and on 3rd January 1922 the body of Mrs Armstrong was exhumed and examined by Bernard Spilsbury who found a lethal amount of arsenic in her body. The trial began on 3rd April 1922 with the major confident of acquittal but his defence wilted under the cross-examination of Mr Justice Derby who showed that Armstrong had no adequate explanation for the small but lethal amounts of arsenic on his person and in his office. He was found guilty and hanged on 31st May 1922.

OPPOSITE LEFT:
Major and Mrs
Armstrong on
their wedding
day (not an
ecstatic-looking
couple).

LEFT: Mr and
Mrs Martin,
whom Armstrong
attempted to
poison and Dr
Hincks, who
first alerted the
Home Office.

RONALD TRUE

MURDER OF GERTRUDE YATES ON 6TH MARCH 1922

TRIAL OPENED 1ST MAY 1922

FOUND GUILTY AND SENTENCED TO HANG BUT REPRIEVED BY THE HOME SECRETARY DUE TO INSANITY

The case of Ronald True is the classic example of the reluctance of a British jury to find a defendant insane. Despite the defence being able to call two psychiatrists and the prison doctor to testify to the insanity of Ronald True the prosecution only had to put the defendant in the witness box to satisfy the jury. British juries tended to believe that however mad the defendant may seem, they were not so mad that they didn't know what they were doing.

Ronald True had experienced a life of failure, folly and petty crime. His rich stepfather had subsidized a career that had included being invalided out of the RAF in the war. He crashed on his first solo flight and suffered brain injuries. True was described as a "very bad pilot" and having a "a feverish air about him ... he seemed deficient in common sense". During the war he acquired a morphine addiction. After leaving the RAF he travelled widely and in New York met and married a young actress, Frances Roberts, with whom he had a son. On returning to Britain his actions became increasingly erratic, criminal and influenced by his growing morphine addiction. His developing paranoia led to a belief that a second Ronald True was stalking him and would bring about his demise.

He became obsessed with a young call girl, Gertrude Yates, who worked under the name of Olive Young. He would turn up at her house late at night and pester to be let in. Fatefully she relented at about midnight on Sunday 5th March. The next morning True walked casually

out of the bedroom when the cleaner arrived and commented that Miss Young should not be woken because they'd had a late night. Eventually the cleaner found a scene of devastation and Miss Young dead. True failed to take any significant measures to hide his guilt and was picked up in the evening at the theatre by the police. His defence attempted to plead insanity but this was rejected by

OPPOSITE LEFT: Gertrude Yates, otherwise known as Olive Young.

LEFT: Miss Emily Steele (middle) who found the body of Miss Yates.

BELOW: Ronald True in court.

the jury, who found him guilty of murder, and he was duly sentenced to death. Juries rarely believed that any murderer did not pass what were known as the McNaughten Rules: "He knew what he was doing and he knew it was wrong." While in prison True was examined again by psychiatrists on the orders of the home secretary and found to be insane. The sentence was commuted to a lifetime in Broadmoor. This kind of intervention by the home secretary was always controversial, with the public having a strong aversion to psychiatrists intervening to save murderers from the gallows.

FREDERICK BYWATERS AND EDITH THOMPSON

MURDER OF PERCY THOMPSON ON 3RD OCTOBER 1922

TRIAL OPENED 6TH DECEMBER 1922

HANGED 9TH JANUARY 1923

The case of Frederick Bywaters' and Edith Thompson's murder of Percy Thompson captivated and appalled Britain. Edith Thompson became one of only 17 women to be hanged in the 20th century. A biased performance from the judge and therefore a mistrial played an important part in the erosion of support for capital punishment. With the trial of Ruth Ellis it would demonstrate the danger of old men with all their insecurities presiding over the trials of young women.

The Thompsons had been married for four years before Freddy Bywaters, a 19-year-old merchant seaman, entered their lives. He was an old school friend of Edith and her sister Avis. The four of them went on holiday to the Isle of Wight. Foolishly, Percy tempted fate by inviting Freddy to lodge with them. Quickly a passionate relationship developed between the romantically inclined Edith and the young and naive Frederick. Percy became aware of the situation and Freddy was forced to leave. However, the relationship continued and Freddy's frequent trips to sea and the correspondence that flowed only seemed to intensify matters. The letters were full of passion, fantasy, plans for the future, allusions to miscarriages or abortions and, most crucially for the future discussions in court, how to get rid of Percy. Interestingly, much of the correspondence was not produced at the trial, presumably because it was judged too salacious with topics such as menstruation and orgasm. Edith would only be charged with murder after the discovery of the letters.

The murder was committed at around midnight on 3rd October as the Thompsons walked back from the station after a night at the theatre. Percy Thompson was confronted and after a short scuffle fatally stabbed. Witnesses reported a woman shouting, "Oh don't, oh don't". At first Edith believed herself to be detained only as a witness but when she saw Bywaters (by police design) at the police station she reportedly said: "Oh God! Oh God! What can I do? Why did he do it? I didn't want him to do it. I must tell the truth." Freddy, when told by the police that he and Mrs Thompson were to be charged with murder, replied: "Why her ... Mrs Thompson was not aware of my movements." The trial opened on 5th December 1922.

Although her counsel advised her not to take the stand Edith was confident that she could carry the day. However, her vanity caused her to overestimate her skills and she appeared as a calculating adulteress who had manipulated the younger man. This overwhelmed other evidence from witnesses; the failure to find any evidence of poisoning from the autopsy and the testimony of Bywaters absolving Mrs Thompson of any blame. By modern standards the summing up

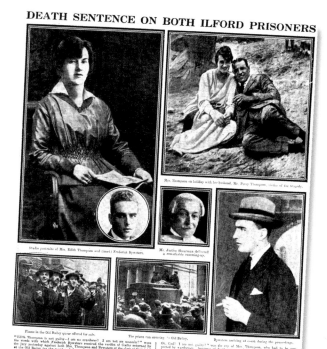

DEATH SENTENCE ON BOTH ILFORD PRISONERS

from the judge was prejudicial, with comments such as "... it means that the love of a husband for his wife is something improper ... and that the love of a woman for her lover, illicit and clandestine, is something great and noble". Both defendants were found guilty and despite a million-signature petition to the home secretary, William Bridgeman, they were both hanged. Edith Thompson was dragged to her execution in a drugged state unable to believe that the sentence was real. The executioner, John Ellis, retired soon after. Many believe that the trauma of the execution was a contributing factor to this decision and his later suicide.

It is perhaps a good moment to reflect on the influence that most home secretaries have had on the cause of justice. Many of the great injustices of the criminal system, including the executions of Edith Thompson, Derek Bentley and Ruth Ellis, were allowed to go ahead by right-wing politicians determined to make an impact with their stern interpretation of the law. It is one of life's ironies that these men hurried through the abolition of the very penalty that they had so stringently upheld.

OPPOSITE LEFT: Mr and Mrs Thompson.

ABOVE RIGHT: Death sentence to both Ilford prisoners.

LEFT: *Daily Mirror* front page, January 1923.

PATRICK MAHON

MURDER OF EMILY KAYE ON OR ABOUT 13TH APRIL 1924

TRIAL OPENED 15TH JULY 1924

HANGED 9TH SEPTEMBER 1924

Patrick Mahon achieved notoriety through the gruesome disposal of his victim, Emily Kaye. By placing her dismembered body in a trunk he created a new fashion for murderers which became especially popular on the south coast. The case led to a development in police procedure. When the pathologist Sir Bernard Spilsbury arrived at the scene he found the police picking up samples with their bare hands because they had no equipment. In the future they would always take a "murder bag" to such scenes.

Patrick Mahon was a married Irishman, who had a way with the ladies and a criminal record from his part in a bank raid. Mahon's life was just starting to become complicated. His wife had become suspicious of his frequent absences and he'd just met a new lover, Ethel Duncan, whom he'd invited to his recently rented bungalow just outside Eastbourne. Already living in Eastbourne was another lover, Emily Kaye, pregnant and looking forward to a new life with Mahon in South Africa. This was to be financed by her £600 savings, which she had already given to him. Unknown to Emily he'd already spent the savings and he didn't want to leave his wife.

He saw his only way out as the murder of Emily Kaye and for that purpose he'd bought a saw and large kitchen knife. Emily was murdered by Mahon around 15th April, probably with the small axe that was later found buried in the coal shed, and her body dragged into the spare bedroom. Mahon would claim at the trial that Kaye had attacked him and in the ensuing struggle had struck her head on the coal scuttle.

The next morning he returned to London to meet his new lover, Ethel Duncan, and invited

OPPOSITE ABOVE LEFT: Emily Kaye, the victim.

ABOVE RIGHT: Patrick Mahon, the muderer.

LEFT: The bungalow.

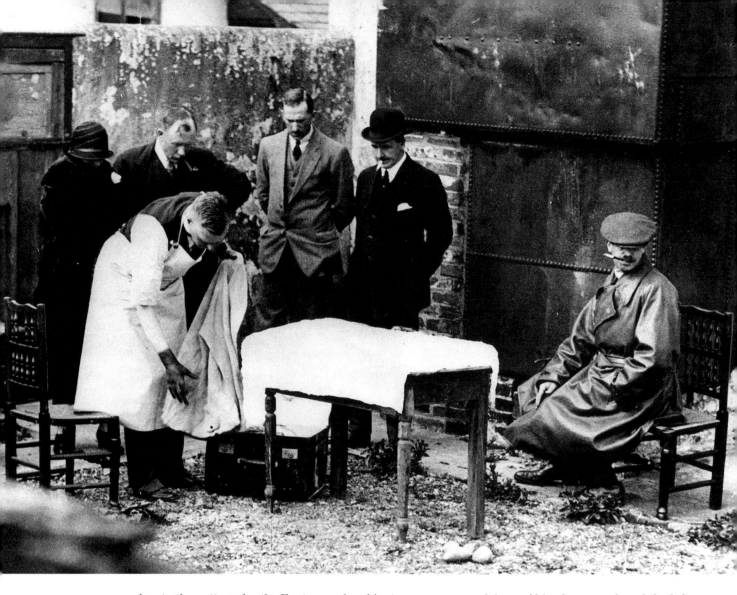

her to the cottage for the Easter weekend just a couple of days later. Good Friday was spent dismembering Emily and putting her in the trunk. Later the same day he met Ethel and brought her back to the cottage and spent the weekend with her. She saw the trunk but Mahon reassured her that it contained valuable books he was storing for a friend. After she left on the Monday he carried on with the disposal of Emily, cutting off her head and burning it on the fire. On his return trip to London he threw parts of the body out of the train window. He made his fatal error by depositing at Waterloo Station the Gladstone bag which had been carrying parts of the body and still contained bloody items of clothing and a knife. Mahon's wife, who by now

was suspicious of his absences, found the left luggage ticket in a coat and gave it to a friend who was a former member of the transport police. He looked at the contents of the bag and informed the police, who returned it to left luggage and waited for Mahon to appear. On his return he was arrested as he left the station. At first Mahon claimed the bloody contents of the bag were the remains of meat he had back for his dogs; but gradually his story spilled out.

The trial was particularly grisly, with some of the jurors being made ill by the graphic evidence and having to be replaced. Sir Bernard Spilsbury testified for the prosecution and demolished Mahon's claims that Emily Kaye's death was an accident. The fortunate

lover Ethel Duncan gave a particularly tearful performance in the witness box. Mahon was quiet and seemed resigned to his fate when the judge was summing up, but on hearing the guilty verdict jumped up and complained of the "unfairness" of it all. He was hanged at Wandsworth on 9th September 1924. The cottage on the coast became famous and was bought by a group of entrepreneurs who did a great trade charging a shilling a visit to ghoulish tourists.

NORMAN THORNE

MURDER OF ELSIE CAMERON ON 5TH DECEMBER 1924

TRIAL OPENED 4TH MARCH 1925

HANGED 22ND APRIL 1925

Elsie Cameron was murdered and dismembered just three months after the hanging of Patrick Mahon. Newspaper cuttings found in Thorne's hut showed that he had taken a close interest in the case. Thorne though lacked the calculation and menace of Mahon. In many ways the domestic tragedy of the case owes more to Crippen without the class, passion and travel. Yet again the recently knighted Sir Bernard Spilsbury was at the heart of the case and his "evidence" was crucial in sending Thorne to the gallows.

Norman Thorne and Elsie Cameron met in 1920, he an 18-year-old electrician and she a 26-year-old typist concerned that her chance of marriage was passing her by. They became engaged and he set up a chicken farm near Crowborough in Sussex. The farm was not a success and Elsie struggled to hold down a job because of what seemed to be psychological problems. She was keen to marry but he was increasingly wary because he'd met a local girl, Bessie Coldicott, who seemed to offer a more simple life. Elsie saw her world disintegrating and put increasing amounts of pressure on Norman to fulfil his responsibilities, telling him that she was pregnant. He was more than a little doubtful on this point as he maintained that they had never fully consummated the relationship. He had been advised by his father to play for time. She walked to the chicken farm on 5th December 1924 determined to stay until she and Norman were married. Elsie was not seen again and when Elsie's father enquired of her whereabouts on 10th December, Thorne denied that she had ever arrived at the farm.

Her father informed the police of her

THE DAILY MIRROR, Tuesday, March 17, 1925.

DENNISTOUN CASE : COLONEL IN THE WITNESS BOX

Daily Mirror

THE DAILY PICTURE PAPER WITH THE LARGEST NET SALE

DEATH PACT OF INVENTOR AND WIFE

No. 6,663   Registered at the G.P.O. as a Newspaper.   TUESDAY, MARCH 17, 1925.   One Penny

THORNE FOUND GUILTY—SENTENCE OF DEATH

Elsie Cameron, the young London typist, and fiancee of Thorne, who yesterday was found guilty at her murder.

Miss Elizabeth Coldicott, the young woman with whom Thorne, in his evidence, stated he was in love.

Mr. Justice Finlay leaving court after passing his first sentence of death.

Norman Thorne, the twenty-four-year-old poultry farmer, sentenced to death.

Miss Elizabeth Coldicott (right) leaving yesterday after Norman Thorne was found guilty of the murder of Miss Elsie Cameron and sentenced to death. Accompanied by a male relative, she made her way towards the station in a state of collapse after hearing the verdict and was followed by a section of the throng assembled outside the court. Some women in the crowd made a demonstration, while others were not in sympathy with this attitude. Two women were in a fracas.

disappearance and on 15th January 1925 they accumulated enough evidence to arrest Thorne. An oxo-cube tin was found containing Elsie's watch and jewellery. Soon after, Thorne admitted that Elsie's dismembered body was buried under the chicken shed. He claimed that Elsie had hanged herself when he'd gone out, but Sir Bernard Spilsbury contradicted his claims by showing that there was no evidence of rope marks on the neck. Although this was challenged by the defence their case was undermined by the gruesome evidence of the dismemberment. It proved impossible to claim that the whole incident was an accident when the jury could see the hacksaw that had been used to dispose of the body. Without the dismemberment Thorne may well have avoided the noose. He was hanged at Wandsworth on 22nd April 1925.

JOHN ROBINSON

THE MURDER OF MINNIE BONATI ON 4TH MAY 1927
TRIAL STARTED ON 11TH JULY 1927
HANGED 12TH AUGUST 1927

John Robinson continues the dubious tradition of dismembering victims and hiding the remains in a trunk. It is surely not a coincidence that Robinson bought the knife he used to dismember Minnie from the same store that Mahon had bought his knife and saw. Strangely, along with Mahon, he also mentioned the coal scuttle as the domestic appliance that had caused the "accidental death" of the victim. A truly remarkable coincidence for a seemingly innocuous object. The case also displays the increasing professionalism of the police, as the investigation required exceptional skills of detection.

Robinson was an estate agent whose business was going bust. He seems to have picked up prostitute Minnie Bonati and taken her back to his office where she was murdered. He then bought a trunk and a knife and proceeded to dismember and parcel up Minnie. The trunk was taken to Charing Cross Station where it was deposited in the left luggage office. A few days later the smell prompted staff to call the police, who opened the trunk and found its grisly contents. The only evidence was a pair of shoes, a handbag and knickers with a tab showing the name P Holt. The knickers were traced to Chelsea to an owner who was still alive. She had employed ten servants over the previous two years, of whom the police traced all but Minnie Bonati who had gone missing on 4th May. The police next traced the trunk back to a

OPPOSITE
LEFT BOTTOM: The trunk
that held the
dismembered
body, shoes
and handbag of
Minnie Bonati.

OPPOSITE LEFT
TOP: Minnie
Bonati.

LEFT: Charing
Cross left
luggage office.

BELOW: The label
that allowed
identification of
the body in the
trunk.

second-hand dealer and traced the taxi driver who had delivered it to Charing Cross. He identified a block of offices, 86 Rochester Row, as the address he had collected the trunk from and the police discovered that one tenant, John Robinson, had gone missing.

They went to his flat in Kennington, but he had left. They did find a telegram directing them to "Robinson, Greyhound Hotel, Hammersmith" where they found a Mrs Robinson who worked there. However, she was not the real Mrs Robinson as she was found to have married John Robinson bigamously. On learning this she agreed to help the police entrap her "husband". He was arrested at the Elephant and Castle on 19th May but denied any involvement and was not identified by any of the witnesses in the identity parades. Chief Inspector Cornish who had led the investigation went back to the contents of the trunk and on a hunch had a duster washed. The word "Greyhound" was

revealed and on a further investigation of the flat a bloodstained match was discovered wedged in a wicker basket. With the evidence accumulating, Robinson broke down and made a statement: "I done it and I cut her up". The trial began on 11th July with Robinson claiming that it was all an accident. When asked why he didn't go to the police, Robinson said: "Because I was in a blue funk and did not know what to do." The jury were again impressed by the evidence of Sir Bernard Spilsbury and found Robinson guilty. He was sentenced to death and hanged on 12th August 1927.

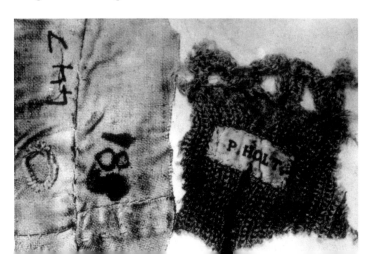

FREDERICK BROWNE AND PATRICK KENNEDY

THE MURDER OF PC GUTTERIDGE ON 27TH SEPTEMBER 1927

TRIAL OPENED 23RD APRIL 1928

HANGED 31ST MAY 1928

The murder of PC Gutteridge marked a coming of age for the science of ballistics with the expert Robert Churchill providing crucial evidence about the exact gun used in the murder. The case also shows the prevalence of the folklore myth of the evil eye. PC Gutteridge was shot through both eyes in the mistaken belief that the eye holds its last image after death.

On the night of 27th September 1927 Doctor Lovell's Morris Cowley car was stolen from his house in Billericay. That same night PC Gutteridge was walking his beat in rural Essex when he decided to wave down a speeding car. The car stopped and he leaned through the window to question those inside. He had a pencil in hand as if to take notes. He was then shot twice and fatally wounded. His assailants

got out of the car and he was shot a further two times through both eyes. The car was driven off and left in Brixton where it was found the next day by the police. They also found an empty cartridge case which ballistics examination later showed had distinctive scarring caused by a fault with the gun. Robert Churchill, the

OPPOSITE LEFT:
PC Gutteridge.

FAR LEFT: Police
at the scene of
the shooting.
The bucket
marks the
spot where PC
Gutteridge was
mudered.

LEFT: Patrick
Kennedy and
Frederick
Browne.

ballistics expert, was also able to show that the shots were fired by a Webley revolver. A huge investigation was launched focusing on well-known South London criminals including Browne and Kennedy who had a string of previous convictions.

Browne owned a garage repair business and employed Kennedy at the time of the shooting. After two months Browne must have felt that he would get away with the murder. He'd been involved with a string of burglaries and car thefts. On return from a trip to Devon the police pounced in connection with a stolen Vauxhall car. They must have received some intelligence because they were well armed. In the garage they found loaded Webley revolvers and cartridges. Kennedy, unaware of Browne's arrest, was picked up a few days later. He attempted to shoot the arresting policeman and only failed because he'd forgotten to release the safety catch. Kennedy gave a long statement regarding his involvement in the shooting of PC Gutteridge and testified in court. Browne always proclaimed his innocence. The ballistics evidence was clear and crucial, and both men were found guilty and condemned to death. They were hanged on 31ˢᵗ May 1928.

FAR LEFT: The
stolen Morris
Cowley.

LEFT: Browne's
revolver.

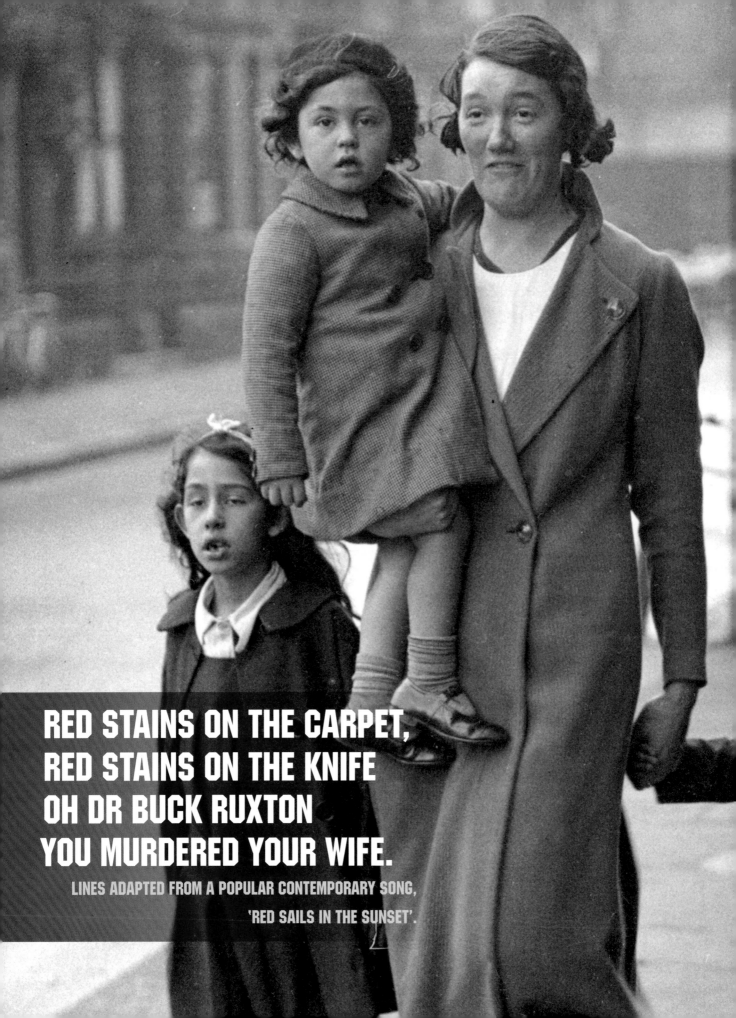

**RED STAINS ON THE CARPET,
RED STAINS ON THE KNIFE
OH DR BUCK RUXTON
YOU MURDERED YOUR WIFE.**

LINES ADAPTED FROM A POPULAR CONTEMPORARY SONG,
'RED SAILS IN THE SUNSET'.

1930-1939

1934 TONY MANCINI: Two bodies in trunks found in one town in a single year. The story of the death of Violet Kaye.

1935 DOCTOR BUCK RUXTON: The murder of his common law wife Isabella Kerr and maid Mary Jane Rogerson.

1935 CHARLOTTE BRYANT: The murder of her husband Frederick by poisoning with arsenic.

1938 EDWARD CHAPLIN: Charged with the murder of his lover's husband.

LEFT: Dr Ruxton's children during the trial.

TONY MANCINI

MURDER OF VIOLET KAYE MAY 1934 (ALSO KNOWN AS THE BRIGHTON TRUNK MURDERS)

TRIAL OPENED DECEMBER 1934

ACQUITTED

The south coast of England has already played a disproportionately large part in this book compared with the rest of the United Kingdom but the year 1934 was to enhance its reputation still further, earning Brighton the title "Queen of Slaughtering Places". Within two months the police had two "dismembered body and trunk disposal" cases to deal with. One has never been solved and the other led to one of the greatest performances by a defence counsel and the acquittal of the relieved suspect.

The first Brighton trunk murder came to light on 17th June 1934 when workers in the left luggage office at Brighton Railway Station complained of a foul smell emanating from a trunk. The police were called and opened the case to discover the torso of a young woman. The next day the legs were found at King's Cross. The post-mortem conducted by Bernard Spilsbury found that she was about 25 years old, fit and five months pregnant. Despite a

THE DAILY MIRROR, Tuesday, July 17, 1934.

Daily Mirror
THE DAILY PICTURE NEWSPAPER WITH THE LARGEST NET SALE

No. 9,559 — Registered at the O.P.O. as a Newspaper. — TUESDAY, JULY 17, 1934 — One Penny

TRUNK CRIME: MAN WITH SCARRED LIP
Have You Seen Toni Mancini—the Dancing Waiter?
POLICE UNABLE TO LINK "CRIME No. 1" AND "CRIME No. 2"

All through the night an intensive police search was carried out for a man usually known as Toni Mancini, who, it is believed, can supply vital information concerning the discovery on Sunday of a second body in a trunk at Brighton.

The man, who has many aliases, is twenty-six and is well-known in Soho, where he has worked as a waiter. He is believed to be in London, although watch for him is being kept at all the ports.

An official police description says that he has a scar above the upper lip. He is very fond of dancing and frequents dance halls.

It has been established that the victim, who was found in an apartment house in Kemp-street, was murdered.

Although she has not yet been officially identified there is no doubt that she was a Mrs. Saunders, who during a long career as a stage dancer used the professional name of Violet or Violette Kaye. She belonged to London and had lately lived in Artillery-street and Lower Rock-gardens, Brighton.

Up to a late hour last night the police had not found any connecting link between it and the discovery of a woman's torso in a trunk at Brighton railway station.

A suggestion that the second might have been an imitative crime is disposed of by the fact that the woman believed to be Violette Kaye was murdered BEFORE the death of the woman found at the station.

Vital Differences

Whoever deposited the trunk containing the body of the young expectant mother in the railway station on Derby Day, June 6, took elaborate precautions to hide the victim's identity. In the latest discovery no such steps had been taken.

In the first case the body had been mutilated with some degree of skill, and although the legs were found on June 18 at King's Cross, the head and arms have never been discovered. In the second case there was no such mutilation.

In order to clarify the position, Scotland Yard yesterday issued the following statement:—

"On July 15, 1934, a trunk containing the complete dead body of a woman was found in a room at Kemp-street, Brighton.

"No attempt had been made to dismember the body, and at the moment it should be clearly understood that there are no grounds, so far as can be seen, to connect this discovery with the original Brighton trunk crime.

"To prevent confusion and loss of public interest in the original Brighton trunk crime it seems necessary that the public should be definitely informed that the head and the arms in the original Brighton trunk crime have not been discovered and that investigations and searches are being continued.

"Again, as a means of preventing confusion, perhaps the original Brighton trunk crime should be Brighton trunk crime No. 1 and the discovery on July 15, 1934, should be known as Brighton trunk crime No. 2."

Man's 5 Aliases

"In connection with the Brighton trunk crime No. 2, the police desire to interview Cecil Lois England, otherwise known as Tony England, Tony English, Antoni Pirillie, Antoni Luigni Mancini, and Jack Noytre.

"Aged about twenty-six years, height 5ft 6in., clean shaven, dark sallow complexion, hair black, well greased, parted on the left and notable scar above the lip on the right side of the mouth.

"Appearance of an Italian but is undoubtedly British; occupation, waiter or kitchen porter, very fond of dancing, frequents cheap cafes and cheap dance halls.

"Dressed in a dark pin stripe jacket with patch pockets, grey worsted trousers, black soft felt hat, brown check shirt with collar attached. Plain white silk tie, black suede shoes, old and shiny, carrying a black overcoat and fairly large expanding suitcase.

(Continued on page 3)

Violette Kaye (Mrs. Violet Saunders), a toe dancer, whose body was found in a trunk in the cellar of a house at Brighton.

The cafe at Brighton where Mancini worked.

Chief-Inspector Donaldson (centre) following Detective-Inspector Pelling, chief of Brighton C.I.D., from the house in Park-crescent where the dead woman lived.

Toni Mancini, the missing waiter, whom the police are anxious to interview.

investigation went no further.

Instead the police discovered another body in a trunk, this time in a flat in the town. They established this to be former dancer and prostitute Violet Kaye, who had been reported missing by one of her clients. Her lover and pimp, Tony Mancini, had been telling her friends and family that she'd left suddenly for Paris. People had been complaining of the unpleasant smell coming from his flat but he'd succeeded in blaming it on the neighbours. However, things were becoming unsustainable when the landlords told Mancini that the flats were to be redecorated. He then took off for London, leaving the painters to report the smell to the police. The police opened the trunk and discovered the unsavoury cause of the smell. Mancini was soon picked up in London, brought

massive police search her identity and the murderer were never discovered. There were rumours that the culprit was an abortionist, Dr Edward Massiah of Hove. The story is that when confronted with the evidence the doctor calmly wrote out a list of the names of the great and good of Brighton, clearly implying that these names would appear in any trial. The

OPPOSITE LEFT:
Daily Mirror
front page from
July 1934.

ABOVE: The
King's Cross
cloakroom.

ABOVE LEFT:
Violet Kaye, the
victim.

back to Brighton and charged with murder. Sir Bernard Spilsbury had reported that Violet had been killed by a blow or blows to the head with a hammer. Mancini's defence was that he'd found Violet dead when he returned to the flat. Mancini was fortunate in having one of the great defence counsels in Norman Birkett. He was the first counsel to sow doubts into the jury's minds about the evidence of Sir Bernard Spilsbury. Birkett created a plausible scenario of an accidental death, arguing that the fracture to Violet's head could have been caused by a fall. If Violet had experienced a violent death why should it have been Mancini who caused it and not one of her clients? In his closing address Birkett claimed that the case was "riddled with doubt".

The jury agreed and found Mancini not guilty. The verdict was not shared by the crowd outside who wanted to lynch Mancini. In later life Mancini gave contradictory interviews but appeared partially to admit his guilt. Whatever the truth, he was a lucky man. Few people escaped the pronouncements of the Home Office pathologist Sir Bernard Spilsbury.

ABOVE: Brighton station cloakroom.

RIGHT: The unfortunate staff of the Brighton left luggage office who had to deal with the trunk murder.

DOCTOR BUCK RUXTON

MURDER OF ISABELLA KERR AND MARY JANE ROGERSON ON 15TH SEPTEMBER 1935

ARRESTED 13TH OCTOBER 1935

TRIAL OPENED 2ND MARCH 1936

HANGED 12TH MAY 1936

The case of Doctor Ruxton is another example of a botched dismemberment and body disposal. So many murderers make one crucial error in the gruesome and, one must suspect stressful, task of body disposal. More than one error backed up by the brilliant application of the latest forensic techniques convicted Doctor Ruxton.

Buck Ruxton was born Buktyar Hakim in India. He changed his name in 1930 on opening his GP practice in Lancaster where he lived with his common law wife, Isabella Kerr, their three children and live-in maid, Mary Jane Rogerson. One could have predicted a sorry end from such a curious choice of name. Ruxton enjoyed a tempestuous relationship with his wife and was frequently consumed by jealous fits of rage which were witnessed by the maid. In one such rage he murdered his wife and the maid, who had had the misfortune of being a witness. He used his surgical skills to dismember the bodies in the bath, taking special care to remove the fingertips. The body pieces were wrapped in newspaper, packed in the boot of his car and driven to Gardenholm Linn, two miles north of

incensed victim took a note of the registration number and informed the police. The doctor was stopped later at a roadblock and must have been relieved that the problem concerned only a traffic incident.

Over the following days questions started to be asked of the whereabouts of Mrs Ruxton and her maid, but the police seemed to accept his explanations. Two weeks later a walker in the Border region found what appeared to be body parts wrapped in paper. At first the police thought they were dealing with five bodies as they had some 70 body pieces. Forensic investigations eventually showed that it was the remains of two female bodies. From the newspapers they found that an edition of the *Sunday Graphic* had been a special slip edition produced only for the Lancaster area. Remarkably, Doctor Ruxton had asked one of his patients to help clean the blood-splattered house and even dispose of a bloodstained suit.

Moffat in Scotland, where they were dumped in a ravine. Ruxton drove back quickly but hit a cyclist near Kendal. He failed to stop but the

OPPOSITE LEFT:
2 Dalton Square, Lancaster where the murders took place.

ABOVE RIGHT:
Doctor Buck Ruxton.

LEFT: The mudered maid Mary Jane Rogerson.

The forensic examination included the use of forensic entomology to study the size of the maggots in the remains and thereby establish the date of death. Forensic anthropology was used to rebuild the face and establish the identity of the remains. Doctor Ruxton was arrested on 13th October. Despite hiring the great Norman Birkett as his counsel, Ruxton was found guilty of murder and hanged. The case captured the imagination of the public sufficiently to have the words to a popular song,

'Red Sails in the Sunset', adapted to:

Red stains on the carpet,
Red stains on the knife,
Oh Dr Buck Ruxton
You murdered your wife.
Then Mary she saw you,
You thought she would tell,
So Dr Buck Ruxton
You killed her as well.

OPPOSITE LEFT:
The bath where
the bodies were
dismembered,
being examined
at the
Department
of Forensic
Medicine,
Glasgow
University.

LEFT: Ruxton
with his eldest
daughter.

CHARLOTTE BRYANT

MURDER OF FREDERICK BRYANT ON 23RD DECEMBER 1935

ARRESTED 10TH FEBRUARY 1936

TRIAL BEGAN 27TH MAY 1936

HANGED 15TH JULY 1936

Charlotte Bryant, like Edith Thompson, was a woman hanged more for her errant lifestyle than the largely circumstantial evidence against her. Her execution left five orphaned children and the whole episode made many people feel uncomfortable about the brutality of the legal system.

Charlotte Bryant was an illiterate Irish girl who met her future husband, Frederick, a British Army soldier, when he was posted to Londonderry in 1922. She was a girl who was known to the troops for her "generous" nature. When Frederick returned to civilian life as a cowhand in the West Country she followed him and they married, settling in a village near Yeovil, Somerset. Life was very quiet and the social life that did exist revolved around the pub. Charlotte spent a lot of her time there where she also earned money through prostitution. In the 13 years of marriage she

THE DAILY MIRROR, Monday, June 1, 1936.

Broadcasting - Page 20

Daily Mirror

THE DAILY PICTURE NEWSPAPER WITH THE LARGEST NET SALE

£100 IN PRIZES FOR THE STORY OF **YOUR ROMANCE** SEE PAGE 10

No. 10,140 Registered at the G.P.O. as a newspaper. MONDAY, JUNE 1, 1936 One Penny

Amusements : Pages 8 and 21

BOY'S LETTER TO MRS. BRYANT

'Mum—When Will You Be Home?'

FROM OUR SPECIAL CORRESPONDENT

STOURMINSTER (Dorset), Sunday.

A LITTLE boy sat writing a letter in this pretty Dorset village to-night. These were the words he penned:—

" Dear Mum,— When are you coming back to see us ? We all want you back. It has been such a long time sins I had see you. Lily is ill. Please come back soon.

" From your loving son, Ernest."

Brown-eyed Ernest Bryant, twelve-year-old son of a murdered father, was writing to his mother in Exeter Gaol, where she lies under sentence of death for killing that father by poisoning.

I saw the boy in the recreation ground here yesterday. He was playing cricket with his school friends.

"Where is Mum ? Is she coming back ? " he asked me. Time and again he asked the question, when I said that I had come from Dorchester.

The Tragic Answer

I had watched the tragic answer to this question, decided by a jury of twelve Dorset men two hours before in the hushed Assize Court at Dorchester.

Mrs. Charlotte Bryant, his thirty-three-year-old mother, had been half-carried from the dock after sentence of death had been passed.

Ernest is his mother's pet

I told the boy as gently as possible that the master of Stourminster Institution has something to tell him.

To Mr. Thomas and the matron fell the task of breaking the news to the boy, and to his ten-year-old sister Lily who is ill in the infirmary.

They were told their mother was not returning last night, as she had planned. Mercifully, the matron did not let the children know at once that Mrs. Bryant had been sentenced to death.

" We just said that she would not be back to-night," Mr. Thomas told me. " They would have heard from other people in the Institution through the wireless in any case.

" It was not until to-day that the boy and girl finally realised what had happened."

"Cried Myself to Sleep"

" I am sure she will be back soon," little Ernest said to me. " Won't she ?

" We have only seen her twice since she was taken away by the police, once when she came here in a big car and then at Dorchester."

" I am sure she will be back." he repeated. It was difficult to look straight at the tear-stained little face.

(Continued on back page)

Lady Edward Spencer - Churchill and Major-General Sir Frederick Maurice with wreaths which they placed on Buxton's war memorial after the morning session of the British Legion conference.

FIVE SWIM TO SAFETY FROM WRECK

FROM OUR OWN CORRESPONDENT

MARGATE, Sunday.

FIVE London men had a thrilling escape near here to-day when a fifteen-ton ketch in which they were attempting to reach the Channel Islands broke up on the rocks at Walpole Bay.

The men swam one hundred yards to shore, as the Margate lifeboat was unable to reach them.

They had left London on Saturday night, and found their ketch unmanageable when the boom was carried away in a strong northerly gale. Their auxiliary engine failed too.

Then the ketch was blown two miles on to the rocks. Within two hours it was a complete wreck.

Responding to distress flares, the Margate lifeboat put out, but was unable to get alongside owing to the sea and swam to safety. The men then dived into the sea and swam to safety.

They were in an exhausted condition, when they reached the shore and were taken to the police station.

The Duke of Saxe-Coburg-Gotha (Germany), between Field-Marshal Sir Philip Chetwode and Major-General Sir Frederick Maurice, leading the foreign delegates at the parade held in connection with the British Legion conference at Buxton yesterday. France, Belgium, Austria, Hungary and Bulgaria were also represented.

Coldest Ever Start to an Overcoat Holiday

BY A SPECIAL CORRESPONDENT

OVERCOAT Whitsun began yesterday in grand style. Resorts declare that it was the coldest Whit Sunday ever.

That did not altogether keep away the crowds, but these felt below expectations.

When they got by the sea holidaymakers did the only thing possible—they kept on walking.

You could crowd the daring souls who went for a bathe, at most of the resorts, on to one photograph; you could count the sun-bathers of the South Coast on the fingers of one hand. Lots of people put one toe into the sea, then dashed back to their bathing huts.

Holidaymakers in the Peak District of Derbyshire had a Christmas-card view of Whit Sunday early yesterday.

Mam Tor, the famous "shivering mountain," was crowned with snow.

The fall came on Saturday evening. On Rushup Edge there was a severe snowstorm, lasting an hour. Snowflakes were as large as shillings.

Better To-day ?

Cheer up, though, June—"flaming June"—gets off the mark to-day, and the weather experts are heralding it with slightly more cheering forecasts.

In any case, yesterday's crowds proved that Britain-on-holiday knows how to enjoy itself, whatever the weather.

They were out in their thousands on the promenades and foreshores. They carried overcoats and raincoats, but they were happy. Largely because they seemed to have more money to spend.

When the sun was friendly enough to take a peep through the clouds it looked down upon little bits of paradise for town-dwellers.

TO-DAY'S WEATHER OUTLOOK

"Cool to cold" in most districts, but some sunny spells likely.

TRAIN DRIVER'S DASH TO SAVE DROWNING BOYS

FROM OUR OWN CORRESPONDENT

CARMILE (near Glasgow), Sunday.

AS a signalman in his box here last night passed an express train through, he saw five boys in grave danger of drowning on a raft at the centre of a nearby pond.

Realising that he could not leave his post he telephoned to a siding a quarter of a mile away where he knew a gang of shunters were at work.

They dashed in their small train to the spot and the driver, Mr. W. Williamson, seeing one of the boys about to go down for the third time, jumped into the water and brought him to safety.

The children were John McGhee, thirteen, and his brother Hugh, eight, of Battlefield-street, Tollcross; James Campbell, ten, of Eversley-street, Tollcross; Eric McAteer, nine, and his brother, Francis McAteer, seven, of Tollcross-road, Glasgow.

The children had wandered from their home to the pond and were playing on rafts.

One of the rafts, which was made of old sleepers and stray pieces of wood, capsized, throwing the children into the water.

The signalman, Mr. James McNiff, said me :

"I could not leave the signal box to go to the children as an express was coming down the main line."

WORKLESS MINERS FIND JOBS IN BEET FIELDS

UNEMPLOYED miners left the hard-hit town of Willington, County Durham, yesterday, for the sugar-beet fields in Norfolk, where they begin work to-morrow.

Expert beet-growers will act as tutors until the men become proficient at their new jobs.

Some of the men have not worked for ten years. Their travelling expenses have been paid and they will receive their union wages.

Ernest Bryant, son of Mrs. Charlotte Bryant.

bore five children. Frederick seemed indifferent to her sexual activities and was grateful for the extra money. In 1933 things became more complicated when Charlotte met Edward Parsons, an itinerant horse trader who moved into the house and relegated Frederick to the sofa. Eventually Parsons was ordered from the house, with Charlotte following to set up home in Dorchester. However, Frederick soon relented and the curious ménage was reinstated. In 1935 Frederick started experiencing regular and severe bouts of illness related to his stomach which culminated in his admittance to hospital and death on 23rd December.

The doctor was immediately suspicious and ordered a post-mortem: this found 4.09 grams of arsenic in the body. The police started to investigate and moved Charlotte and her children into a workhouse. They took 150 samples from the house, of which 30 were found to contain arsenic. However, they failed to find a positive identification for Charlotte buying the arsenic. Despite this she was arrested on 10th February 1936 and charged with murder. Charlotte commented: "I haven't got poison from anywhere and that people know. I don't see how they can say I poisoned my husband." Central to the police case was an empty tin of weedkiller that was found in some ashes from the boiler which had then been disposed of in the garden. At the trial it was stated that high levels of arsenic of 149 parts per million were found in the ashes that contained the weedkiller tin. Doctor Roche the expert said that 49 parts per million was more normal. The evidence was circumstantial but what was probably more damaging was evidence of her promiscuity and loose living. She was found guilty and sentenced to hang. After the trial evidence was received from a Professor Bone who had read about the trial in the Sunday papers and stated that an arsenic ratio of 149 parts per million was quite normal for ashes. The appeal court decided that this was new evidence and not a correction of wrong evidence, and the judgment stood. Charlotte Bryant was hanged on 15th July 1936.

OPPOSITE LEFT: *Daily Mirror* front cover from June 1936.

LEFT: A young Frederick Bryant in army uniform.

BELOW: Charlotte Bryant with child.

EDWARD CHAPLIN

MANSLAUGHTER OF PERCY CASSERLEY 23RD MARCH 1938

TRIAL OPENED 24TH MAY 1938

SENTENCED FRIDAY 27TH MAY 1938 TO 12 YEARS' PENAL SERVITUDE. RELEASED 1946

The manslaughter of Percy Casserley by his wife's lover Edward Chaplin demonstrated that in domestic murder cases the attitude of judges and juries had changed in the 16 years since the Bywaters and Thompson trial. In this case the jury were reminded by the judge that they could record a manslaughter verdict if they believed that Casserley had been shot in the "heat of passion". Judges, however, still had a poor opinion of married women involved in affairs, which was made clear by the judge's comments at the end of the trial: "Your case has aroused the most ridiculous nonsense. A great many people have treated you as though you were some sort of heroine. You were a participator in a vulgar and sordid intrigue... Now please go."

The Casserleys married in 1927. Percy was 20 years older than his wife and a successful businessman. By 1937 Percy was 57 and his health had deteriorated due to alcoholism and an unspecified operation which meant that the

couple no longer enjoyed a sexual relationship. He had given up work in September 1937, probably due to his alcoholism. Next door to the Casserleys a 35-year-old builder, Edward Chaplin started work in the spring as foreman on a house renovation. A sexually frustrated Ena Casserley invited the young foreman over for a cup of tea and an affair began. The affair deepened when Percy Casserley went into hospital for treatment for his alcoholism. It was while in hospital that Percy discovered his wife was pregnant and wanted a divorce. He replied to his wife's request: "Do you think I am such a fool as to give you up for someone else?" Percy returned from hospital on 22nd March and by the 23rd was dead.

There are various accounts of the events of the night of the 23rd given to the court. It is clear that Ena wanted her child legitimized and that her husband had refused to give the divorce that she wanted. Chaplin called at the house on the evening of 23rd March and there was a scuffle during which Percy was severely beaten and fatally shot. At first Ena claimed to the police that her husband had been assaulted by a burglar and she'd discovered him dying on her return from a walk. Her story changed under questioning as it became clear that the police did not believe the burglary story. Chaplin was questioned and admitted there had been a violent struggle between himself and Casserley as they wrestled for a gun that was kept in the house. The shooting had been an accident. Both Chaplin and Ena were arrested, with Chaplin being charged with murder and Ena with being an accessory. Sir Bernard Spilsbury appeared for the prosecution and observed that there were 17 bruises on the victim's body and none on Chaplin's. The prosecution case was that this was premeditated murder, while the defence led by Norman Birkett told the story of a long struggle. The judge reminded the jury that if they believed the death of Casserley to be an accident, "in the heat of passion", a verdict of manslaughter was possible. The jury took the guidance and Chaplin was duly found guilty of manslaughter and sentenced to 12 years' penal servitude. Ena Casserley was sentenced to a nominal 11 days and immediately released with a severe censure. Chaplin was released in 1946 after serving eight years and met by Ena at the prison gates. They married immediately.

OPPOSITE LEFT: Mr and Mrs Casserly.

LEFT: Edward Chaplin.

BELOW: The house at Tadworth, Surrey, where Ena and Edward Chaplin lived after his release.

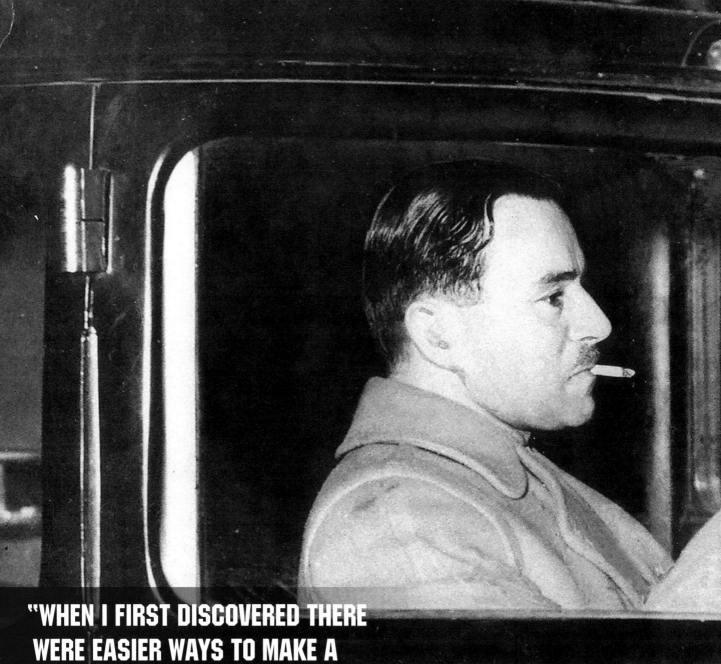

"WHEN I FIRST DISCOVERED THERE WERE EASIER WAYS TO MAKE A LIVING THAN TO WORK LONG HOURS IN AN OFFICE, I DID NOT ASK MYSELF WHETHER I WAS DOING RIGHT OR WRONG. THAT SEEMED TO ME TO BE IRRELEVANT."

WRITTEN BY JOHN HAIGH AFTER HIS ARREST IN 1949 FOR CONSPIRACY TO DEFRAUD.

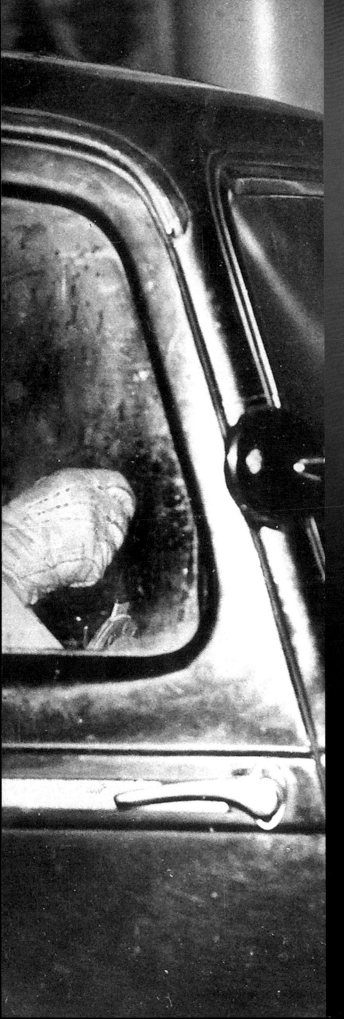

1940-1949

1942 GORDON CUMMINS: The murder of four women in one week earned him the name of the "Blackout Ripper".

1944 KARL HULTEN AND ELIZABETH JONES: The senseless murder of taxi driver George Heath in what became known as the cleft chin murder.

1946 NEVILLE HEATH: The brutal murder and mutilation of two young women.

1949 JOHN HAIGH: The murder of five people made even more infamous by the method of body disposal.

LEFT: John Haigh in his car.

GORDON CUMMINS

MURDER OF EVELYN OATLEY AND THREE OTHER WOMEN IN 1942

TRIAL BEGAN 27TH APRIL 1942

HANGED 25TH JUNE 1942

Gordon Cummins was a 28-year-old airman who earned the name of the "Blackout Ripper" for the murder of four women in London in 1942. The murders looked back to the tradition of Jack the Ripper in the East End of London in the 1880s and in many ways prefigure the anonymous murder by the serial killer that has become prevalent from the 1960s to the present day.

Cummins was a well-educated young man who'd married a theatre producer's secretary in 1936. Called up to the RAF Cummins was regarded as slightly eccentric by his colleagues, with a false Oxford accent and belief that he descended from an aristocratic line which earned him the nickname of the "duke" or "count". In the new year of 1942 he was billeted in a block of flats in St John's Wood. Over six days in the second week of February four women were murdered and there were two attempted murders. The first murder on the Saturday night was of 40-year-old Evelyn Hamilton who, although her clothes were disarranged, had not been sexually assaulted. She had been robbed of £80. On the Sunday night a 35-year-old showgirl and prostitute, Evelyn Oatley, was found in her flat strangled, her throat cut and she had been sexually assaulted with a tin opener.

From this murder the police discovered that the murderer was left-handed. He'd also left a fingerprint. The next day 43-year-old Margaret Lowe was murdered and her body slashed with both a knife and a razor. Her body wasn't

found until three days later and examined by Sir Bernard Spilsbury who described the killer as a "savage sexual maniac". On the Wednesday Doris Jouannet was found murdered in the two-bedroom flat she shared with her husband in Sussex Gardens. She had been strangled and her body sexually mutilated. On the Friday Greta Hayward was attacked near Piccadilly Circus but saved by a delivery boy who interrupted the attack. Cummins left behind his gas mask with a serial number. The same evening, as the police were tracking him down, he attacked another prostitute, Catherine Mulcahy, in her flat in Paddington. Her resistance was so effective that he left behind his belt and gave her an extra £5. Cummins was arrested on the Sunday. He of course professed his innocence and claimed that his billet passbook showed that he'd been in barracks at the time of the attacks. It was soon shown that the aircraftmen were signing each other out and in, and the billet was searched. Various items from the victims were found and Cummins' fingerprint matched that found in Evelyn Hamilton's flat. The trial on 27th April 1942 only lasted a day and Cummins was found guilty and sentenced to hang. The sentence was carried out at Wandsworth Prison on 25th June. Two other unsolved murders at the time were later attributed to him.

OPPOSITE LEFT AND LEFT: The four victims, Margaret Lowe (top), Evelyn Hamilton (middle), Doris Jouannet and Evelyn Oatley (left).

ABOVE: Gordon Cummins.

KARL HULTEN AND ELIZABETH JONES

MURDER OF GEORGE HEATH (CLEFT CHIN MURDER) ON 6ᵀᴴ OCTOBER 1944

TRIAL BEGAN 16ᵀᴴ JANUARY 1945

HULTEN HANGED ON 8ᵀᴴ MARCH 1945. JONES, ALTHOUGH SENTENCED TO DEATH, WAS REPRIEVED AND RELEASED IN 1954

What became known as the "cleft chin murder" was decried by George Orwell for embodying the decline of the English murder. He wrote of it: *There is no depth of feeling in it. It was almost chance that the two people concerned committed that particular murder, and it was only by good luck that they did not commit several others. The background was not domesticity, but the anonymous life of the dance-halls and the false values of the American film.*

Orwell believed the crime would soon be forgotten because of its lack of "depth of feeling". How wrong could he be? The "cleft chin murder" would provide the template for the most notable crimes in the second half of the 20ᵗʰ century. Murder from now on would become largely anonymous and motiveless. The classic age of British murder was over.

Karl Hulten, an American army deserter, and Elizabeth Jones, a Welsh waitress and barmaid-cum-stripper at the Panama and Blue Lagoon clubs, indulged in six days of crime culminating in the murder of taxi driver George Heath. The two met in a café in Hammersmith through a mutual friend. She had been married at the age of 16 to a Welsh soldier 10 years her senior but had separated on their wedding day after he assaulted her. He had recently been reported missing in action. She said that she wanted excitement, to be a "gun moll". He claimed to have been part of the mob in Chicago. They were both fantasists acting out a drama. He stole an American army truck and they drove to Reading, knocking a nurse off her bike on the way and robbing her. A couple of nights later there was an unsuccessful hold-up of a taxi and an attack on a girl hitchhiker which ended with her being knocked unconscious and a derisory amount stolen.

The following night they decided to rob a taxi, and Jones flagged down a private hire car driven by George Heath in Hammersmith. Just

OPPOSITE LEFT: Elizabeth Maud Jones, the 18-year-old Welsh girl who wanted to be a gun moll.

BELOW: The parents of Elizabeth Maud Jones.

HULTEN LAUGHS AS JUDGES SEAL HIS DOOM

Karl Gustav Hulten, 22,
American paratrooper;
death sentence stands.

Elizabeth Maud
("Marina") Jones, 18½,
strip-tease girl;. the Old
Bailey jury recommended
mercy.

By Your Special Correspondent

KARL GUSTAV HULTEN and Elizabeth Maude Jones both lost their appeal yesterday against the sentence of death passed upon them for the murder of George Heath, the "Cleft Chin" taxi-driver. Both took the blow quietly.

Mr. Justice Macnaghten's almost inaudible summing-up took precisely an hour. During that hour the pair stood at the back of the jury-box where they sat for two days, mutely listening and watching while their fate was decided.

At the final word "Dismissed" all was still for the space of a heartbeat. Then the two wardresses swung "Marina" Jones round like a doll and led her away.

Hulten walked out as he had walked in, smiling slightly and joking with his guards.

Hulten lost none of his self-confidence as this worst of all ordeals dragged on minute by minute. During that part which concerned himself, he watched the Judge carefully, though even then his attention wandered from time to time; and he glanced round the court from the corners of his eyes.

Stood With Head Bowed

Jones, on the other hand, looked very nearly spent. She entered the court with her head dropped so low that the brown crown of her hair showed over the bleached pompadour.

She kept her eyes closed and never raised her head at all.

Now and again the tall wardress at her side glanced kindly at her.

When Mr. Justice Macnaghten said, "The jury might well have come to the conclusion that this was not a case of mere killing in the act of robbery, but one of cold-blooded murder," her head rolled as if she were going to faint.

Two of the wardresses gripped her by the arms and did not leave go of her again.

In the body of the court, Mr. Casswell, K.C., counsel for the girl, rested his cheek on his hand and watched Mr. Justice Macnaghten fixedly. His assistant, Mrs. Lloyd Lane, wrote continuously.

Mr. Maude, K.C., counsel for Hulten, was not present.

Behind counsel sat the girl's parents. Mr. Baker, wearing a worn navy-blue suit, sat quietly with his hands folded.

Mrs. Baker, her mother, wearing deep black, leaned forward in her seat, growing greyer and greyer in the face. Once she put her hand to her mouth and glanced at her daughter.

Mr. Justice Croom-Johnson wrote composedly, Mr. Justice Wrottesley fidgeted with his glasses, shuffled papers.

The blanket of silence became almost too heavy to bear as the quiet, halting voice of Mr. Justice Macnaghten continued, on and on.

Hulten scarcely moved at all, standing erect, hands loosely clasped. His police guard seemed more moved than he.

But "Marina" Jones, "18 years and 7 months old," as Mr. Macnaghten commented, approached nearer and nearer to collapse.

The wax-like face glistened more and more yellow under the glaring lights. As minutes passed, she leaned more and more heavily against the wardress until the Judge ceased.

after the Chiswick roundabout Hulten asked the driver to stop and when he bent down to open the door, shot him. Heath was pushed out of the driver's seat and Hulten drove on to Staines, with Jones searching Heath's pockets for valuables and discarding out of the car window anything she considered unimportant. His body was dumped near Staines. The crime would yield a miserable £8 in cash which would be squandered at the dogs the following evening. George Heath's body was found the next day and the police put out a search for his car. Foolishly, Hulten continued to use the stolen car, which was spotted by a diligent constable, PC William Walters, who was patrolling on the beat. He helped arrest Hulten when he next used the car. A cocked Remington pistol was found in Hulten's pocket.

The American authorities were informed and Hulten's identity and desertion established. Hulten used Jones as an alibi for the night of the murder and took the police to her flat. At the time the police had not linked Jones to the shooting of

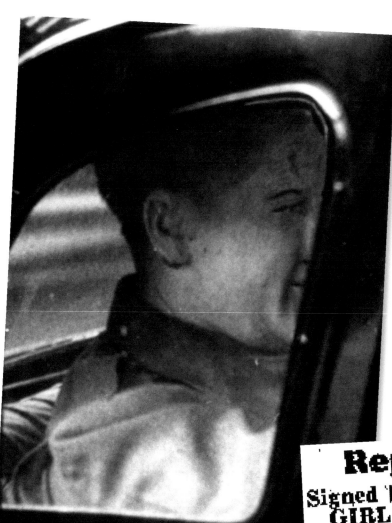

Hulten and he appeared in a British court with Jones. A curiosity is that Jones was the first person to be defended by a female barrister in a capital case. Both were found guilty and sentenced to hang. Jones, controversially, had her sentence commuted two days before it was due to be carried out. There were numerous letters of complaint in the press especially from women in South Wales. She was released on licence 8 years later in 1954. Hulten hanged on 8th March 1945, aged 23.

Heath, and Jones was allowed to leave after giving a statement. But she was only an 18-year-old and rattled, and when she met an old acquaintance, Harry Kimberley, who commented on her haggard appearance, she blurted out: "If you had seen someone do what I have seen done, you wouldn't be able to sleep at night." Kimberley was a wartime reserve constable and reported the conversation to the police who called on Jones later in the day. When confronted by the police she made a full confession blaming Hulten for the tragedy. When Hulten heard this he admitted the murder and blamed Jones for encouraging him "to do something exciting".

The Americans waived their right to try

Reprieve

Signed by FIFTY ATS GIRLS in Wales:

We have come to the conclusion that the girl Jones, in the Cleft Chin murder case, was more to blame than the man Hulten. It is not right for him to have been hanged and she not to have been.

We have received more than 400 letters in the same strain, the signatures on which run into several thousands. Your Two Codgers are in agreement with them all.

NEVILLE HEATH

MURDER OF MARGERY GARDNER ON 20TH JUNE 1946 AND DOREEN MARSHALL ON 3RD JULY 1946

ARRESTED 5TH JULY 1946

TRIAL BEGAN 24TH SEPTEMBER 1946

HANGED 26TH OCTOBER 1946

Neville Heath is typical of many murderers found in this book, with his early life characterized by petty crime, deception both of self and others, betrayal, vanity and laziness, reaching a chilling climax with murder.

Heath, born in 1917, joined the armed services in 1934 and was employed by them intermittently for the next 12 years during which he managed to be court-martialled three times, sent to borstal, marry, divorce and emigrate to South Africa. In 1945 his last court-martial, for undisciplined behaviour and wearing medals to which he was not entitled, ended with his dismissal from the RAF and return to Britain. Spring 1946 found Heath in London staying at the Pembridge Court Hotel in Notting Hill. A few weeks earlier he'd met Margery Gardner, a film extra with a predilection for masochistic sex. He'd also promised marriage to and spent the night with 19-year-old Yvonne Symonds.

When she had safely returned to her parents in Sussex he called Margery Gardner and arranged a date for later that week. After an alcohol-fuelled evening out they staggered back to the Pembridge Court Hotel. The following afternoon a maid opened up Heath's room and found the body of Margery Gardner bound by her ankles, gagged and sexually mutilated. There

SEE
SCHEME

were 17 whip marks on her face which had left a diamond pattern. The examination by pathologist Professor Keith Simpson showed that the horrific injuries were inflicted before her death by suffocation. He was reported to have said: "Find that whip and you've found your man".

The morning after the murder Heath contacted his "fiancée" Yvonne Symonds and travelled to Worthing to meet her and her parents who were suitably impressed by this smart young man. Bizarrely, at dinner the next evening he admitted knowing details of the murder and that he'd been staying in the room where the body was found. When her parents read the details of the murder in the paper the next day and learned that the police were looking for 6ft tall Neville Heath they were understandably concerned. Wonderfully innocent Yvonne phoned her fiancée at his

hotel and reported their worries to which he replied in the ultimate understatement: "Yes I thought they would be". Fortunately for Yvonne she would not see Heath again until the trial later in the year. Heath rapidly decamped to Bournemouth where he booked in to the Tollard Royal Hotel under the name of Group Captain Rupert Brooke.

On 3rd July he met 21-year-old Doreen Marshall and arranged to have dinner with her. At about 11pm, after dinner, Doreen asked for a taxi to be called but was countermanded by Heath who said that he would walk her back to her hotel. The night porter reported that she seemed distressed and when Heath said that he would be half an hour she retorted: "No, quarter of an hour". One can only surmise that there had already been a disagreement about the future of the evening. Doreen never made

OPPOSITE LEFT: A young Neville Heath.

LEFT: Margery Gardner, the first victim.

BELOW: Wanted poster.

POLICE GAZETTE

PUBLISHED BY AUTHORITY.

NEW SERIES   TUESDAY, JUNE 25, 1946   No. 147   VOL. XXXIII

Manuscript for publication should be addressed "THE COMMISSIONER OF POLICE, NEW SCOTLAND Yard, S.W.1" with "C.R.O. (P.G.)" in top left corner.

HAROLD SCOTT
The Commissioner of Police of the Metropolis.

Special Notice

MURDER

M.P. (FH). It is desired to trace the after-described for interview respecting the death of MARGERY GARDNER, during the night of 20th–21st inst.—NEVILLE GEORGE CLEVELY HEATH, alias ARMSTRONG, BLYTH, DENVERS and GRAHAM, C.R.O. No. 28142-37, b. 1917, 5ft. 11½in., c. fresh, e. blue, believed small fair moustache, h. and eyebrows fair, square face, broad forehead and nose, firm chin, good teeth, military gait ; dress, lt. grey d.b. suit with pin stripe, dk. brown trilby, brown suede shoes, cream shirt with collar attached or fawn and white check sports jacket and grey flannel trousers. Nat. Reg. No. CNP 2147191.

Has recent conviction for posing as Lt.-Col. of South African Air Force. A pilot and believed to possess an "A" licence, has stated his intention of going abroad and may endeavour to secure passage on ship or plane as passenger or pilot. May stay at hotels accompanied by woman.

Enquiries are also requested to trace the owner of gent's white handkerchief with brown check border, bearing "L. Kearns" in black ink on hem and stitched with large "K" in blue cotton in centre.

it back and two days later the hotel reported her missing. The police quickly traced "Group Captain Rupert Brooke" as her last contact and they noticed his resemblance to the missing Neville Heath wanted for murder in London. The police found a left luggage ticket from Bournemouth Railway Station in Heath's jacket.

When it was redeemed they found a suitcase containing articles with the name Heath marked on them and a riding whip with a distinctive cross-pattern. Professor Simpson had been correct. The police had found the whip and their man. When told of the finds and that he was to be detained further Heath exclaimed, "oh all right" and began to dictate a statement. The next morning Doreen Marshall's body was found in a wooded area near the sea. She had been sexually assaulted in a similar manner to Margery Gardner.

The trial in September focused on attempts by Heath's counsel to show that he was insane. His counsel didn't allow him to take the stand because his demeanour was regarded as too aloof and sane. The judge summed up the case with: "A strong sexual instinct is not of itself insanity. Mere love of lust, mere recklessness are not in themselves insanity. Inability to resist temptation is not in itself insanity." It took the jury an hour to find him sane and guilty; he hanged on 26th October 1946.

LEFT: Police examining the scene where Doreen Marshall's body was found.

OPPOSITE BELOW INSET: Doreen Marshall with her family.

BELOW: Neville Heath: a man at peace with his pipe.

JOHN GEORGE HAIGH

MURDER OF WILLIAM DONALD MCSWANN ON 9TH SEPTEMBER 1944, HIS PARENTS JULY 1945, DOCTOR AND MRS ANDERSON FEBRUARY 1948 AND MRS DURAND-DEACON ON 18TH FEBRUARY 1949

ARRESTED 28TH FEBRUARY 1949

TRIAL OPENED 18TH JULY 1949

HANGED 6TH AUGUST 1949

Haigh was a petty criminal who decided during the Second World War that the days of being imprisoned for trivial crimes had to come to an end. However, instead of starting on a path of virtue he chose a path of cold-blooded murder. His initial success led to overconfidence and his eventual demise.

Born in 1909, Haigh was the only child of a family involved with the Plymouth Brethren sect. The sect practised a lifestyle that turned its back on most of modern life and convenience. In 1934 he married, dropped out of the Brethren and was sent to prison for 15 months for fraud. His wife left him, the Brethren rejected him and he set out on a life of crime. By 1944, after his release from prison for the third time, Haigh met up with William Donald McSwann, a man he'd known in the 1930s. He'd also known McSwann's parents well.

On the night of 9th September 1944 the two men went back to a basement flat at

79 Gloucester Road where Haigh had been repairing a pinball machine for McSwann. There he coshed and robbed him and put his body in a water butt filled with acid. He told McSwann's parents that their son had gone into hiding to avoid a military call-up. In July the following year he repeated the process with McSwann's parents and then, posing as the missing son, disposed of the estate worth £4,000. In 1948 he murdered a couple whom he'd met through a property deal, Doctor and Mrs Henderson, and disposed of their bodies in acid baths that had been installed at a workshop in Crawley. He placated their relatives with forged letters.

Haigh should now have been a relatively wealthy man but by January 1949 all the money had been squandered on gambling. For a number of years he'd been living at Onslow Court Hotel in South Kensington.

LEFT: William Donald McSwann.

BELOW: Inside the workshop in Crawley.

He was overdrawn and owed the hotel money. He needed quick cash and saw the opportunity to make it in the form of fellow resident, 69-year-old wealthy widow Mrs Durand-Deacon. She enquired whether Haigh could help her with an idea for making artificial fingernails. He took his chance and invited her down to his workshop in Crawley.

There he shot her, took her fur coat, cash and jewellery before putting the body in the tank full of acid. He was back in London for 11pm that evening and claimed that Mrs Durand-

Deacon had failed to turn up for their meeting. With concern growing among the hotel residents over the next couple of days, Haigh agreed to go with Mrs Durrand-Deacon's friend Mrs Lane to Chelsea Police Station. They were interviewed by policewoman Sergeant Lambourne who instinctively distrusted Haigh. Her suspicions were confirmed when she discovered Haigh's previous convictions.

Meanwhile, unconcerned by the police attention, Haigh continued to check the decomposition in the tank and dispose of the jewellery and fur coat. He decided that the acid had done its work and tipped the contents into the yard. The handbag was still intact so he hid it behind a fence. Haigh still seemed confident but eventually the police arrived at the workshop in Crawley and found an array of implements including rubber gloves, gas mask and gun. Haigh was called in again for questioning by the police and eventually confessed with the immortal lines: "I've

ABOVE: Police investigating the murder of the McSwann family in the flat on Gloucester Road.

RIGHT: Police looking for evidence at the workshop in Crawley and inset, Doctor and Mrs Henderson.

Whether Haigh drank the blood of his victims will never be known but it's clear that from the start of the police investigation he had intended to use insanity as his defence . One of his comments was: "Tell me frankly what are the chances of anyone being released from Broadmoor?" The jury and judge were not impressed and Haigh was found guilty and sentenced to death. He was hanged on 6th August 1949.

LEFT: Mrs Durand-Deacon.

BELOW: *Daily Mirror* Vampire Horror story.

destroyed her with acid ... You'll find the sludge that remains at Leopold Road. Every trace has gone. How can you prove murder if there's no body?" Unfortunately for Haigh there was more than enough left of Mrs Durrand-Deacon, including her dentures and handbag.

He gave a full confession, including confessing to the other murders, and embellished the story with tales of drinking the blood of his victims. The press loved this and christened him "the vampire killer".

"LET'S BE FRANK ABOUT IT;
MOST OF OUR PEOPLE HAVE
NEVER HAD IT SO GOOD."

HAROLD MACMILLAN, SPEECH AT BEDFORD FOOTBALL
GROUND 1957.

1950-1959

1952 MILES GIFFARD: The murder of his parents by a love struck youth.

1952 DAVID BENTLEY AND CHRISTOPHER CRAIG: A botched break-in leads to the murder of PC Miles. Bentley is hanged even though he was under arrest when the shot was fired.

1953 JOHN CHRISTIE AND TIMOTHY EVANS: The murder of Mrs Evans and other women by John Christie and the hanging of an innocent man.

1955 RUTH ELLIS: The murder of David Blakely in a London street. The great *crime passionnel* of the century.

1956 JOHN BODKIN ADAMS: The sensational acquittal of the Eastbourne doctor on the charge of the murder of Edith Morrell.

1958 PETER MANUEL: The first man in Britain to be described as a serial killer. He murdered at least eight people.

1959 GUENTHER PODOLA: The shooting of DS Purdy while resisting arrest.

LEFT: Ruth Ellis and David Blakely.

MILES GIFFARD

Miles Giffard was clearly an immature and mentally unbalanced 26-year-old from a profoundly dysfunctional family, and he murdered his parents in what appears to be a drunken tantrum. His hanging was the first of a series of pointless executions that helped to undermine support for capital punishment, especially amongst the political class.

Miles Giffard lived with his wealthy parents in a beautiful house on a cliff top near St Austell in Cornwall. He was a problem child who, despite his public school education, had been seeing a psychiatrist since the age of 14 and found it impossible to hold down a job. If he'd been born 15 years later his lifestyle might have been accepted. In the Fifties living off one's parents was not acceptable and as Miles became older the tensions in the house grew. Things came to a head when Miles met 19-year-old Gabrielle Vallance from Chelsea and fell in love. She persuaded him that he had to move away from his parents and sent him back to Cornwall to collect his clothes.

After a three-day hitchhike he arrived back in Cornwall on 31ˢᵗ October 1952 and had a huge row with his father who wanted him to resume his studies and threatened to "cut him off without the

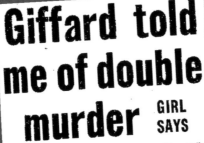

Giffard told me of double murder GIRL SAYS

From Howard Johnson, St. Austell, Cornwall, Thursday.

A NINETEEN - YEAR-OLD girl from Chelsea, Gabrielle Vallance, told the magistrates here today that ex-public schoolboy Miles Giffard confessed to her outside a public house that he had murdered his mother and father.

The story of a five-week friendship between twenty-six-year-old Giffard and Miss Vallance came soon after the prosecution had opened their case against Giffard—accused of double murder

Witnesses had been called to trace the twenty-four-hour drama that followed the finding of the bodies of Giffard's parents beneath a 120-foot cliff near their clifftop home at Porthpean

Then a court officer called. "Miss Vallance." Dressed in a simple, high-necked bottle-green coat, the fair haired Chelsea girl from fashionable Tite-street, entered the tiny court-room.

Miles Giffard, who had been sitting with head bowed between two police officers, sat up and looked keenly in her direction. She smiled quickly towards him.

Miss Vallance then told the court—the same court where for twenty - three years Miles Giffard's fifty-three-year-old solicitor father had sat as Clerk to the Magistrates — that on Friday night, November 7, Miles had phoned her from his home in Cornwall to say that he was definitely coming up to London and would borrow his father's car.

The night of November 7 was the night that Mr. and Mrs. Giffard met their death. Mr. Giffard's car had disappeared from the garage; and three valuable pieces of jewellery had vanished from the dressing-table in Mrs. Giffard's bedroom, the prosecution said.

She Sobbed

In a voice little more than a whisper, Miss Vallance—she described herself as of independent means — occasionally sobbing and dabbing her eyes with a handkerchief, then told the story of Saturday, November 8.

At noon, Miles rang her and asked her to meet him at Leicester-square at 2 p.m. She met him there with her mother. Together the three of them went for a drink and then to see the picture "Limelight."

After the film Miss Vallance's mother left them,

GABRIELLE VALLANCE
Drinks and a cinema.

and she and Miles went to have a meal and then to Shepherd's Bar.

"We had a gin each," she said, "and then Miles said that his feet ached, he was dreadfully tired and wanted to go.

"I said I thought it was early to have to go, and we went to the Star in Chesham-mews."

proverbial penny". Prophetically, he wrote to Gabrielle: "Short of doing him in, I see no future in the world at all." On Friday 7th November at 5.30 he phoned Gabrielle and told her that his father had lent him the car and he was driving up to London to meet her. At 9.30pm the same evening, the Giffards' maid returned to find a blood-splattered kitchen. Miles had bludgeoned his father to death in the garage and then walked through to the kitchen and knocked his mother unconscious. The bodies were then placed in a wheelbarrow, taken to the nearby cliff edge and tipped over.

Miles was in London by the next morning, pawning his mother's jewellery and taking Gabrielle for a good day out culminating in a pub crawl during which he told her about the double murder. She didn't believe him. By the time they arrived back at her parents' house the police were waiting and Miles was arrested. His only explanation was: "I can only say that I have had a brainstorm... I cannot account for my actions. I had drunk about half a bottle of whisky on the Friday afternoon before all this happened. It just seemed to me that nothing mattered as long as I got back to London and my girlfriend. She just fascinated me." The defence tried the plea of insanity quoting evidence of schizophrenia, but the judge seemed determined that Miles should hang and the jury duly found him guilty. Gabrielle stood by him throughout and visited him just before the execution in Bristol. The whole affair has a tragic, pathetic quality which makes the sentence seem doubly brutal. Miles was hanged on 25th February 1953.

OPPOSITE LEFT TOP: Giffard's mother and father.

OPPOSITE LEFT BELOW: *Daily Mirror* article.

LEFT: The family home.

BELOW: The headland from which the bodies were tipped into the sea.

CRIMES OF THE CENTURY MILES GIFFARD

DEREK BENTLEY AND CHRISTOPHER CRAIG

MURDER OF PC MILES ON 2ND NOVEMBER 1952

TRIAL BEGAN 9TH DECEMBER 1952

BENTLEY HANGED 28TH JANUARY 1953

The case of Bentley and Craig is the most celebrated in the history of the campaign to end capital punishment in Britain. Bentley was hanged for the murder of PC Miles despite not being the man who pulled the trigger, despite having been under arrest for 15 minutes before the shooting, despite having a mental age of 11, despite his 16-year-old accomplice escaping with a gaol sentence and despite a petition signed by 200 MPs. Bentley was a victim of political expediency. An example had to be set to discourage violent young men.

FAIRFAX

The calm courage of five policemen— by a magistrate

JACKS   HARRISON   McDONALD   MILES

THEY BRAVED SHOTS

FIVE policemen showed "calm courage" on a warehouse roof on the cloudy and wet November night when Police-Constable Sidney Miles was shot dead a magistrate said yesterday.

"Their behaviour," he added, "reflects the bravery of the police force in this country as a whole.

The magistrate, Mr. F. L. Richardson, chairman of the Croydon (Surrey) bench, had just committed Christopher Craig, 16, and Derek Bentley, 19, for trial on a charge of murdering Police-Constable Miles, one of the five men whose courage he commended.

This, according to the prosecution, was what these five men did:—

Detective-Constable Fairfax clambered up a drainpipe to the roof, was shot in the shoulder, but arrested Bentley and later went back on the roof with a revolver to face Craig.

Police-Constable Miles kicked open the stair-case door to the roof, went fearlessly forward and was shot between the eyes. Police-Constable Harrison, forced by shots to retreat along the gutter beside a sloping roof, followed Police-Constable Miles up the staircase and hurled his truncheon, a milk bottle and a block of wood at Craig.

He Tried Twice

Police-Constable McDonald tried twice to climb the drainpipe to aid Detective Fairfax and succeeded at the second attempt. Police-Constable Jacks also reached the roof by the drainpipe.

Craig in hospital with a fractured back and other injuries after falling from the roof, was alleged to have told police: "If I hadn't cut a bit off the barrel of my gun, I would probably have killed a lot more policemen.

"That night I was out to kill because I had so much hate inside me for what they had done to my brother."

Mr. David Nelson, for Craig, told the magistrates there might be a question about Craig's mental state.

The fact that he was only sixteen was also a matter that would cause concern.

Craig and Bentley both pleaded not guilty and reserved their defence.

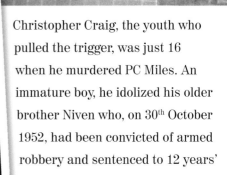

Christopher Craig, the youth who pulled the trigger, was just 16 when he murdered PC Miles. An immature boy, he idolized his older brother Niven who, on 30th October 1952, had been convicted of armed robbery and sentenced to 12 years' imprisonment. Craig had been in court for the sentencing. On the afternoon of 2nd November Craig and his girlfriend had seen the film *My Death is a Mockery*, in which the hero is hanged after shooting a policeman. Craig had developed a hatred of the police and a love of American gangster culture. Later that day Craig called for 19-year-old Derek Bentley and the two eventually caught a

contested. Fairfax detains Bentley who shouts the fatal line: "Let him have it Chris". Fairfax's shoulder is grazed by a bullet. Meanwhile police reinforcements have arrived led by PC Miles who kicks open the roof door and steps onto the roof where he is instantly killed by a bullet to the head. The police account has Craig uttering many lines of gangster-inspired rhetoric, including: "I'm Craig. You've just given my brother 12 years. Come on you coppers. I'm only 16." When his ammunition ran out Craig jumped 25ft head first off the roof. He was jumped on by another policeman and was reported to have said: "I wish I was fucking dead. I hope I killed the fucking lot." It would have saved a lot of trouble if he were dead but instead he had fractured his spine and other bones. Meanwhile Bentley had been quietly led away.

Both boys were charged with murder under the concept of joint enterprise. Craig was under the age of 18 when PC Miles was shot and therefore could not be hanged, while Bentley was 19 and could be.

bus to West Croydon. Craig had given Bentley a knuckleduster. It is not known if Bentley knew that Craig was armed. They found a wholesale confectioner's which they decided to break into by scaling a drainpipe and climbing in through the roof. However, they were seen by a neighbour who alerted the police.

First on the scene was Detective Constable Fairfax who clambered up and demanded they give themselves up. Here the story becomes

LEFT: The site of the crime and, inset, PC Miles.

OPPOSITE LEFT: *Daily Mirror* article.

BELOW LEFT: Christopher Craig on an ambulance stretcher.

BELOW RIGHT: The gun.

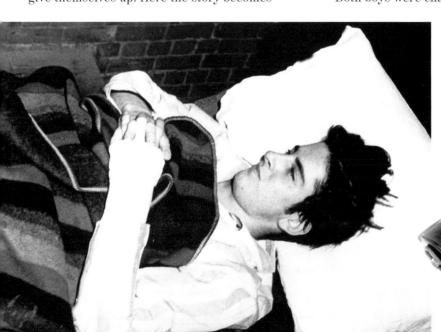

WILL BENTLEY HANG ?

"DAILY MIRROR" REPORTER

THOUSANDS of people last night were wondering whether Derek Bentley, the nineteen-year-old youth sentenced to death yesterday at the Old Bailey, will hang.

Bentley was sentenced after he and gunman Christopher Craig, 16, were found guilty of the murder at Croydon, Surrey, of Police-Constable Miles.

Craig was ordered to be detained during Her Majesty's pleasure.

It was Craig's shot that killed the policeman that night last month when both youths were cornered on a warehouse roof. Bentley did not have a gun.

And yesterday, the jury, finding him guilty of murder recommended him to mercy.

Wherever people last night were discussing: "Will he hang?" these two points were being mentioned.

The official attitude of the Home Secretary—who has to decide Bentley's fate—was defined in a memorandum the Home Office laid before the Royal Commission on Capital Punishment.

It said: "The Home Secretary always attaches weight to a recommendation to mercy by the jury. He would be very reluctant to disregard such a recommendation if it is concurred in by the Judge."

Out of every 100 murderers convicted between 1900 and 1948, but recommended to mercy. Home Secretaries reprieved seventy-five.

Later evidence by the Home Office before the Royal Commission said that in very occasional cases the Home Secretary granted a reprieve because he felt that in spite of the verdict there was a shadow of doubt of the prisoner's guilt.

Christopher Craig's punishment means that he will be in prison without knowing how many years he has to serve.

Because of the injuries he received when he dived off the warehouse roof after shooting Police-Constable Miles, he will be in Wormwood Scrubs prison hospital for some time. When he is fit he may be transferred to a gaol like Wakefield or Maidstone.

Craig smiles as he is sentenced—see Centre Pages.

Bentley's fate was sealed. The defence was unable to argue for the lesser charge of manslaughter because the "malicious intent" of the burglary was transferred to the shooting. A plea of insanity was not possible, because although the boys were of limited intelligence there was at that time no defence of diminished responsibility. The case was heard by the Chief Justice,

Lord Goddard, a man of strong conservative disposition with a stern approach to sentencing. He saw it as the role of the judiciary to defend the country from a tide of lawless young men. The defence counsel had a very short time to master the brief.

There were significant holes in the police case, especially in the ballistics evidence. The police were not sure how many shots had been fired. They never produced the bullet that killed PC Miles. Many years later it emerged that the fatal bullet was of large calibre such as those used by the police. Craig always believed that he shot PC Miles but he commented many years later to the investigative writer David Yallop: "What I've never been able to understand is how I shot him between the eyes when he was facing away from me and was going the wrong way." Goddard made an extraordinary 250 interventions from the bench, almost all of them prejudicial to the defendants such as this comment on the evidence of the police: "Those three officers in particular showed the

---

ABOVE LEFT: *Daily Mirror* article.

ABOVE RIGHT: Bentley's mother and sister the day before his execution.

RIGHT: A letter from Bentley to his mother.

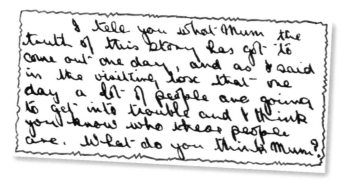

THE LAST ACT

NINETEEN-YEAR-OLD Derek Bentley must die tomorrow for his part in the murder committed by sixteen-year-old Christopher Craig. A horrifying crime now proceeds to its horrifying outcome. It has brought sorrow for everybody, including the Home Secretary, Sir David Maxwell Fyfe, a humane man who has had to take a terrible decision. He has not found it possible to allow Bentley to escape the consequences of his act.

Capital punishment is retained in this country because of Parliament's belief in its deterrent value. The fate of Bentley must be read as a warning that there will not be leniency towards anyone who goes along with a man who carries a gun.

HMP WANDSWORTH

Under the Prison Act 1952 it is an offence for any person

to help a prisoner to escape or attempt to escape: the maximum penalty is 5yrs. imprisonment (section 39 as amended by the Criminal Justice Act 1961):

without authority to convey or attempt to convey into a prison or to a prisoner intoxicating liquor or tobacco: the maximum penalty is 6mths. imprisonment or a £50 fine or both (section 40):

without authority to convey or attempt to convey into or out of a prison or to a prisoner any letter or other article or to place it outside the prison intending it to come into a prisoner's possession: the maximum penalty is a £50 fine (section 40).

highest gallantry; they were conspicuously brave. Are you going to say that they are conspicuous liars?"

The jury took only 75 minutes to find both youths guilty but with a recommendation of mercy for Bentley. Craig, because of his age, was sentenced to be detained at his majesty's pleasure. Bentley was sentenced to hang. There was a major campaign by the Bentley family, including a petition signed by 200 MPs which was presented to Home Secretary Sir David Maxwell-Fyfe. It was to no avail and Bentley was hanged on 28th January 1953. The family campaigned tirelessly to clear Derek's name, leading to the Court of Appeal setting aside his conviction in 1998.

Shortly before his death the retired Lord Goddard blamed the home secretary for failing to commute Bentley's sentence.

ABOVE LEFT: Christopher Craig's mother leaving court.

ABOVE RIGHT: *Daily Mirror* editorial.

LEFT: Bentley's sister Iris, laying a wreath outside Wandsworth Prison.

JOHN REGINALD CHRISTIE

THE MURDER OF:

RUTH FUERST AUGUST 1943

MURIEL EADY AUTUMN 1944

MRS CHRISTIE 12TH DECEMBER 1952

BERYL EVANS AND GERALDINE EVANS NOVEMBER 1952 (AT FIRST ATTRIBUTED TO TIMOTHY EVANS)

RITA NELSON JANUARY 1953

KATHLEEN MALONEY JANUARY 1953

HECTORINA MACLENNAN MARCH 1953

TRIAL OPENED 22ND JUNE 1953

HANGED 15TH JULY 1953

The murders committed by John Christie present one of the most complex and intractable cases in British criminal history. The two men involved, John Christie and Timothy Evans, were both inveterate liars and self-delusional.

The murders were committed over a 10-year period, with a long interval between the first pair of murders and the last five. The police investigation of the murders of Beryl and Geraldine Evans was seriously flawed and almost certainly led to the wrongful conviction and hanging of Timothy Evans. It is a classic example of the police finding a convincing narrative and ignoring all evidence to the contrary. This, tragically, led to the hanging of one innocent man and left John Christie to commit a further four murders. No wonder that the judicial establishment attempted to prevent a full investigation of the case.

Christie, a Yorkshireman born in 1898, had a long history of petty crime, imprisonment and domestic violence before he turned to murder. He moved to London in 1923, leaving his wife in Yorkshire. After a last period in prison in 1933 his estranged wife agreed to live with him again and moved to London. In 1938 they settled at 10 Rillington Place, a rundown terrace turned into

flats on the edge of Notting Hill.

Over the next 15 years, seven women and a child would be murdered in this house. The first was a young Austrian nurse, Ruth Fuerst, whom Christie had met in his work as a special constable. He strangled her in Rillington Place, engaging in sexual intercourse during or after her death. Because he was expecting his wife back that evening he put the body under the floorboards of the kitchen before transferring it to the garden under the cover of darkness. Christie met his next victim, Muriel Eady at his new employers. He'd been forced to leave his previous work as special constable when a soldier cited him in a divorce case. Christie lured Muriel back to his flat with the promise of a cure for her catarrh, and there he gassed and strangled her and engaged in sexual intercourse with her comatose or dead body, which was then buried in the garden. Things now go quiet for many years until the arrival of the Evans family. Timothy Evans was an inadequate young Welshman with a rudimentary education which had left him almost illiterate. He married Beryl Thorley in September 1947 and moved into 10 Rillington Place when Beryl again became pregnant in 1948. A daughter, Geraldine, was born in October, and life proceeded normally, although neighbours claimed there were a

OPPOSITE LEFT: John and Ethel Christie.

LEFT: Rillington Place street scene.

ABOVE: 10 Rillington Place.

large number of rows. In October 1949 Beryl became pregnant and told her husband that she intended to have what was then an illegal abortion. Accounts vary widely about what happened next. All we know for certain is that

ABOVE: Muriel Eady and Beryl Evans.

RIGHT: Ethel Christie.

OPPOSITE TOP: Kathleen Maloney, Rita Nelson and Hectorina MacLennan.

OPPOSITE RIGHT: Christie in his special constable's uniform.

Mrs Evans and her baby daughter Geraldine died at some time in the second week of November 1952.

Timothy Evans alone gave four different accounts of Beryl's death in statements to the police. All of them can be shown to be false in some way. The first statement made voluntarily and unsolicited to police in Wales claims that he found his wife dead after a failed abortion attempt and that he disposed of the body in the drain. The police followed this up and had to employ three policemen to remove the drain cover. Therefore it was impossible for the relatively small Evans to have disposed of the body in the drains. In the second statement, and the one the evidence shows to be the most plausible, Evans claims that Christie had attempted an abortion which failed and led to Beryl's death. Because of the circumstances Christie persuaded Evans not to go to the police but instead stored the body in an empty flat, with Christie promising to dispose of it in the drain the next day. Evans then went to work the following day leaving Christie to look after the baby. On Evans' return Christie claims to have given the baby away. Beryl's body had been moved and Christie persuaded Evans to leave London. This statement tallies with what Evans had been told by Christie and would explain some of the errors in his early statements.

The third and fourth statements made after the bodies had been found do not stand up to examination. They fail to mention Christie and have the bodies left in the wash shed at a time when it was still being used by workmen. They also require the baby to have been left unattended for 12 hours on two days without anybody hearing cries. The third and fourth statements read as if they have been dictated by

innocence and blamed Christie but was unable to provide any motive. He was not to know that Christie was a man who gained sexual gratification from the murder of women and that that was all the motive he would need. For legal reasons Evans was only tried for the murder of his daughter Geraldine, although it was possible to use evidence relating to the murder of Mrs Evans. Christie delivered his evidence at the trial in a quiet measured way and the prosecution was able to gloss over his earlier criminal record as the aberrations of a young man which should not be held against the responsible mature man with war service in the police who was now in front of them. The evidence given by Evans was contradictory and his demeanour was that of a liar. Evans was found guilty and went to the gallows remarkably cheerfully but still protesting his innocence.

The Christies continued living at Rillington Place but with a new Jamaican landlord and neighbours. Because of the evidence that came out during the court case Christie lost his job with the Post

the police. It also seems that Mrs Christie must have lied to protect her husband. She would have been more likely to do this if she thought Mrs Evans had died in a failed abortion than if her husband had been engaged in a sexually motivated murder.

At the trial Evans always maintained his

Office and, along with his wife, suffered from poor health. On 14th December 1952 Christie strangled his wife, claiming that he couldn't bear to see her suffer. There was no convincing explanation for the murder. It might have been just to get her out of the way so that the sexually motivated murders could take place.

Possibly Mrs Christie realized that she was living with a murderer and had threatened her husband with exposure. Christie interred her body under the floorboards in the front room. Running out of money Christie sold off most of the furniture.

Over the next three months he murdered and sexually assaulted three women and interred their bodies in an alcove behind the kitchen. By mid-March 1953 Christie had run out of money and as a last resort sublet the flat, receiving three months' rent as a deposit. With this money in his pocket he left and started living in homeless refuges around London. Unfortunately for the new tenants the landlord threw them out and allowed an existing tenant to use the kitchen. While renovating the kitchen he discovered the papered-over entrance to the alcove and peering inside saw a naked back. The police found the bodies of the three missing

of having two stranglers in one house caused some self-questioning among the legal establishment, and a rapid and patently inadequate report was presented by a leading QC. It concluded that Evans had killed both his wife and daughter. This laughable whitewash did not make the doubts disappear and the case was often quoted in debates about capital punishment and was a significant contributor to its end. In 1966 the case was retried and Evans was found not guilty of murdering his daughter but guilty of murdering his wife. This judgment seems bizarre. Why would Christie murder the daughter if he didn't murder Mrs Evans? Surely the only reason to murder the daughter was to avoid detection for the first murder. It

OPPOSITE LEFT: Evans arriving at Paddington Station with police.

OPPOSITE BELOW: Police checking the back garden of Rillington Place.

LEFT: Christie with police.

BELOW: Christie arriving at the back of Notting Hill Police Station.

women and later the body of Mrs Christie in the front room. An alert was put out for Christie and he was soon found. Christie admitted to all the murders except for that of the baby, Geraldine. He was a vain self-serving man who always attempted to place his actions in the best possible light, depicting the women as being depressed or too sexually assertive. Killing a baby couldn't be fitted into this fantasy. The closest he came to admitting his guilt for the murder of Geraldine was a comment in a statement that if somebody said that he'd done it he must have, "but I want to know the truth as much as you do".

Christie's only hope was to plead insanity but it was to no avail: and he was found guilty and sentenced to hang. The sentence was carried out on 15th July 1953. The unusual coincidence

seems that the judges couldn't face accepting that an innocent man had hanged and had to implicate Evans for murder even if it wasn't the one for which he was sent to the gallows.

RUTH ELLIS

MURDER OF DAVID BLAKELY 10TH APRIL 1955

TRIAL BEGAN JUNE 1955

HANGED 13TH JULY 1955

Ruth Ellis became famous for being the last women to be hanged in Britain. The case ostensibly simple showed once again the inadequacies of the British judicial system and the lottery caused by political control of the granting of reprieves. Nine out of ten women sentenced to be executed in the 20th century had their sentences commuted, but political expediency ensured that Ruth Ellis hanged. A more just judicial system would have recognized the many signs of mental illness that Ellis displayed. A more rigorous trial might have investigated the provenance of the gun Ellis used to shoot Blakely.

The Ellis family with their five children moved to London in 1941. At the age of 14 Ruth left school to begin work as a waitress. In 1944 at the age of 17 Ruth fell pregnant by a married Canadian soldier and gave birth to a son who would be known as Andy. The next year the soldier returned to Canada leaving Ruth devastated and suspicious of men. Ruth started working in nightclubs and her talent was recognized by nightclub owner Maurice Conley who promoted her to "hostess". It was in his clubs that she met her future husband, an alcoholic dentist, George Ellis. Ruth seemed attracted to abusive and alcoholic men. Many years later her sister would claim that she'd been sexually abused by her father and there is reason to believe that the same happened to Ruth. Ruth and George Ellis married in 1950 and had one daughter, Georgina, whose paternity George always doubted.

They had a highly unstable relationship

dominated by his alcoholism, the infidelities of both partners and the jealousies that arose from them. On a visit to a hospital where George Ellis was being treated for his alcoholism Ruth became abusive and violent and had to be restrained by the staff. She received sedation from the psychiatrist Dr T P Rees who would continue to treat her until her arrest. In 1951 George Ellis filed for divorce and in 1953 Ruth became manager of the Little Club on Brompton Road. David Blakely, a part-time racing driver, heavy drinker and serial womanizer, became a regular customer and soon moved into Ruth's flat above the club. Despite his wealthy background, the cost of racing, the development of his car, "The Emperor", and a hectic alcohol-fuelled social life always

seemed to leave him short of money. From the start the relationship was turbulent, with frequent arguments and fights. Ruth was jealous of Blakely's other relationships, including that with Carole Findlater and her nanny. In retaliation she would leave him to spend time with other men, especially Desmond Cussen. When Ruth left the Little Club in late 1954

she stayed at Cussen's flat, assuring Blakely that she wouldn't sleep with him. The ménage became a little more complicated when Cussen financed the deposit on a new flat for Ruth and Blakely. In March of 1955 Ruth had a miscarriage after being punched by David Blakely. The relationship came to its fatal conclusion over the Easter weekend. Blakely had spent much of it at the Findlaters' flat where Ruth was convinced he was having an affair with the nanny. She was often outside shouting and demanding that Blakely show himself. She eventually caught up with Blakely the next day, 10th April outside the Magdala Tavern where she fired six shots into him. Blakely was fatally wounded. One shot missed and the ricochet slightly wounded a passer-by, Mrs Gladys K. Yule. Ruth made no attempt to escape and surrendered herself to an off-duty policeman who had been drinking in the pub.

ABOVE: Ellis at Brands Hatch.

RIGHT: Ellis and Blakely with Mr and Mrs Findlater.

The trial took only one and a half days and the verdict was clear from the answer given to the only question asked by the prosecution counsel: "Mrs Ellis, when you fired that revolver at close range into the body of David Blakely what did you intend to do?" Her counsel would have coached her to respond with anything other than: "It is obvious that when I shot him I intended to kill him." Ruth Ellis effectively ended the trial. The judge, Lord Justice Havers ruled out the defence of provocation saying that there was no evidence to allow it. The concept of diminished responsibility at that time was not allowed in British courts. It would be introduced a couple of years later, largely in response to the trial. The jury took just 20 minutes to find her guilty. The verdict and capital sentence caused an outcry, with a 50,000-signature petition and pleas for clemency to the home secretary. The mood was summed up by William Connor writing in the *Daily Mirror* under his pen name

ABOVE: Bullet hole in the wall at the Magdala Tavern.

RIGHT: Clive Gunnell during the Ellis, Blakely trial.

Cassandra, in one of his most powerful pieces in condemnation of the hanging: "The one thing that brings stature and dignity to mankind and raises us above the beasts will have been denied her – pity and the hope of ultimate redemption." Against this the innocent bystander who was injured wrote in the *Evening Standard*: "If Ruth Ellis is reprieved, we may have other vindictive and jealous young women shooting their boy friends in public places and probably innocent blood on their hands. *Crime passionnel* indeed." A French reporter commented: "Passion in England, except for cricket and betting, is always regarded as a shameful disease."

It was only in 1999 when Home Office records were released that it became clear that the murder was a more complicated tale than depicted in the trial. Desmond Cussen had arranged for a solicitor friend, John Bickford, to defend Ellis. He had suppressed evidence which showed that the gun was supplied by Desmond Cussen and that he had driven Ruth Ellis to the Magdala Tavern. Two days before the execution her lawyers submitted new evidence of the abuse she had suffered but to no avail. The Conservatives had just won the General

Daily Mirror

THURS JULY 14 1955

1½ FORWARD WITH THE PEOPLE
No. 16,048

Millions of people are worried about the fate of RUTH ELLIS. Today we ask our readers—

SHOULD HANGING BE STOPPED ?

RUTH ELLIS . . . HER EXECUTION HAS SET THE WHOLE WORLD TALKING.

YESTERDAY was not a happy day in Britain. The sun shone but the nation was upset.

At 9 a.m. in Holloway Gaol a woman of twenty eight suffered death by hanging. Her body was later buried within the precincts of the prison.

Mrs. Ruth Ellis was not a virtuous woman. She admitted shooting one of her two lovers because she thought he was unfaithful. This was the gruesome end to a sordid affair.

Yet who in Britain yesterday felt happy that this mother of two children should lose her life — even though she herself had taken life?

Do the people of Britain believe that the punishment for murder should be CAPITAL PUNISHMENT?

M.P.s would not go past the prison

Are Members of Parliament satisfied that hanging is the expression of the public will?

Some M.P.'s were NOT happy yesterday. Some who were to drive past Holloway Gaol on their way to the House of Commons took a different route to avoid the prison.

Five months ago M.P.s debated capital punishment. On a free vote they decided against a suggestion that the death penalty should be suspended FOR AN EXPERIMENTAL PERIOD OF FIVE YEARS and replaced by life imprisonment.

But did this vote mean that the majority of M.P.s were in favour of hanging? They voted against its suspension — not against its abolition

One man had to decide her fate

How would they have voted on the straight question Should we abolish the death penalty for good?

How would they vote today?

Because there is a death sentence, one man has a terrible responsibility. In court the witnesses give evidence, the jury return a verdict, the judge passes sentence. They all represent the public conscience. All did their duty at the trial of Ruth Ellis.

But one man — a professional politician who happens to be Home Secretary — had to decide whether this woman should be reprieved.

What an unenviable task

While this young woman waited in her prison cell one man had to decide whether there should be visited on her the retribution prescribed in a pitiless Biblical phrase:

"And thine eye shall not pity, but life shall go for life, eye for eye, tooth for tooth, hand for hand, foot for foot."

These words from the Old Testament Book of Deuteronomy were written probably 2500 years ago, before the birth of Christ by an unknown Jewish scribe.

And the enlightened British nation today still follows the teaching of all those centuries ago.

It is understandable why people in

Britain felt uneasy yesterday. In the rush of life the particular case of Ruth Ellis will be forgotten. But the problem of capital punishment remains.

Some murderers attract much public sympathy. There has been more talk about the fate of PRETTY YOUNG Ruth Ellis than there was about the similar fate of UGLY Mrs. Christofi, aged fifty-three, who strangled her daughter-in-law.

But is it unnatural if the execution of a pretty young mother causes public distress?

One fact remains:

Whether a murderess is pretty or ugly. Whether a murderer is young or old. Whether a killer attracts public sympathy or not—the lawful penalty is death by hanging.

Time for a change in the Law?

What the Ruth Ellis case has done is to focus attention on the whole problem of capital punishment.

People are asking

Is hanging degrading to a civilised nation? Has the time come for hanging to be abolished in Britain?

—or—

Should hanging be retained as the just penalty for taking life?

The "Mirror" believes that the public should be able to voice its views.

Today we ask readers to give their verdict. There is a voting form in the Back Page.

Please express your opinion on the voting form in the Back Page

THIS is the Gin...

... FOR A PERFECT GIN AND TONIC

Undoubtedly the coolest, cleanest drink in the world with a subtle flavour of its very own. Best results are easily obtained by simply mixing Gordon's and tonic water in a goodish sized glass, add a thin slice of lemon and relax. Then you'll have proved to yourself that there's nothing absolutely nothing so good as a Gordon's Gin and Tonic.

"ASK FOR IT BY NAME

Gordon's

Stands Supreme

WAR PRICES: BOTTLE 33/9d : ½ BOTTLE 17/2d : 1 NIP: 4/5d : MINIATURE 5/9d. U.K. Tax 1

'Capital Punishment Amendment Act, 1868'

(31 & 32 *Vict.* c. 24, s. 7)

...e sentence of the law passed on ...

...ound guilty of murder, will be carried into execution at   a.m. to-morrow.

Election on a strongly pro-capital punishment platform and had no intention of letting down their supporters. In the words of an adviser to the home secretary: "It would be a bad day for this country if we adopted the doctrine of *crime passionelle*. This was a deliberately planned and cold-bloodedly executed murder."

Ruth Ellis hanged on 13th July 1955. She left behind two children, Georgina, who was adopted and Andy, who was aged 10 at his mother's death. He never recovered from the trauma and committed suicide in a squalid bedsit in 1982. It is said that leading figures involved in the trial helped with the upkeep of the family. A slither of humanity in a tragic, brutal story.

JOHN BODKIN ADAMS

TRIED FOR THE MURDER OF EDITH MORRELL IN 1956. FOUND NOT GUILTY. OTHER POSSIBLE MURDER CHARGES WERE NOT PROCEEDED WITH. HE WAS LATER SUCCESSFULLY PROSECUTED FOR FAULTY RECORD-KEEPING OF DRUGS AND FALSIFICATION OF CREMATION CERTIFICATES AND FINED £2,500

The name John Bodkin Adams should be as infamous in the annals of murderers as those of Doctors Crippen and Shipman. If he'd been found guilty of murdering elderly widow Edith Morrell his alleged involvement in the deaths of about 160 people would have been fully exposed. Instead, after Adams was cleared of the murder of Mrs Morrell, the Crown in the form of Sir Reginald-Mallingham Buller decided not to prosecute in relation to any of the other possible murder charges. This decision, along with many others concerning the trial, has provoked widespread allegations of an establishment conspiracy to save Bodkin Adams.

Adams was born into the Plymouth Brethren. He shared this allegiance with the acid bath murderer John Haigh. His early medical career was mediocre and it was recommended that he go into General Practice. In 1922 he moved to Eastbourne, which was known then, as now, for its large number of wealthy elderly residents. By 1929 Adams had persuaded an elderly resident to lend him £2,000 to buy an 18-room mansion. By the middle of the 1930s rumours were circulating in Eastbourne about the deaths and legacies of Dr Bodkin Adams' patients. He was being sent postcards accusing him of "bumping off" patients. The rumours were sufficient for the other Eastbourne GPs to refuse to include him in a pool system organized during the war to cover the patients of doctors who had been called up. By the mid-Fifties he was rumoured to be the wealthiest

GP in England with a large number of rich and influential patients including magistrate Sir Roland Gwynne, policemen including the chief constable of Eastbourne, Richard Walker, and his deputy Alexander Seekings, and aristocrats such as the Duke of Devonshire. He also had strong personal relationships with Gwynne and Seekings who shared Bodkin Adams' homosexuality.

In 1956 the Eastbourne police received a complaint about the death of a patient of Doctor Adams, Gertrude Hullett. The case was transferred to the Metropolitan Police in the form of the dynamic and successful Detective Superintendent Herbert Hannam. He examined cases going back to 1946 and found 163 to be suspicious, with nurses describing special injections where the drugs were not known, of being excluded from the room when the doctor administered injections and of relatives being excluded from the patient. At first the BMA reminded the local GPs of their duty of confidentiality, effectively instructing them not to cooperate with the investigation. The Attorney-General Sir Reginald Mallingham-Buller spoke with the BMA and showed them

LEFT: Bodkin Adams with police.

OPPOSITE BELOW: *Daily Mirror* front cover.

BELOW: Bodkin Adams with the family of Mrs Hullett. Front row: Bodkin Adams is on the left, Mrs Hullett is in the centre.

ABOVE: Mrs Morrell.

RIGHT: Mrs Hullett at a wedding 16 days before her death, and inset Mr Hullett.

OPPOSITE TOP: From left to right: nurses Ellis, Stronach and Randall, whose evidence was undermined by the defence counsel.

OPPOSITE BELOW: The exhumation of the body.

the prosecution case, causing them to relax their position. When the police examined Bodkin Adams' house they found chaos: there was no Dangerous Drugs Register and food was mixed in with the medicine. Adams attempted to obstruct the police by hiding two bottles of morphine but was caught and challenged by the police. Adams would later be found guilty of obstructing the police and not keeping a Dangerous Drugs Register.

Adams was eventually arrested on 19th December 1956 and charged with the murder of Gertrude Morrell. The Attorney-General could have chosen a number of deaths to prosecute and it was a mystery to the police why he chose the murder of Mrs Morrell as her body had been cremated, making cause of death far more difficult to prove.

Edith Morrell had suffered a stroke in 1948.

Since then Bodkin Adams had prescribed increasing amounts of morphine and adding heroin until she became addicted. She died on 13th November 1950 of what Adams certified to be a stroke. He inherited among other things a Rolls-Royce but stated on her cremation form that he had no pecuniary interest in her death and that therefore a post-mortem was not necessary. Mrs Hullett died of a barbiturate overdose on 23rd August 1956. Adams had been prescribing the dangerous drug since the death of her husband in spite of the risks raised by her frequently stated desire to commit suicide. On 21st July Mrs Hullett wrote a cheque to Adams for £1,000. He processed it rapidly to ensure that the money was in his account before her possible death. On 23rd July she was found in a coma and despite his knowledge of her suicidal state Adams failed to investigate a possible overdose and instead diagnosed a cerebral haemorrhage. When a pathologist, Doctor Sher, proposed that the coma might have been caused by an overdose, Adams argued against investigation. Adams had even tried to organize a private post-mortem before Mrs Hullett's death. At the inquest the coroner stated that he found it "extraordinary that the doctor, knowing the past history of the patient"

did not "at once suspect barbiturate poisoning". After the inquest the cheque disappeared. Adams inherited a Rolls-Royce worth almost £3,000. Mrs Hullett was buried.

The trial in the new year was one of the

"trials of the century" and lasted 17 drama-packed days. The prosecution depended upon the testimonies of the nurses who tended Mrs Morrell. At the opening of the trial the defence produced notebooks of the medicines prescribed at the time. These would have more credibility than the nurses' memories but the prosecution had never seen them. Their provenance was never questioned and, strangely, Sir Reginald Mallingham-Buller failed to ask for an adjournment to allow the prosecution to read the notebooks. With the body cremated the notebooks were crucial. Their very existence was surprising considering the dearth of other records kept by Adams. The prosecution's expert witnesses were not totally convincing and the notebooks raised questions about the testimonies of the nurses. Adams did not give evidence, surprising both the prosecution and the judge. He was found not guilty. Remarkably, the prosecution failed to bring charges on the deaths of Mr and Mrs Hullett, entering a *nolle prosequi*. This was very rare and normally only used when the defendant was too ill to face a further trial. The trial judge, Patrick Devlin, would later describe this as an abuse of process. Adams left the court in triumph. He was later prosecuted successfully for relatively minor offences and struck off by the BMA for a number of years but by 1961 was reinstated as a GP. He eventually died in 1983 leaving an estate of over £400,000.

The question remains as to why Adams was treated in such a generous way by the judicial system. Undoubtedly he was very well connected in Eastbourne society, with evidence that a network of gay friends in the police and among magistrates helped subvert the prosecution. The disappearance of the

£1,000 cheque from Mrs Hullett followed by the disappearance and reappearance of the notebooks would prove crucial in the trial. The uncharacteristic reticence of Sir Reginald Mallingham-Buller in the prosecution of the case might have been explained by his being related to one of Adams' patients. The general political situation at the time was not conducive to hanging doctors. Morale was low in the recently formed NHS and a guilty verdict might have led to a wave of resignations. The country was embroiled in the Suez crisis and Prime Minister Sir Anthony Eden had been forced to resign and was replaced by Harold Macmillan. The new government was highly unstable and did not need any further scandal. It is said that Adams would have named names if the verdict had been different and the case had gone to appeal. I think that we can conclude that Doctor Bodkin Adams was quite fortunate.

PETER MANUEL

MURDER OF NINE PEOPLE: ANNE KNIELANDS 1956, MARION AND VIVIENNE WATT AND MARGARET BROWN 1956, SYDNEY DUNN 1957, ISABELLE COOKE 1957, PETER, DORIS AND MICHAEL SMART 1958

TRIAL OPENED MAY 1958

HANGED 11TH JULY 1958

Peter Manuel was the first of the modern killers. His crimes were impersonal and not motivated by greed. They were the actions of a calculating psychopath, a personality type which would haunt the next 50 years. He needed attention above everything and only murder could sate the craving.

Peter Manuel was born in 1927 in the United States into a Scottish family who had just emigrated. They returned to Scotland when Peter was five. From an early age he was involved in petty crime, increasing to burglary and low-level sexual assaults. There were frequent clashes with the police and periods in reform school. The incidents culminated in an assault with a hammer on a woman in her own house, having woken her up first so that she could experience the horror of the attack. The attack had the hallmarks of his method of operation: the brutal violence, the invasion of the victim's personal space and the attempt at humiliation by exposure of the body. He was sent to Peterhead Prison for nine years for this attack and other similar ones. For much of this time he was kept in solitary confinement after misbehaviour designed to impress the long-term prisoners with whom he was incarcerated. He didn't succeed and was regarded as an outsider and never gained the attention and respect that he craved. After his release the crimes escalated until in 1956 he started to commit murder.

The first murder was of 17-year-old Anne Knielands whose battered body was left on a golf course. Later in the same year he shot three women, Margaret Brown, her sister Marion Watt and daughter Vivienne. Vivienne's clothes had been raised to leave her exposed. Manuel was questioned by the police about both

118

LEFT: Marion Watt, Vivienne Watt and Margaret Brown.

OPPOSITE LEFT: Anne Knielands the first victim.

BELOW: William Watt (bending over) at the funeral of his wife and daughter.

the police were now onto Manuel.

The method of operation and evidence was clear and the hunt was on. Even Glasgow gangland had turned against him and provided information that eventually led to his being apprehended at the home of his parents. He denied all the charges until his mother intervened and told him that he should tell

these crimes but released because of a lack of evidence. Within weeks he was in prison again for burglary and annoyed to discover that the police had remanded Mr Watt, the husband of Marion Watt and father of Vivienne. Manuel began to write to Watt's counsel explaining that another prisoner had confessed to the crime. As more letters arrived it became clear that the correspondent had to be or know the murderer and that Mr Watt was innocent. Manuel was now again out of prison and about to start on his last murder spree. On a trip to Newcastle-under-Lyme in early December 1957 Manuel shot dead and slit the throat of taxi driver Sydney Dunn. Later in the month he murdered 17-year-old Isabelle Cooke. His last murderous frenzy led to him breaking into the house of the Smart family, shooting Peter Smart, his wife Doris and their 10-year-old son Michael. Doris Smart's clothes had again been pulled up and her lower body exposed. After the murder Manuel had made himself a meal and fed the cat. He even returned to the house to open and shut the curtains so that the discovery of the bodies was delayed. However,

the truth, which he then proceeded to do. The confession included murders not previously associated with him and moments of great theatricality such as the discovery of the body of Isabelle Cooke. Manuel had taken the police to a field and when asked where she was replied: "I'm standing on her now".

The trial provided huge drama. On the first day Manuel dismissed his counsel and defended himself, which he did in an effective and stylish manner. The judge commented in his summing up that he had conducted his defence with a skill that was "quite remarkable". However, despite this performance the jury found him guilty and he was sentenced to hang. While awaiting

ABOVE: Watt, who had been charged with the murder of his own family, being driven away.

RIGHT: The Smart family home.

execution Manuel confessed to a further nine killings, although they have not been attributed to him. Perhaps it was just more of his vanity and craving of attention.

There has been much debate since about whether Manuel was mad and should have

been sent to a secure mental institution for the rest of his life. He was clearly a psychopath but almost certainly not mad by the criteria of the MacNaughten rules. He was conscious of his actions and the murders were carried out with unnerving calm. Few people have deserved the ultimate sanction as much as Manuel.

LEFT: Manuel at Barlinie.

BELOW: *Daily Record* front cover.

BOTTOM: The ploughed field where Isabelle Cooke's body was buried.

Daily Record

FRI MAY 30 1958

SCOTLAND'S NATIONAL NEWSPAPER

2½d

No. 19,333

SENTENCED TO DEATH

PETER ANTHONY MANUEL, WHOSE PICTURE IS ON RIGHT, WAS SENTENCED TO DEATH AT GLASGOW HIGH COURT

He was found:-

Not guilty of the murder of Anne Kneilands.

GUILTY of the capital murders of Marion Watt, Margaret Brown, and Vivienne Watt.

GUILTY of the murder of Isabelle Cooke.

GUILTY of the capital murders of the Smart family.

GUILTY of stealing the Smarts' car.

GUILTY of breaking into a house at Bothwell, and firing a gun into a mattress.

GUILTY of breaking into a house at High Burnside, and stealing jewellery and other items.

Not proven on a charge of breaking into a house at North Mount Vernon.

● PETER MANUEL . . . found guilty of seven murders

121

GUENTHER PODOLA

MURDER OF D S PURDY ON 13TH JULY 1959

ARRESTED 16TH JULY 1959

TRIAL OPENED 10TH SEPTEMBER 1959

HANGED 5TH NOVEMBER 1959

Guenther Podola was a German immigrant who shot a policeman in the course of his duty. He feigned amnesia but the jury did not believe him and he was sent to the gallows. He was the last person to be executed for the murder of a policeman. It can have been little surprise that a German (the newspapers referred to him as Fritz) who gunned down a policeman in cold blood could expect little mercy with the war still so recent.

Daily Mirror

WED SEPT. 23 1959

2½d FORWARD WITH THE PEOPLE No. 17,347

PODOLA

LOSS OF MEMORY IS NOT GENUINE

—SAYS JURY

Trial for murder begins today

TURN TO PAGE 13

GUNTHER PODOLA

Fit and sane to stand trial.

ROMANCE and I—by CALLAS

OPERA star Maria Callas is pictured at London Airport last night. She had just flown in from Rome.

Before leaving Italy, she said that there was no romance between herself and the Greek millionaire shipowner Aristotle Onassis with whose name her own had been linked.

"There is no romance," she insisted, adding: "A woman in my position could do with a little romance."

She and the Onassis family were simply "friends."

Her separation from her husband, she said, was being held up by difficulties over money.

On landing in Britain she agreed that she was short of cash. "But I'm not broke," she said.

The opera star is here to appear at the Royal Festival Hall and on ITV before leaving for Berlin.

Advertiser's Announcement

The Marquis and the model

THEY'RE together everywhere. Nightclubbing. Motor-racing. Party-going. A handsome, titled, moneyed man-of-the-world ... and a girl who was tapping a typewriter two years ago. How did she do it? How did she acquire poise ... earn the admiration of men and the envy of women ... develop the ability to model fabulous clothes? First, she had the basic beauty that is in all women. Second, she had faith in her ability. Oh yes, she had luck, too. But above all she made the most of herself. She had a lovely figure ... and she accentuated it. Lovely hair ... and she high-lighted it. Lovely teeth ... and she made sure they gleamed always. We can't tell you what make of bra she wears or what she uses on her hair. But we can tell you what makes her smile so devastating. Her own personal magnetism, of course, but it's brought out, made more radiant, more telling, by a simple, yet brilliant beauty aid, a make-up toothpaste called Cosmetic. Give yourself that extra touch of glamour by using every day and before every date Gordon-Moore's Cosmetic—the ruby-red toothpaste of the stars. You'll be able to see for yourself how Cosmetic toothpaste—the only toothpaste with rougeryl—polishes your teeth to dazzling whiteness. You'll be able to see for yourself how it subtly tints your gums, making your teeth whiter still by contrast. *Get Gordon-Moore's Cosmetic toothpaste at your local chemist or store today. Beauty Box Size 1/10½d. Also large Celebrity Size only 2/11½d.*

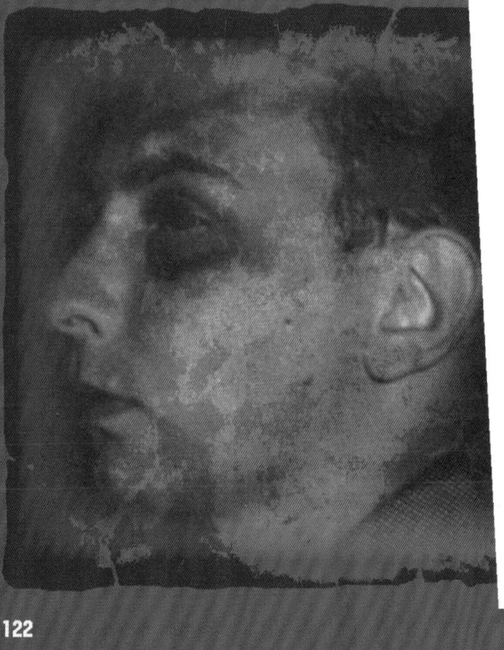

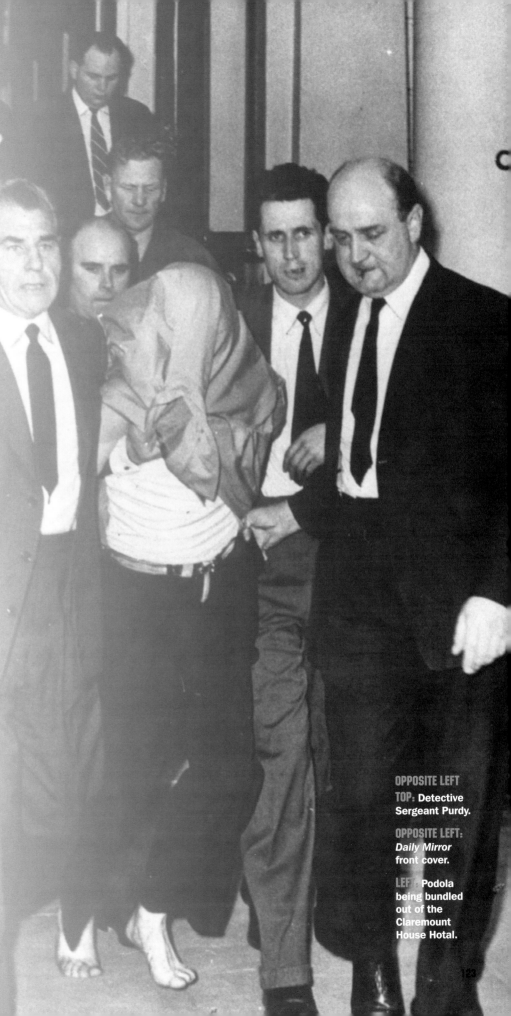

Podola was born in Berlin in 1929 and was brought up there during the traumatic period of the Second World War, in which his father died. In 1952 he escaped from East Berlin to the West and emigrated to Canada where he stayed for six years until deported in 1958 after being imprisoned for petty crime. In 1959 he appeared in London affecting a gangster persona and carrying out a number of burglaries. One of these was of a model, Mrs Verne Schiffman, from whom he stole furs and jewellery with a value of about £2,000. A couple of days later she received a letter blackmailing her and she informed the police. The police tapped her phone so that when she was called again on 13th July they were able to trace the call to a phone box at South Kensington Tube Station. The nearest police were scrambled and at 3.50pm Mrs Schiffman heard a scuffle at the other end of the line. Somebody said, "OK lad, we're police officers", followed by: "Mrs Schiffman, this is Detective Sergeant Purdy. Remember my name." Unfortunately for all concerned the events of the next hour would ensure that nobody would forget DS Purdy's name.

Podola was arrested by DS Purdy and DS John Sandford

OPPOSITE LEFT TOP: Detective Sergeant Purdy.

OPPOSITE LEFT: *Daily Mirror* front cover.

LEFT: Podola being bundled out of the Claremount House Hotal.

but broke free as they took him up the steps to the street outside. The officers chased Podola to a block of flats in Onslow Square where he was cornered and recaptured, but as DS Purdy turned away for a moment to talk to his colleague Podola pulled out a gun and shot the policeman dead. As DS Sandford went to assist his colleague Podola made his escape. The next two days saw a massive police hunt which eventually tracked Podola down to the Claremont House Hotel on Queensgate.

On the afternoon of 16th July the police broke down the door of Podola's hotel room knocking him out in the process. Forty-five minutes later, after some medical attention, he was led out, with a towel over his head, to the police car and taken to Chelsea Police Station. The next day he was admitted to hospital. Podola claimed that he could not remember any of the events of the shooting because of the amnesia caused by the blow to his head during his arrest. Over the following weeks Podola was examined by doctors to establish the truth of the amnesia claims.

Because of these doubts the trial in September was split into two parts. The first was spent establishing the truth of the amnesia claims and lasted nine days, with doctors having opposing opinions. The jury decided that the amnesia was feigned and that Podola should face trial. They were then discharged and a new jury brought in for the second half which

ABOVE: Podola, still with a black eye from his arrest, is taken from hospital to court.

lasted only two days. Podola made a statement: "I do not remember the circumstances leading up to the events or to this shooting. I do not know if I did it or whether it was an accident or an act of self-defence. For those reasons I am unable to admit or deny the charge against me ..." It took only half an hour for the jury to find him guilty. He hanged on 5th November 1959.

MURDER IS WRONG. HANGING IS STATE MURDER

"THEY WERE THE BEST YEARS OF OUR LIVES. THEY CALLED THEM THE SWINGING SIXTIES. THE BEATLES AND THE ROLLING STONES WERE RULERS OF POP MUSIC, CARNABY STREET RULED THE FASHION WORLD ... AND ME AND MY BROTHER RULED LONDON. WE WERE FUCKING UNTOUCHABLE."

RONNIE KRAY WRITING ABOUT THE SIXTIES IN HIS AUTOBIOGRAPHY.

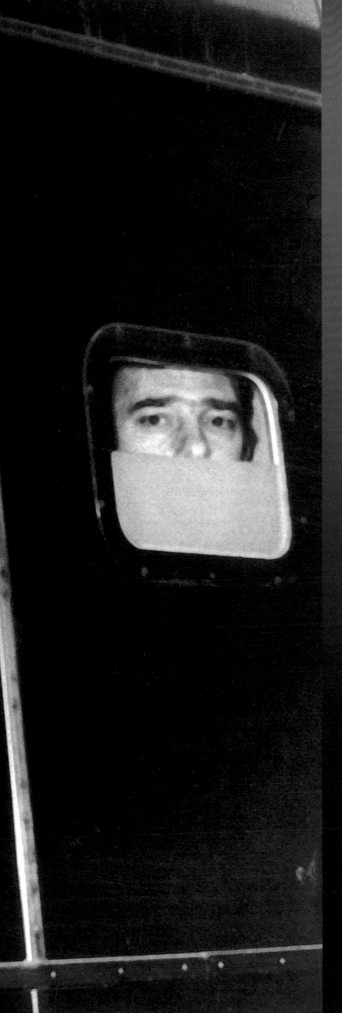

1960-1969

1963 THE GREAT TRAIN ROBBERY: The most creative crime of the century but fatally undermined by small errors.

1964 GWYNNE OWEN EVANS AND PETER ANTHONY ALLEN: The pointless murder of John West in an inept robbery leaves the perpetrators the last men to be hanged in England.

1965 IAN BRADY AND MYRA HINDLEY: The murder of children.

1966 HARRY ROBERTS, JOHN DUDDY AND JACK WITNEY: The ruthless murder of three policemen.

1967 RONALD AND REGINALD KRAY: The murders of George Cornell and Jack McVitie.

1968 MARY BELL: The murder of two children.

1969 BIBLE JOHN MURDERS: The murder of three women in 1960s Glasgow.

LEFT: Ronnie and Reggie Kray are driven away after being sentenced to 30 years' imprisonment.

THE GREAT TRAIN ROBBERY

8TH AUGUST 1963

AT THE TIME, THE LARGEST ROBBERY IN BRITAIN IN MONETARY VALUE

THE GANG MEMBERS WE KNOW OF WERE: BRUCE REYNOLDS, RONNIE BIGGS, CHARLIE WILSON, JIMMY HUSSEY, JOHN WHEATER, BRIAN FIELD, JIMMY WHITE, TOMMY WISBEY, GORDON GOODY, BUSTER EDWARDS, ROGER CORDREY, BOB WELCH AND THREE MEN ONLY KNOWN AS 'NUMBER 1', 'NUMBER 2' AND 'NUMBER 3'

The Great Train Robbery has long held a special place in the history of British crime. If Doctor Crippen's is the definitive murder, The Great Train Robbery holds the same position for theft. It is not because of the amount stolen, although for the time it was a huge theft. It was not for the violence, because although the train driver Jack Mills was badly injured when hit by an iron bar no guns were used. It is the ambition of the enterprise that appeals.

To stop a train in the middle of the night with 70 workers on board, move it to a siding, knock out communications and unload a large number of mail bags packed with over £2 million of used banknotes was a magnificent organizational achievement. But in a very British tradition there are all the minor cock-ups which led to the capture of most of the gang, followed by daring escapes, hideouts across the world and ending with a return to Britain of the gang's most famous member so that he can enjoy one last pint of bitter. Forty five years after the crime Ronnie Biggs has only recently been released on compassionate grounds.

At 3.30am on 8th August 1963 the Glasgow to London Mail Train was stopped in Buckinghamshire at Sears Crossing by a red light rigged up by Roger Cordrey, the electrician in the gang.

DAILY MIRROR, Friday, September 13, 1963   PAGE 13

IED

Nine people who may be able to assist the police with their Great Train Robbery inquiries

RONALD CHRISTOPHER EDWARDS
32-year-old ex-boxer and florist, whose picture was released by the Yard yesterday. He is 5ft. 6in. tall, has fresh complexion, dark brown hair, small scar on left side of nose. Known as "Buster."

JUNE ROSE EDWARDS
attractive wife of "Buster" Edwards — another picture circulated by the police yesterday. She is 31, 5ft. 3in. tall, with striking black hair. She has a daughter aged two-and-a-half.

ROY JOHN JAMES
28, known as "The Weasel," is 5ft. 4in. tall, has light brown hair, hazel eyes, bow legs. Is a keen racing driver and fond of gambling.

BRUCE RICHARD REYNOLDS
pictured, left, with his wife Frances. Reynolds, 41, is 6ft. 1in. tall, has light brown hair, grey eyes, cleft in chin, wears glasses. Speaks with Cockney accent.

JOHN THOMAS DALY
pictured, right, with his wife Barbara. Daly, 32, is Irish, 5ft. 11in. tall, broadly built with dark brown wavy hair, blue eyes. Drinks double Scotches, smokes big cigars.

JAMES WHITE
43, 5ft. 10in. Slim. Right forearm tattooed with Royal Artillery crest.

CHERRY WHITE
wife of James White. Aged 34, 5ft. 2in., olive or Mediterranean type complexion.

SEARS CROSSING

The train driver, Jack Mills was overpowered and, although injured forced to drive the train and the front two carriages that had been decoupled a further 800 yards to Bridgeco Bridge. There the rest of the gang were waiting to unload the haul from the high-value carriage which was the robbers' target. The workers inside were overcome and the gang spent the next three hours unloading the huge number of bags of cash. They had £2,631,784 in cash, far more than expected. The gang returned to a farmhouse 27 miles away, planning to stay there a couple of

OPPOSITE LEFT BELOW: *Daily Mirror* most wanted.

ABOVE: The lorry used to transport the haul and inset, the traindriver, Jack Mills.

LEFT: Sears Crossing from the air.

weeks. However, it quickly became clear from the furore in the press that the huge police operation would discover them and the gang decided to split. It was now that the carefully conceived plan started to unravel. The farmhouse at which they had been staying, both before and after the raid, was not cleaned up properly and the police found a huge number of fingerprints and other evidence.

OPPOSITE LEFT:
The bridge where the train was unloaded from the air and ground level.

LEFT:
Leatherslade Farm.

BELOW LEFT:
Biggs arrested in 1963.

BELOW RIGHT:
Mirror, Britain's 12 most guarded. The irony of this headline would soon become apparent.

The purchase of the farm had also been poorly organized, allowing the police to track down members of the gang. The police had assigned their top men, Detective Chief Superintendent Tommy Butler and Detective Jack Slipper, to find the robbers. Within a day of the police tracking down the farm they arrested Roger Cordrey, followed a week later by Charlie Wilson and a month after by Ronnie Biggs. The police had found their fingerprints at the farmhouse. Within a couple of months

Tommy Wisbey, Jim Hussey and Bob Welch had been arrested.

At the end of March they were sentenced to between 24 and 30 years in prison. On 12th

THROUGH
TRAPDOOR
IN ROOF

INTO
GETAWAY
CARS

August 1964 Charlie Wilson escaped from Winsome Green Prison, followed a year later by Ronnie Biggs from Wandsworth Prison. Biggs was smuggled to France where he had plastic surgery and acquired a new identity and passport before moving on to Australia where his family joined him. Meanwhile Bruce Reynolds, Jimmy White and Buster Edwards were arrested in 1968 and sentenced to long

ABOVE: Biggs escape route and inset, Bruce Reynolds.

RIGHT: Charles Wilson being led away.

UP ESCAPE
LADDERS

ON TO
VAN FLOOR

LEFT: Biggs celebrates 25 years since the Great Train Robbery. Later the thought of a beer would lure him back to the UK.

BELOW: Buster Edwards.

escalating cost of health care drove him back to the UK. He was returned to prison for eight years before being released on compassionate grounds in 2009. Bruce Reynolds, widely regarded as the mastermind of the operation, has made a new career as a commentator on organized crime. Buster Edwards became a flower seller and suffered the indignity of being portrayed by Phil Collins in the film *Buster*. He committed suicide in 1994. Jack Mills, the injured train driver, never worked again and died of leukaemia in 1970. There is no evidence that the injuries incurred in the robbery played any part in his death.

terms in prison, although they were much shorter than those handed out in 1964.Biggs realized with the arrests in the UK the hunt would be renewed for him and he moved to Brazil via Panama and Venezuela.He would remain there for the next 30 years, thwarting all attempts to extradite him until he returned voluntarily in 2001 claiming that he just wanted to "walk into a Margate pub as an Englishman and buy a pint of bitter".

Less romantic observers argue that the

GWYNNE OWEN EVANS AND PETER ANTHONY ALLEN

MURDER OF JOHN WEST ON 7TH APRIL 1964

TRIAL OPENED JULY 1964

HANGED 13TH AUGUST 1964

For centuries men and women had gone to the gallows in England. In many cases it was for the most appalling of crimes, there had been many miscarriages of justice and many cases when the sentence should have been commuted. It seems so strange that all this human drama and tragedy should end with such a banal case and that the names of the last men to hang in England, Evans and Allen, should be largely unknown. Centuries of state barbarism came to an end on 13th August 1964 and nobody seemed to notice.

A delivery driver, John West, was bludgeoned to death in his home in Workington in the small hours of 7th April 1964. The purpose of the crime was robbery but the yield was tiny and the murder completely unnecessary. It was also incompetent because the murderers left behind a medallion with the name of Evans inscribed

Daily Mirror

TUES MAR 13 1956

2D FORWARD WITH THE PEOPLE
No. 16,252

"Wicked tongues are sniping at my marriage"
—SAYS AUDREY HEPBURN

FILM star Audrey Hepburn, 26, pictured above with her American husband, Mel Ferrer, 38, said in Hollywood yesterday: "WICKED TONGUES ARE SNIPING AT MY MARRIAGE."
Then she hit back at American gossip columnists who have been saying that her husband dominates her. She said her husband did not run her life or her career. She had never been happier.
Audrey and Mel were married in 1954, she for the first time, he for the fourth time. "MEL IS NOT A SVENGALI."—See Page 3

Jack Dunkley's talking horse says—

TROUBLE TROUBLE TROUBLE BUT THERE'S NOTHING TO WORRY YOU IN—

CYPRUS JORDAN MIDDLE EAST CRICKET IN PAKISTAN

Racing Mirror

It's the trouble-free guide to the Flat season which starts next Monday—all you want to know in a handy tear-out page, every day in the Daily Mirror.

AGAIN IT'S YES— ABOLISH HANGING

FOR the second time in less than a month the House of Commons last night voted in favour of abolishing the death penalty for murder.

This time, Mr. Sydney Silverman's Bill to end hanging was before the House. An amendment to reject it was defeated, and the Bill, without a further vote, now goes forward for detailed consideration by a committee of the whole House.

HOW THE M.P.s VOTED

Abolish death penalty	286
Keep it	262
Majority	24

The major vote when hanging was debated last month was on a Government motion for its retention. This was beaten by 293 to 262, a majority of 31.

One feature of last night's vote was the unchanged total of 262 in favour of retention of hanging.

The fact that the vote against hanging was down by 7, suggests that most of the 48 Tory M.P.s who voted for abolition last month stuck to their decision.

The debate is reported on the Centre Pages. What the 'Mirror' says—Page 2.

Daily Mirror

WED JULY 11 1956

2ᴰ FORWARD WITH THE PEOPLE ✦ ✦
No. 16,354

The great hanging debate

LORDS HANG ON TO ROPE

The dapper young Duke

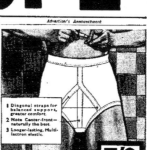

THE Duke of Kent, 20, set a new fashion in morning clothes yesterday.
With his sister, Princess Alexandra (above), he went to a London wedding immaculate in morning coat, pearl grey waistcoat, silk tie —and bold CHECK trousers instead of the usual stripes.

The Duke was among 600 guests at the wedding in St. James's Church, Piccadilly, of the Marquis of Hertford, who married the Comtesse Louise de Caraman-Chimay, from Belgium.
The general verdict on the Duke's trousers was: "Quite attractive."

In Savile-row, home of men's exclusive tailoring, one tailor, whose prices for morning suits start at 45 guineas, said: -
"We do not yet know whether check trousers are 'correct' with morning wear, but it was very individual of the Duke to wear them."

THE HOUSE OF LORDS LAST NIGHT THREW OUT THE BILL TO ABOLISH HANGING.
The vote: 238 to 95—a majority of 143.
As soon as the result of the vote was known, Sir Anthony Eden called a Cabinet meeting for today.

Crowded Chamber

Drama and tension mounted as M.P.s crowded into the Chamber in the closing stages of the two-day debate.
The sponsor of the Bill, Mr. Sydney Silverman, who had piloted it through the Commons, stood at the bar of the House for nearly the whole of the debate.
Lord Salisbury, Leader of the House, hinted that the Government might introduce a Bill providing for special categories for murder for which hanging should be kept.

Debate: See Back Page.

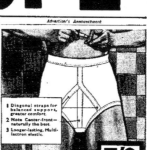

Advertiser's Announcement

Man alive!
WHY PAY MORE?

FULL SUPPORT puts spring in a man's step. Adds inches to his stride. Leaves more money in his pocket too—if it's Activity "Snugs" he's wearing. Five and sixpence all sizes! And they last through literally hundreds of washings.
Why pay more?
Once you've worn Activity Center-front, you'll never want any other. Most good men's outfitters stock them.

1 Diagonal straps for balanced support, greater comfort.
2 Note Center-front— naturally the best.
3 Longer-lasting, Multi-lactron elastic.

5/6
SNUGS & SINGLETS
ALL SIZES

SINGLETS 5/6

Activity
MADE IN ENGLAND
CENTER-FRONT

ACTIVITY TEXTILES LTD., STOCKTON-ON-TEES

on it and a memo from a former girlfriend with her address. Within two days the police had arrested the two men and charged them with capital murder under the Homicide Act of 1957. Although the number of crimes allowing a capital sentence had been much reduced, it was still available for murders committed in pursuance of a robbery.

Evans was found with West's watch in his pocket but blamed Allen for beating the victim to death. The jury found them both guilty and they were sentenced to hang. The executions occurred simultaneously in Strangeways and Walton prisons on 13th August 1964.

Hanging in Britain in the 20th century

The last 200 years saw a gradual reduction in the number of crimes punishable by death. By the end of the 19th century capital punishment was reserved for murder and treason. In 1908 the minimum age for capital punishment was

---

Daily Mirror

Tuesday, November 9, 1965
Telephone: FLEet-street 0246

No-Hanging Bill becomes law.. and two murderers take their place in history

DEATH CELL IS ABOLISHED

Junction-land vicar defends that TV play

By MIRROR REPORTER

A VICAR at Clapham, London—setting of the BBC's controversial television play "Up the Junction"—said yesterday that he had refused to sign a petition protesting about the programme.

The play, based on a book by Nell Dunn, was about sex, violence and abortion in the Clapham Junction district.

The vicar—the Rev. Stanley Evans, of St. Mark's, Battersea Rise—said yesterday:

"I was approached by East Hill Congregational Church, Wandsworth, to sign a protest petition. I refused to have anything to do with it.

"I thought the play was a perfectly true picture of a certain section of the community round here."

'Tired'

Mr. Evans, chairman of Battersea Moral Welfare Committee went on:

"Because I'm a vicar I can't condone extra-marital sex. But I'm tired of seeing the Church heading down in a bomb-proof shelter of piety and miniatures.

"If unmarried people want to have sex who is the church to say they are right or wrong?

"If contraceptives are used, and venereal disease is avoided, extra marital sex is NOT against Christian principles.

"It's time we ministers that there are worse things in life."

STAND BACK ON PAY—BROWN

ECONOMICS Minister Mr. George Brown said last night that the Government had tried to ensure a fairer distribution of income.

Speaking at Hammersmith, London, he said: "Some of our people have got to get it into their heads that they may have to stand back a bit until others catch up and we get a fairer distribution of income."

'Squeeze' hits new HP business

THE credit squeeze has caused a sharp drop in new "never-never" business.

In the July-September quarter of this year, it fell to only one-fifth of last year's average.

The Board of Trade said last night that in these three months the total hire purchase debt rose by only £8,000,000.

This compares with increases of £31,000,000 and £44,000,000 in the second and first quarters of the year.

TANK DEATH: 3 ARE RAPPED

A NAVAL officer and two Royal Marine officers have been censured over the death of a soldier drowned in a Centurion tank when a secret landing craft capsized on trials in Poole Harbour, Dorset.

The Ministry of Defence announced the censure last night, but the names of the officers were not disclosed.

The parents of the soldier, Lance Corporal Thomas Rylance, 23, of Barnsley, Yorks, received a letter from the Ministry saying that there had been "inadequate preparation for trials."

PLAN TO BEAT THE WILDCATS

By
BRIAN MORTON-SMITH

A PLAN to outlaw unofficial strikes in return for compulsory trade union membership has been put before the Royal Commission on trade unions and employers' organisations.

It comes from the 1,000,000-strong Amalgamated Engineering Union—the first major union to submit evidence to the Commission—in a memorandum published today.

The AEU chiefs suggest that, if the Government would introduce legislation to enforce the "closed shop" principle, trade unions would agree to outlaw all unofficial strikes.

With compulsory trade union membership, says the memorandum, unions could exercise far more disciplinary power over their members. This would act as an effective deterrent against wildcat strikes.

The AEU men go on to say that such a system would also mean the unions giving up some of their disciplinary powers to an independent body.

Catalyst

"If expulsion from a union means the loss of a person's livelihood," the memorandum continues, "it would be reasonable to deny unions the absolute right to expel a member unless and until it had been proved to everybody's satisfaction that the expulsion was justified."

The AEU describes the union as an ever-present catalyst for industrial unrest." But it repudiates employers who brand all

shop stewards as trouble-makers. The memorandum says that bloody-minded employers have no one but themselves to blame if they find that they have to deal with bloody-minded shop stewards.

"It is our experience," the type of shop steward their outlook reflects," the AEU adds.

THE No-Hanging Bill became law yesterday—and two men waiting in death cells became part of history.

The two men are David Wardley, 19, and David Chapman, 23.

Phone calls to two jails sent officials to their cells shortly after 2.30 p.m.

At that time the Bill abolishing the death penalty for murder was

By EDWARD VALE

given the Royal Assent in the House of Lords.

And Wardley and Chapman were told: "Your death sentences have been commuted to life imprisonment."

Wardley was sentenced last month for the murder of Detective Sergeant James Stanford of Wolverhampton.

Chapman got the death sentence at Leeds on November 1 for murdering a night watchman.

They are the last convicted murderers to occupy condemned cells.

Guarded

Until yesterday, both were guarded day and night by two warders.

The drama of the death cells ended a years-long

campaign by Mr. Sydney Silverman, Labour M.P. for Nelson and Colne, who successfully piloted the Bill ending hanging for murder through Parliament.

Last

The last people to hang in Britain were Gwynne Evans, 24, and Peter Allen, 21. They were executed on August 13, 1964, for the murder of John West, 53, found battered to death at his home at Seaton, Cumberland.

Victor Knight writes:

The no-hanging law was one of six Bills which received the Royal Assent yesterday.

Among the others were Mr. Richard Crossman's "Fair Rents" Bill and the new law to make incitement to race hatred an offence.

A long list of new Bills will be announced today when the Queen opens the new session of Parliament.

M6—speed blamed for fog deaths

By PATRICK MENNEM

DEATH crashes on a fogbound motorway last week were caused by speed, the police told the Transport Ministry yesterday.

Five people died, and fifty-six were hurt in crashes on the M6 in Staffordshire and Lancashire last Friday night.

Yesterday, senior police officers from the two counties reported to Mr. Stephen Swingler, Joint Parliamentary Secretary at the Ministry of Transport.

Mr. Swingler said later: "The report from the officers confirmed that it was excessive speed by drivers, in very bad conditions, that caused the accidents and the casualties.

Special

"No other abnormal factors have been indicated."

The police made a special report to lorry drivers who go too fast and run into fog.

Mr. Swingler added:

"I shall be reporting to the Minister tomorrow—and will suggest that we make an immediate review of all the rules and regulations covering conditions on the motorways."

David Wardley . . . a phone call yesterday ended his death-cell wait.

BLUNDER AGAIN BY U.S. JETS

A MERICAN planes have again accidentally bombed friendly South Vietnamese people, U.S. officials said last last night.

One woman was killed and ten other people injured when U.S. Marine Skyhawk jets dropped eight 250lb. bombs on Loc Thuong, 240 miles north of Saigon, capital of South Vietnam.

The error was made because a map reference figure was incorrect. An inquiry has been started.

Ten days ago, American aircraft killed forty-eight people by bombing the wrong village.

Several US pilots were sent home from South Vietnam last month for accidentally bombing friendly villages.

US Navy bombers yesterday struck again at missile sites 60 miles south of Hanoi, North Vietnam's capital.

Open up the Party Season with sparkling Babycham

BABYCHAM
Champagne Perry

Invitation
Babycham at home
any night you fancy!

raised to 16 and then to 18 in 1933. In 1922 the charge of infanticide replaced murder for mothers killing children below the age of one year. Before the Second World War there was a proposal for an experimental suspension of capital punishment for five years but its introduction was postponed by the war. After the war the House of Commons passed the bill but it was rejected by the House of Lords. A Royal Commission was set up to examine the issue but with public opinion still strongly in favour of hanging the Commission declined to end the practice. In the Fifties a series of decisions undermined support. The cases of Timothy Evans, Derek Bentley and Ruth Ellis showed the arbitrary nature of the punishment and highlighted possible miscarriages of justice. In 1957 the Homicide Act restricted hanging to six categories: in the course or furtherance of theft; by shooting or explosion;the murder of a policeman;the murder of a prison warder by a prisoner; while resisting arrest or during an escape;the second of two murders committed on separate occasions within the UK.

Hanging was also retained for treason and some military-related offences. In 1965, with the recent election of a large number of new Labour MPs, a lifetime campaigner for the abolition of hanging, Sydney Silverman, introduced a private member's bill suspending capital punishment for five years. It was passed by a large majority and the abolition was made permanent in 1969.

The abolition of capital punishment was an important element in the general liberalizing and civilizing of British society. If George Orwell had still been alive, surely he would have approved of this less barbarous nation.

IAN BRADY AND MYRA HINDLEY

MURDER OF FIVE YOUNG PEOPLE BETWEEN 1963 AND 1965:

PAULINE READE 12TH JULY 1963

JOHN KILBRIDE 23RD NOVEMBER 1963

KEITH BENNETT 16TH JUNE 1964

LESLEY ANNE DOWNEY 26TH DECEMBER 1964

EDWARD EVANS 6TH OCTOBER 1965

BRADY ARRESTED 7TH OCTOBER 1965, HINDLEY 11TH OCTOBER 1965

TRIAL OPENED APRIL 1966

BOTH SENTENCED TO LIFE IMPRISONMENT WITH A MINIMUM TARIFF OF 30 YEARS.

The crimes committed by Brady and Hindley were a new development in British murder. Brady was a narcissistic psychopath who murdered as a personal statement in the same way as another person might create a work of art.

Most murders before the late 1950s, however gruesome and savage, had a primary motive such as revenge, lust or money. Peter Manuel in the late Fifties started the trend towards murder as an end in itself and in a perverted way Ian Brady perfected the form. They were to set a horrifying trend for the rest of the century, exemplified by the murders carried out by Nilsen, Fred and Rose West and Harold Shipman.

Ian Brady was born in Glasgow to single mother Peggy Stuart who gave her son up for unofficial adoption at the age of four months

to a family with the surname Sloane. He would have a difficult childhood, developing a fascination with Nazi philosophy and art while slipping into petty crime and causing his adoptive parents to return him to his natural mother. She had moved to Manchester with her husband called Brady whose name Ian took. Despite the change of circumstances the crime continued and resulted in his being sent to Strangeways Prison in Manchester. The fascination with Nazism developed into sadomasochism and the psychology of domination. On leaving prison Brady had a series of mundane jobs and then started work at Millwards Merchandising as a stock clerk. There he met a girl four years his junior, Myra Hindley. She found his intelligence and style attractive but it took him about a year to notice her. However, by the new year of 1961 they were in a relationship, with Hindley working hard to fulfil Brady's far from conventional sexual requirements. She'd become obsessed with him and would do anything he requested, even up to and including rape and murder.

The first victim, Pauline Reade, was lured into Hindley's car and taken onto Saddleworth

ABOVE:
Saddleworth
Moor in May
1966.

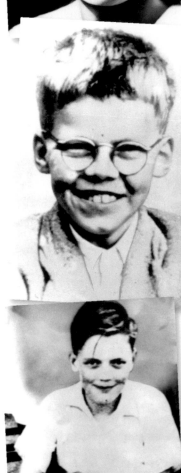

Moor on the pretext of looking for a lost glove. Brady followed on a motorbike and jumped Reade from behind, raping and then murdering her before burying her body on the moor. In November 12-year-old John Kilbride was lured from Ashton-under-Lyme market by Hindley and driven to Saddleworth Moor for the waiting Brady who raped and murdered him. In June the following year Keith Bennett was lured in a similar way and murdered. His body has never been found. The next victim, 10-year-old Lesley Ann Downey, was abducted and taken to the house that Hindley shared with her grandmother. There she was raped, tortured and eventually murdered, with the events recorded on audiotape and in photographs taken by Hindley. The voices

THE HUNT

Beagles aid big search for John, 12

A 25-STRONG beagle pack went hunting across a gale-swept moor yesterday . . . for a missing boy.

They were brought in to aid the massive search for 12-year-old John Kilbride, who vanished ten days ago.

The Holme Valley Beagles were out for

JOHN KILBRIDE

their annual fox-clearing on a 3,000-acre estate near Ashton-under-Lyne, Lancs.

Mr. Maurice England, from Morley, near Leeds, who was in charge of the hounds, agreed to their hunting for the boy too.

But they searched in vain for John, of Small-shaw-lane, Ashton.

of Lesley, Brady and Hindley can be heard clearly on the tape. They buried her body on the moor the next day. Fortunately, Brady's insanity grew sufficiently for him to make the mistake that would bring the campaign to an end. It would, however, cost the innocent life of Edward Evans who was lured to Hindley's home from the railway station. David Smith, Hindley's brother-in-law, was invited around for the evening to witness the murder. Evans was bludgeoned 14 times by the blunt end of an axe before being strangled. Smith was told to help move the body upstairs which he did, fearing that he would be the next victim. Hindley spent

S ON.. FOR A BOY

OPPOSITE LEFT:
Pauline Read,
Keith Bennett,
John Kilbride
and Lesley Ann
Downey.

LEFT: Article
in the *Mirror*
on huntsmen
helping in the
search for John
Kilbride.

BELOW: Police
searching
houses for
missing John
Kilbride.

the hunt that set out after foxes searches barren moorland for clues to a missing boy.

her time making jokes about the mess caused. When David Smith got home he told his wife the awful tale and they went straight to the police, who fortunately believed them. The next day the police raided the house, found the body and immediately arrested Brady who attempted to keep Hindley out of the story. Hindley wasn't arrested for another four days while the police searched the house and car, finding a detailed plan for the murder of Evans. Smith had told the police of Brady's boast of bodies on the moor and a search of Saddleworth Moor was launched, resulting in the discovery of the body of Lesley Ann Downey and, 11 days later,

that of John Kilbride. A more detailed search of the house revealed a left luggage ticket. On redeeming it the police found sadomasochistic equipment, photographs of a naked and bound Lesley Ann Downey and the horrific audiotape of her last hours. Despite this overwhelming evidence Brady and Hindley denied their guilt and tried to implicate David Smith. The couple were found guilty at the trial and sentenced to life imprisonment. The trial judge described Brady as being "wicked beyond belief". They are the most hated people in the British criminal system, having combined sadistic murder with crimes against children. Hindley finally admitted her part in the murders of all five victims. Information from her helped the police to find the remains of Pauline Reade in 1987. It is unlikely Hindley would ever have been released despite any repentance and her rediscovery of the Catholic faith. The attempt to escape with her lesbian prison officer lover showed how little she really understood and repented of her crimes. Her death of a heart attack in 2002 at the age of 60 saved a future home secretary any difficult decisions. Ian Brady claims that he never wants to be released. I am sure that his wish will be fulfilled. He has been back to Saddleworth Moor in attempts to locate the remaining body of Keith Bennett. It is not clear how genuine he was in those efforts. In 1985 Brady was diagnosed with a severe psychiatric problem and transferred to Broadmoor. In 1999 he went on hunger strike demanding that he be allowed to die and was

ABOVE: Edward Evans and the terrace house where he was bludgeoned to death.

RIGHT: David Smith and his wife.

OPPOSITE RIGHT TOP: Letter from Myra Hindley to the mother of Lesley Ann Downey.

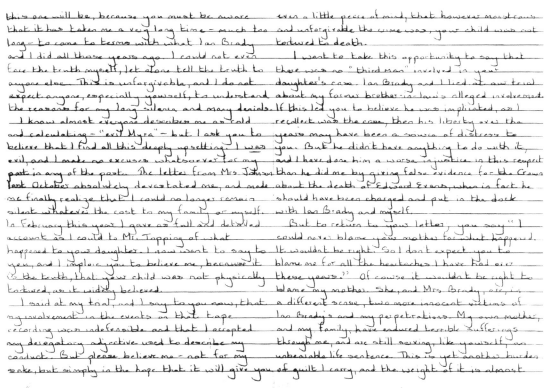

this one will be, because you must be aware that it has taken me a very long time – much too long – to come to terms with what Ian Brady and I did all those years ago. I could not even face the truth myself, let alone tell the truth to anyone else. This is unforgivable, and I do not expect anyone, especially yourself, to understand the reasons for my long silence and many denials.

I know almost everyone describes me as cold and calculating – "evil Myra" – but I ask you to believe that I find all this deeply upsetting. I was evil, and I make no excuses whatsoever for my part in any of the past. The letter from Mrs Johnson last October absolutely devastated me, and made me finally realize that I could no longer remain silent whatever the cost to my family or myself. In February this year I gave as full and detailed account as I could to Mr. Topping of what happened to your daughter. I now want to say to you, and I implore you to believe me, because it is the truth, that your child was not physically tortured, as it is widely believed.

I said at my trial, and I say to you now, that my involvement in the events on that tape recording was indefensible and that I accepted any derogatory adjective used to describe my conduct. But please believe me – not for my sake, but simply in the hope that it will give you

even a little peace of mind, that however monstrous and unforgivable the crime was, your child was not tortured to death.

I want to take this opportunity to say that there was no "third man" involved in your daughter's case. Ian Brady and I lied at our trial about my former brother-in-law's alleged involvement. If this led you to believe he was implicated, as I recollect was the case, then his liberty over the years may have been a source of distress to you. But he didn't have anything to do with it, and I have done him a worse injustice in this respect than he did me by giving false evidence for the Crown about the death of Edward Evans, when in fact he should have been charged and put in the dock with Ian Brady and myself.

But to return to your letter, you say "I could never blame your mother for what happened. It wouldn't be right. So I don't expect you to blame me for all the heartaches I have had over these years." Of course it wouldn't be right to blame my mother. She, and Mrs Brady, are, in a different sense, two more innocent victims of Ian Brady's and my perpetrations. My own mother, and my family, have endured terrible sufferings through me, and are still serving, like yourself, an unbearable life sentence. This is yet another burden of guilt I carry, and the weight of it is almost

BELOW LEFT: Brady assisting Police in 1988. Brady is centre back.

BELOW: inset, *Mirror* headline from July 1987 and Winnie Johnson, mother of Keith Bennett digging on Saddleworth Moor in an attempt to locate her child's body. It has yet to be found.

force fed in Ashworth Psychiatric Hospital. It is surely a painful and ironic end for a follower of a philosophy predicated on the concept of the "triumph of the will". Brady is now as powerless as his victims, unable to even die.

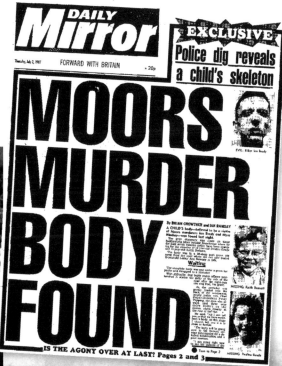

HARRY ROBERTS, JOHN DUDDY AND JACK WITNEY

MURDER OF THREE POLICEMEN: DS CHRISTOPHER HEAD, DC DAVID WOMBWELL AND PC GEOFFREY FOX ON 12TH AUGUST 1966

TRIAL OPENED 6TH DECEMBER 1966

FOUND GUILTY AND SENTENCED TO LIFE IMPRISONMENT WITH A RECOMMENDATION THAT THEY SERVE A MINIMUM OF 30 YEARS. JOHN DUDDY DIED IN PRISON IN 1981. JACK WITNEY WAS RELEASED IN 1991 BUT WAS MURDERED IN 1999. HARRY ROBERTS IS STILL IN PRISON HAVING BEEN DENIED PAROLE ONCE. HE IS THE LONGEST-SERVING PRISONER IN THE UK HAVING BEEN IN PRISON FOR 42 YEARS

The murder of policemen is very rare in the UK and the last time that three had been killed in the same incident was 65 years earlier in the botched jewellery raid in 1910 at Houndsditch.

Friday 12th August 1966 was another fine warm day in west London. England was basking in the glory of winning the Football World Cup and the three police officers in Q car Foxtrot Eleven patrolling East Acton and Shepherd's Bush were expecting a quiet day. They had a call at 3.10pm to collect a colleague from Marylebone Court. On the way there they passed Wormwood Scrubs and saw a suspicious blue Vanguard car. The police were always aware of cars near the prison walls and the possibility they could be used to help prisoners escape. The police flagged it down and Head and Wombwell got

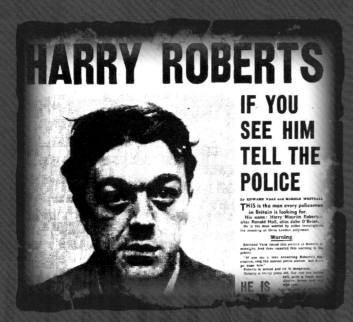

out to investigate. Inside were three small-time crooks who had been looking for a car to steal to use on another job. One of the occupants, Harry Roberts, had a fear of returning to prison. He was carrying guns and knew that he was looking at a 15-year sentence. When it became clear that the police would not be leaving quickly and were likely to search the car Roberts decided to act. Pulling out his revolver he shot DC Wombwell in the head. He leaped out of the car and shot the fleeing DS Head. Meanwhile, Duddy had taken the other gun and shot PC Fox as he attempted to reverse the car out of the ambush. The three policemen lay dead and the three gunmen made their escape at high speed. However, the speeding car was noticed by a member of the public who noted the registration, PGT 726. The car was traced to its owner, Jack Witney, who concocted a story of the car being sold to an unknown man for £15. He had hidden the car in a garage in Vauxhall but unfortunately for him a member of the public had seen it being driven in.

The garage was found to be rented by Witney, who quickly confessed and led the police to the homes of Duddy and Roberts. He was clearly terrified of Roberts and only agreed to help after receiving assurances from the police about the safety of his family. Meanwhile, Roberts and Duddy had gone on the run, Duddy to Glasgow and Roberts, using the training that he'd received in the army, disappeared into the woods around London. The next day, 16th August, photographs of Roberts appeared in the press and £1,000 reward was soon announced. Duddy was quickly caught but Roberts evaded a huge manhunt for three months. He was finally apprehended in November near Thorley Wood, three miles to the north of Epping Forest, and confessed to murdering Head and Wombwell. He pleaded guilty to their murder at the trial in December. All three were sentenced to life imprisonment with a recommendation that they spend at least 30 years in prison. Roberts is still in prison.

OPPOSITE LEFT: A policeman lies dead in the road at the scene of the shooting and (below) *Mirror* front page.

ABOVE: The entrance to the garage in Vauxhall where the body was found.

LEFT: Police examine the car and the reward notice.

RONALD AND REGINALD KRAY

MURDER OF GEORGE CORNELL AND JACK MCVITIE

ARRESTED 9TH MAY 1968

TRIAL OPENED JANUARY 1969

CONVICTED AND SENTENCED TO LIFE IMPRISONMENT WITH A MINIMUM TARIFF OF 30 YEARS

The Kray twins are the iconic gangster figures in British culture, gaining them cult status in some sections of society. The combination of brutal violence with celebrity culture is unique in the history of British crime. However, the model never made business sense and the drama was only going to end with death or imprisonment. Reggie had tried to move *the firm* on to a more business-orientated trajectory when Ronnie was imprisoned in the early Sixties. He might well have become an almost legitimate club owner and now be celebrated for his business prowess. It was not to be, and Ronnie's return propelled the gang towards its inevitable destruction.

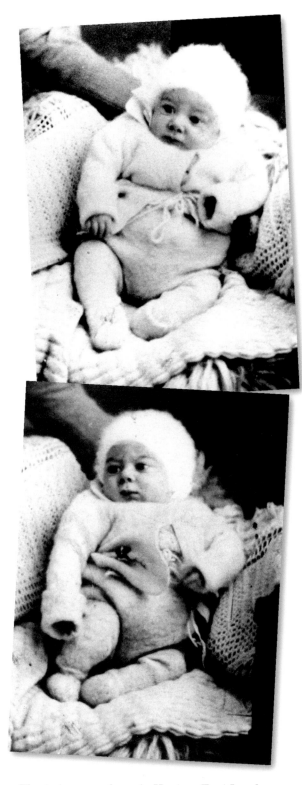

The twins were born in Hoxton, East London to Violet and Charles Kray in 1933. They were from an early age constant rivals, forcing each other never to back down. Even in their early teenage years their reputation for extreme violence was established. By the age of 16

OPPOSITE LEFT:
Reggie and
Ronnie as
babies.

LEFT: Reggie,
Charlie and
Ronnie.

they had bought their first gun and by 17 were professional boxers. Their careers were interrupted by National Service, which resulted in battles with the military police and periods in military prison. As their conduct became more bizarre and violent the army eventually gave them a dishonourable discharge. They left the army with contacts throughout the criminal underworld.

On release from military prison they acquired a billiard hall in Mile End which they used to run their fast-evolving criminal empire. Even at this early stage it was Ronnie who was driving the extreme violence. When confronted by Reggie for shooting a rival in the leg, Ronnie's riposte was: "You couldn't shoot a man if you tried". The violence led in 1956 to Ronnie being sentenced to three years' imprisonment

for GBH administered to Terence Martin. The Martin family's club was mysteriously burnt down. Ronnie's incarceration allowed *the firm* to develop as a business, with new clubs and car lots being acquired. In Wandsworth Prison Ronnie was going insane and was transferred to a mental hospital where he was diagnosed with paranoid schizophrenia. Reggie organized a swap with Ronnie on a visit to allow him to escape and, in theory, be cured. However, the family realized that he was so ill that he had to be returned to Wandsworth. He was released in 1958 but prison had made him even

ABOVE: Reggie on the phone.

RIGHT: Ronnie with boxer Billy Walker.

CRIMES OF THE CENTURY RONALD AND REGINALD KRAY

more violent and brutish. Reggie knew that Ronnie's homicidal behaviour would destroy the business. He was said to have commented: "He's ruining us ... I know we ought to drop him. But how can I? He's my brother and he's mad." The business had been growing fast and was moving into the West End. The progress was interrupted by Reggie's imprisonment for 18 months, leaving Ronnie in charge. With *the firm* established in the West End Ronnie felt free to be open about his homosexuality and developed a wide range of contacts among show business personalities and the political class. As the power and influence grew, Ronnie's violence, drinking and drug-taking increased. There were run-ins with the press and the law but these battles were won and the victories celebrated with extravagant parties, enhancing the twins' feeling of invulnerability. Ronnie was later to write in his autobiography: "They were the best years of our lives. They called them the swinging Sixties. The Beatles and the Rolling Stones were rulers of Pop Music, Carnaby

Street ruled the fashion world ... and me and my brother ruled London. We were fucking untouchable." As the twins' influence increased they started bumping up against other major London gangs, including the Richardsons.

At Christmas 1965 there was an altercation at the Astor Club when George Cornell, a henchman of the Richardsons, called Ronnie a "fat poof". An all-out gang war ensued, involving the shooting of Richard Hart, a Krays associate, at Mr Smith's Club in Catford. Although the Krays had not been directly involved Ronnie decided that decisive action was necessary and went to the Blind Beggar in Whitechapel. The pub had only a few customers, including George Cornell drinking at the bar with two friends. Ronnie Kray walked in and shot Cornell between the eyes. Nobody in the pub identified Ronnie during the police investigations. Although the twins seemed to be getting away with the murder, their lives and business were starting to spiral out of control. Reggie's wife, Frances Kray, committed suicide, which drove Reggie to drink. Frank Mitchell, who had been sprung from Dartmoor Prison, became difficult and was murdered. Ronnie's driver, Frost disappeared, and there were a large number of non-fatal shootings and stabbings.

ABOVE LEFT: Ronnie with Victor Spinetti.

ABOVE: Leslie Holt with Ronnie and Lord Boothby. Holt attempted blackmail and became one of the very few people to fail to survive the removal of a wart in hospital.

Events culminated with the murder of Jack "the hat" McVitie for a lack of respect to the Krays and for owing them money. He was lured to a basement flat in Stoke Newington by the promise of a party with booze and girls. As he staggered through the door Reggie went to shoot him in the head but the gun jammed. Jack was grabbed by Ronnie who pinioned him and shouted for Reggie to kill him. Reggie, now armed with a carving knife, stabbed Jack in the face, chest and stomach and with a final blow through the neck impaled him on the floor. The body was never found. Despite the wall of silence that greeted the disappearance of Jack McVitie the position of *the firm* deteriorated.

A month earlier the police had set up a task force under Detective Superintendent Leonard Read to take the Krays off the streets. They had a 200-page statement from an associate of the Krays, Leslie Read, but nothing to back it up. More material came from Alan Cooper and Paul Elvey who had been employed to murder a nightclub owner. It wasn't really enough to convict but Read went ahead and arrested the twins on 9th May 1968 along with 16 members of *the firm*. With the Krays and their associates off the streets the police had an opportunity to get people to talk. Criminals were offered immunity from prosecution, and others, such as the barmaid of the Blind Beggar, felt safe to speak. The Krays had no real defence and after a 39-day trial were found guilty and sentenced to life imprisonment with a minimum tariff of 30 years. The judge, Mr Justice Melford Stevenson, memorably said: "In my view, society has earned a rest from your activities." Ronnie died in prison and Reggie was only released when he had two weeks to live.

OPPOSITE LEFT

TOP: Frankie Fraser outside the Blind Beggar and (right) Jack McVitie.

LEFT: Reggie Kray's funeral cortège.

OPPOSITE BOTTOM: The team that caught the Krays: Detectives Daphne Robeson, Carole Liston, Janet Adams; Sergeants A Gallacher, A Trevette; Commander John Du Rose, Superintendent Leonard Nipper Read, Inspector Frank Cater, Superintendent Henry Mooney and Sergeant Algernon Hemmingway.

MARY BELL

THE MANSLAUGHTER OF TWO BOYS, MARTIN BROWN ON 25TH MAY 1968 AND BRIAN HOWE ON 31ST JULY 1968

TRIED WITH NORMA BELL FOR MURDER. TRIAL OPENED DECEMBER 1968

NORMA BELL WAS ACQUITTED AND MARY BELL FOUND GUILTY OF MANSLAUGHTER ON THE GROUNDS OF DIMINISHED RESPONSIBILITY. MARY BELL WAS SENTENCED TO BE DETAINED AT HER MAJESTY'S PLEASURE

The murder of children and murders by children cause far greater shock to people than any other type of murder. The murders carried out by Mary Bell are even more shocking because of the calculating intelligence that she displayed in her attempts to deflect the guilt onto other children. Despite the horror of such incidents it must be remembered that in the vast majority of cases children are injured parties to adult violence.

Betty Bell was only 16 when she gave birth to Mary. The father is unknown. Betty was often away working as a prostitute during Mary's early life. Mary Bell alleges in her autobiography that she was sexually abused from an early age. Despite her deprived background she was clearly highly intelligent. The day before her 11th birthday the body of four-year-old Martin Brown was found in a derelict house in Scotswood, Newcastle. The

police at first believed that the death of Martin Brown was accidental, an opinion they maintained even when a local nursery was vandalized and notes claiming responsibility for the death left behind.

Three months later the body of three–year-old Brian Howe was found on waste ground in the

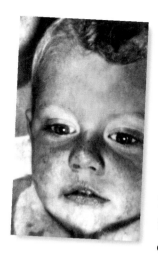

same area. His body had an "N" which had been altered by another hand into an "M" carved onto his stomach. With the second death the police launched a massive investigation focusing on local children. When Mary Bell implicated an eight-year-old boy who could not have been responsible suspicion fell on her. Mary showed huge self-awareness and composure when questioned by the police. She made comments such as: 'I'll phone for some solicitors, they will get me out. This is being brainwashed." She had considered a number of defences including amnesia and madness but decided on a planned defence because there was "no one in the police clever enough to prove she was guilty".

In the trial she attempted to deflect the blame on to her friend Norma Bell. Despite being older Norma was described as being of limited intelligence and easily led. The court was told that Mary Bell had a psychopathic disorder which needed treatment. The trial in December found Mary Bell not guilty of murder but guilty of manslaughter on the grounds of diminished responsibility. She was sentenced to be detained "at Her Majesty's Pleasure". She was released 12 years later when she was regarded as no longer a danger to the public. She has since gone on to have a daughter of her own and the identity of both is protected, allowing them to live something approaching a normal life.

OPPOSITE LEFT: Mary Bell *Mirror* article.

LEFT: Martin Brown.

BELOW: The site of Brian Howe's murder and inset, Eric Howe, the father of the murderd Brian.

CRIMES OF THE CENTURY MARY BELL

BIBLE JOHN

THE MURDER OF THREE WOMEN: PATRICIA DOCKER 22ND FEBRUARY 1968, JEMIMA MCDONALD 16TH AUGUST 1969, HELEN PUTTOCK 30TH OCTOBER 1969

NOBODY HAS BEEN BROUGHT TO JUSTICE FOR THESE CRIMES

Despite thousands of hours of police time, 50,000 statements, a number of witnesses and now strong forensic evidence, nobody has been brought to justice for the series of murders that terrorized Glasgow in the late Sixties. The combination of the murder of women at a nightclub with a murderer quoting the Bible has kept the cases alive in the media and popular imagination for almost 40 years, and the police have not given up hope of closing the file.

All the victims had spent the evening at Glasgow's Barrowland Ballroom. Patricia Docker was seen to leave with a man. She was found the next morning strangled with her own stockings and her handbag stolen. Things were quiet for over a year until the body of Jemima McDonald was found in a derelict building. She, too, had been strangled with her own stockings, her handbag stolen and, like Patricia Docker, was having her period. Jemima had been seen dancing with a tall man in a blue suit for most of the evening. Other people saw them walking away from the club together. Despite a massive police effort few leads were found.

The murder of the next victim, Helen Puttock, was to prove more productive for the police. Helen had been concerned at the murders but felt confident she would be safe as she was with her sister Jean. She'd spent the evening dancing with a tall young man called John who had invited himself into the sisters' taxi

taking them home. During the taxi ride he'd spoken about his strict religious upbringing, that at Hogmanay he prayed rather than drank and that his father regarded dance halls as dens of iniquity. When the taxi got to Scotstoun Jean got out and the taxi continued to Earl Street where Helen lived. This was the last time she was seen alive. Her body was found in the early hours by a man walking his dog. She had been strangled, her handbag stolen and she'd been menstruating.

The police launched one of the biggest investigations in Scottish criminal history, helped by some semen stains and a bite mark left on the body. The police had a huge amount of information, including a widely distributed artist's impression of the killer, which makes it very strange that he wasn't caught. The press loved the case and christened the killer "Bible John". Hundreds of men across Scotland fitting the description were pulled in for questioning but to no avail; the trail went cold. There were no more cases and it seemed that the killer's identity would never be known. However, forensic developments gave new hope to the police. In 1996 the body of Scots Guard John Irvine McInnes was exhumed and the newspapers of the time prematurely declared the case solved. Unfortunately, the DNA analysis proved inconclusive. Hopes were raised again in 2004 when a DNA sample provided an 80 per cent match, but nothing was conclusive. The most recent link is with convicted rapist and serial killer Peter Tobin. He claims to have killed up to 48 women. When questioned by police his response was: "Prove it!"

OPPOSITE TOP TO BOTTOM: John Beatie in 1974: the man who launched the Bible John investigations. Patricia Docker, Jemima McDonald and Helen Puttock.

ABOVE: Police at the Patricia Docker murder scene.

LEFT: Bible John poster and part of the vast media coverage.

155

"ALL MEN DREAM, BUT NOT EQUALLY. THOSE WHO DREAM BY NIGHT IN THE DUSTY RECESSES OF THEIR MIND WAKE IN THE DAY TO FIND THAT IT WAS VANITY. BUT THE DREAMERS OF THE DAY ARE DANGEROUS MEN, FOR THEY MAY ACT THEIR DREAM WITH OPEN EYES, TO MAKE IT POSSIBLE."

T E LAWRENCE, 'THE SEVEN PILLARS OF WISDOM'

1970-1979

1970 ARTHUR AND NIZAMODEEN HOSEIN: The incompetent kidnap and murder of Mrs McKay.

1971 GRAHAM YOUNG: A terrible error by psychiatrists leads to the release of a poisoner who kills again.

1975 PATRICK MACKAY: Failures by the psychiatric services lead to at least three murders.

1975 DONALD NEILSON: The murder of three postmasters and the kidnap and murder of Lesley Whittle.

LEFT: A line of police cars and vans in a Newcastle Street, 1974.

ARTHUR AND NIZAMODEEN HOSEIN

THE KIDNAP AND MURDER OF MRS McKAY JANUARY 1970

TRIAL OPENED 14ᵀᴴ SEPTEMBER 1970

FOUND GUILTY OF MURDER AND KIDNAP AND SENTENCED TO LIFE IMPRISONMENT

This is perhaps the most incompetent kidnap in 20th-century British criminal history. The kidnap seems to have been conceived on a whim with minimal planning. The brothers kidnapped the wrong person and demanded a ludicrous ransom. Alick McKay, her husband, made a tragic misjudgement, probably born of his newspaper background, by informing the media as soon as the kidnap occurred. This turned the investigation into a circus, swamping the police with false leads and bogus kidnappers. There was even a Dutch clairvoyant who accurately predicted the kidnap area. Police efforts to meet with the kidnappers were beset by bad communications and bad luck. Suffering through all this was the cold and terrified figure of Mrs McKay waiting to be murdered by the buffoons who had taken her. A truly tragic case.

Arthur Hosein, the driving force behind the kidnap, was an Indian from Trinidad. He dreamed of being an English gentleman and, not content with being a successful tailor, bought a farm in the Hertfordshire countryside. However, lack of money always constrained his ambitions. One evening watching television the brothers saw that Rupert Murdoch had just bought the *News of the World* and surmised that his wife would be a good source of funds if kidnapped. So was conceived the hare-brained scheme that would end in tragedy. They discovered the identity of Murdoch's Rolls-Royce, followed it to a house in Wimbledon and made their plans. The only problem was that the Murdochs had returned to Australia, loaning the Rolls to the new deputy chairman of the *News of the World*,

Alick McKay, and it was his home that the brothers had staked out.

On 28th December Alick McKay returned home to find his wife missing and the phones ripped out. He phoned the police, who encamped in the house, closely followed by the press who had been informed of events early on. On the evening of the kidnap the Hosein brothers phoned the McKay house to announce the kidnap and demand one million pounds. By Tuesday 30th the *Sun* was running the headline, "Mystery of press chief's missing wife". Newspaper man Alick McKay was convinced that all publicity was good publicity, yet the standard police procedure is to provide a news blackout and it's not clear why this was not followed. It surely would have given a better chance of a happier outcome. The publicity grew by the day and with it the flood of false information that was to dog the efforts of the police. The most infamous contribution was from a Dutch clairvoyant, Gerard Croiset, who stated that the victim was being held on a white farm near an airfield north of London, with the worrying injunction that if she were not found within 14 days she would die. The police reluctantly followed up the lead, which took them within a few miles of Rooks Farm.

For all the useful leads there were

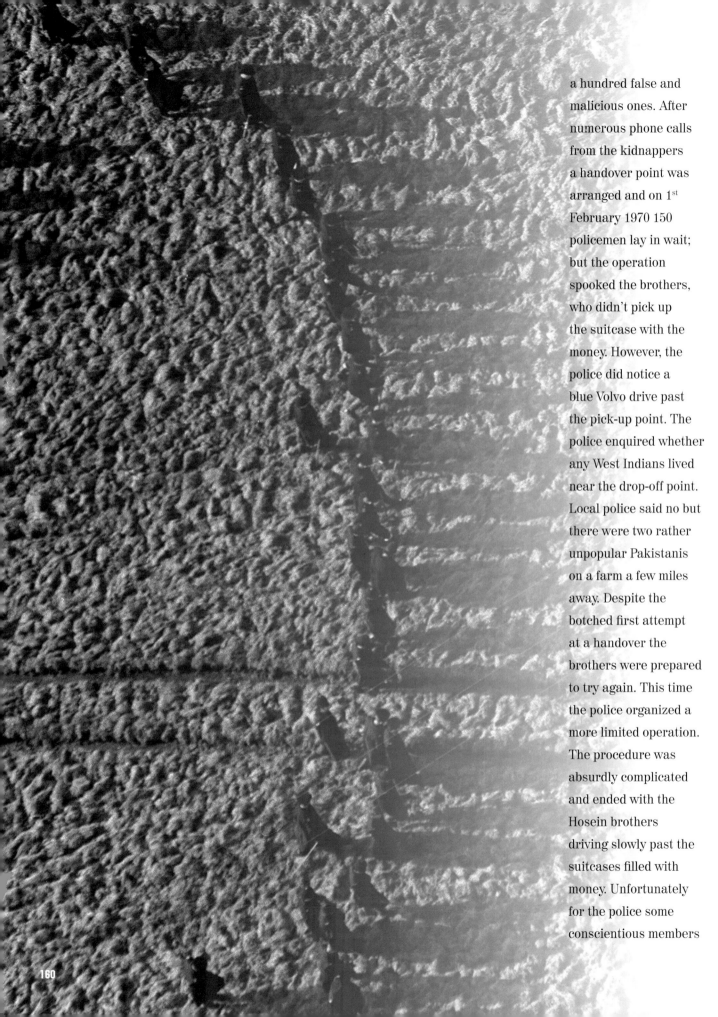

a hundred false and malicious ones. After numerous phone calls from the kidnappers a handover point was arranged and on 1st February 1970 150 policemen lay in wait; but the operation spooked the brothers, who didn't pick up the suitcase with the money. However, the police did notice a blue Volvo drive past the pick-up point. The police enquired whether any West Indians lived near the drop-off point. Local police said no but there were two rather unpopular Pakistanis on a farm a few miles away. Despite the botched first attempt at a handover the brothers were prepared to try again. This time the police organized a more limited operation. The procedure was absurdly complicated and ended with the Hosein brothers driving slowly past the suitcases filled with money. Unfortunately for the police some conscientious members

OPPOSITE LEFT:
Police checking
open land.

LEFT: Rooks
Farm.

BELOW LEFT:
Police
poster and a
remarkably
happy
Nizamodeen
Hosein.

BELOW RIGHT: The
Hosein brothers
are taken away
from court.

METROPOLITAN POLICE
HAVE YOU SEEN THIS WOMAN?

Missing from her home at Wimbledon since evening of 29th December, 1969.

Height 5ft. 9in., medium build, dark brown hair, brownish green eyes, dark complexion, Australian accent.

Wearing black cashmere reversible coat, fawn coloured wool on reverse side, no button. Green jersey suit. Cream patent shoes, square toes, 1½in. heel, yellow metal chain across instep.

IF YOU HAVE SEEN Mrs. McKay since 5 p.m. on 29th December, 1969, please inform Wimbledon Police Station at 01-946 1113, or your nearest Police Station.

of the public mentioned the suitcases by the side of the road to the local police, who had not been informed of the operation. They were more than a little surprised when they opened them up. Although the operation had failed again the police had again observed the blue Volvo and it was cross-referenced to the previous operation. The car was traced to Rooks Farm and the brothers were arrested. The police found enough evidence to link the brothers with the kidnap of Mrs McKay, and even though her body was never found they were successfully charged with kidnap and murder.

GRAHAM YOUNG

MURDER OF THREE PEOPLE, THE FIRST HIS STEPMOTHER IN 1962 WHEN ONLY 14, AND TWO WORK COLLEAGUES, BOB EGLE AND FRED BIGGS IN 1971

ARRESTED 21ST NOVEMBER 1971

TRIAL OPENED 19TH JUNE 1972

SENTENCED TO LIFE IN PRISON

Graham Young in 1962, at the age of 14, was the youngest person committed to Broadmoor. He had been poisoning his family although they were reluctant to admit the fact even when Graham's stepmother died. His father tended to attribute the frequent bouts of illness that afflicted the family to his son's carelessness with the chemistry set. The same sense of denial would cause the psychiatric profession to ignore potential dangers and release him back into the outside world – with disastrous consequences. The case would provoke a major review of the way mentally ill prisoners were released and monitored on their return to the outside world.

Graham's mother died when he was only a few months old and so he was brought up by his aunt. When his father remarried two years later he was reunited with Graham. From an early age Graham Young behaved strangely. He was fascinated by Nazism and the occult. At school the only subject to take his interest was chemistry and. more specifically. toxicology. With his burgeoning knowledge came a desire to employ it practically, and the first to suffer, other than mice, was a fellow student, Christopher Williams, who experienced attacks of vomiting. The experience proved frustrating for Young who couldn't follow his victim to his sickbed to monitor the effects.

To rectify the problem he moved on to his family, who frequently became ill. Although his father was suspicious he was reluctant to link his son's interest in toxicology to the suffering of his family. This continued even when

MIRROR COMMENT

GRAHAM YOUNG: The tragic error

THE case of Graham Young, found guilty yesterday of two murders by poison, raises deeply disquieting questions.

It is now revealed that Young had a history of morbid fascination with poison.

In 1962, at the age of fourteen, he was sent to Broadmoor for administering poison to his father, his sister and a school friend.

Last year he was released. The doctors who had been treating him believed that his disordered mind had been restored to normal. And Mr. Maudling, the Home Secretary, accepted their advice. Obviously a tragic mistake was made. And the question worrying everyone must be how to ensure that such a mistake is not made again. What has to be faced

is that the only CERTAIN guarantee would be NEVER to release a patient with this kind of background.

But such an inflexible rule would be too harsh. The Home Secretary must remain free to order a release when he believes that this is safe. The dilemma is

how to combine a degree of supervision that safeguards others while not making a normal life for the released patient impossible.

For example, what chance of a job would there be if a potential employer was told about the background?

After Graham Young's release there seems to have been very little supervision. This is one of the most disturb-

ing aspects of the affair. Mr. Maudling has sensibly set up two inquiries.

One is into the more immediate problem of safeguarding the public—and on the basis of this case there is a lot that needs to be done.

The other inquiry, under Lord Butler, that wise elder statesman, is into the more fundamental question of how abnormal offenders should be treated.

Public alarm over the case of Graham Young is inevitable and understandable. But it IS an exceptional case.

Mr. Maudling gave the figures: more than 300 releases from Broadmoor in the last twelve years and only one other murder by a released patient who was still under supervision.

The Mirror repeats: there can be no total guarantee against mistakes unless all such offenders, without exception, are incarcerated for life. And in a humane society that would be intolerable.

MURDER BY POISON

GUILTY SECRET OF THE MAN IN BLACK

GUILTY. A jury delivered this verdict on poisoner Graham Young yesterday and then they heard a startling revelation: The man in the dock had done it all before.

Young, 24, had poisoned people on a considerable scale in his childhood, the twelve-man jury was told.

● As a 14-year-old schoolboy he was sent to Broadmoor for poisoning his father, sister and a young pal. All survived.

● The judge at the schoolboy's trial had recommended that he should be kept at Broadmoor for at least fifteen years.

● But he was actually released after eight years and seven months.

All these facts had to be kept secret during the nine-day trial at the Crown court in St. Albans, Herts, because a jury must not be told of an accused's previous convictions.

Yesterday Young, dressed in a black suit and white shirt, stood expressionless as the jury's verdicts were delivered.

Calmly, the foreman announced:

GUILTY of two murders.

GUILTY of two attempted murders.

GUILTY of two charges of administering poison.

Duty

Then came the speech from Sir Arthur Irvine, the tall defence Q.C., who is also a Labour MP for Liverpool Edge Hill.

He said: "I consider this is a duty to my client and I mention it with the utmost reluctance.

"It was only possible for Graham Young to commit

By EDWARD LAXTON

these offences because he had been released on licence.

"This release may appear in the light of evidence we have heard here to have been a serious error of judgment."

Sir Arthur went on : "The authorities had a duty to protect Young from himself as well as a duty to protect the public . . .

"Young himself thinks that a prison sentence would be better for his condition than a return to Broadmoor.

"The Broadmoor experience thus far has had the tragic consequence of which we have learned in this trial."

The judge, Mr. Justice

Eveleigh, nodded his agreement—and he passed four sentences of life imprisonment for the murders and attempted murders.

Young went off last night to Brixton jail.

The jury foreman then said: "We consider it to be our duty to draw the attention of the authority concerned to the apparent failures in the present system whereby dangerous poisons may be obtained by the public.

"We ask that the present procedure be reviewed . . ."

BROADMOOR has a population at the moment of more than 900.

Twenty years ago, the number of releases was

about thirty a year. In recent years, it has increased to about ninety annually.

All patients are released into the care of a person or an organisation who can satisfy the Home Office that they can take responsibility for the man's behaviour.

Stages

If they feel they cannot fulfil the responsibility because of the man's behaviour, they tell Broadmoor and he is taken back.

Other patients are transferred to ordinary mental hospitals for final stages of treatment when they are no longer thought to be a danger to the public.

The condition of parole patients is reviewed regularly.

Graham's stepmother died in agony. It was only when, three months later, his chemistry teacher informed the police of the strange contents of his pupil's desk that the poisoner was apprehended. Young admitted his guilt and was sentenced to be held at Broadmoor for a minimum of 15 years. During this time there were a number of poisoning incidents, including one death.

Young continued to secretly study toxicology. He was warned that adverse behaviour would impair the chance of his release. Somehow the psychiatric profession failed to notice his continuing obsession with poison and he was released in February 1971 despite a recorded

comment to a nurse that he intended to murder a person for every year of his incarceration. There quickly developed a suspicious amount of stomach illness at the hostel he was sent to. He was able to stock up on poisons and take a job at a photographic laboratory which was awash with dangerous substances. Despite receiving a reference from Broadmoor the unfortunate company was not informed that their new store manager was a poisoner. Two staff were to die

OPPOSITE LEFT: Young aged 14 (centre), with friends.

ABOVE: *Mirror*, murder by poison.

because of this and over 70 became ill. They had no reason to question why Graham Young was so willing to make his colleagues a cup of tea.

Young was only discovered when a doctor, who was attempting to reassure staff, was questioned by Young in front of other workers about why he'd failed to consider thallium poisoning. Surprised by the storeman's depth of knowledge the doctor reported the

incident to the management who, in turn, informed the police. The police found Young's diary describing the dosages and times of administration, quantities of poison and his prison record.

He was arrested in possession of thallium on 21st November while visiting his father. Although he verbally admitted his guilt he never confessed and he went to full trial. His previous

experiences of the British legal and medical professions clearly filled him with confidence and he expected to be acquitted. He relished his time in court and the opportunity to be in control and the centre of attention, but he did resent the press labelling him "the tea cup poisoner". Not the right tone for a Nazi hero. Fortunately the jury had no trouble in seeing the guilt of the accused and he was sentenced to life imprisonment. He was incarcerated in Parkhurst where he formed a friendship with fellow Nazi psychopathic murderer Ian Brady.

Young died aged 42 of a heart attack, although there is speculation that he was poisoned by his fellow inmates who considered him as too mad and bad even for them.

OPPOSITE LEFT: Young at trial getting into a van.

LEFT TOP TO BOTTOM: Fred Biggs, Bob Egle and the father of Young, reading the paper.

BELOW: *Daily Mirror* cover.

PATRICK MACKAY

MURDER OF THREE PEOPLE: ISABELLA GRIFFITHS IN 1974, ADELE PRICE AND FATHER CREAN IN 1975

ARRESTED FEBRUARY 1975

MACKAY CLAIMED UP TO 11 MURDERS

FOUND GUILTY AND SENTENCED TO LIFE IMPRISONMENT. HE HAS A WHOLE OF LIFE TARIFF AND WILL NEVER BE RELEASED

The case of Patrick Mackay shows a justice and psychiatric system in chaos. A man whom the system knew to be a potentially dangerous psychopathic killer was allowed to wander in and out of the prison and mental health system until eventually he killed – and then decisive action was taken. At least three people, and some claim many more, would die because of the failure of the legal and mental health systems to take responsibility.

Patrick Mackay's father died at the age of 42 when Patrick was only 11. Though a violent alcoholic, who regularly attacked his son, his death tipped what was an already psychologically fragile boy over the edge, and from then on he would be known for his violence and anger. At the age of only 15 a Home Office psychiatrist, Doctor Leonard Carr, described Mackay as likely to evolve into a cold psychopathic killer and therefore he was sentenced to spend four years at Moss Side Hospital. During this period his fascination with Nazism and other ideologies grew until, in a bizarre twist, he demanded that he be known as Franklin Bollvolt the First.

In 1972, at the age of 20, he was released from Moss Side. There now began a period of moving from one job and house to another. During this time Mackay met Father Crean, a monk who believed that love and compassion could turn around most lives. They formed as much of a relationship as Mackay could manage, and met regularly. However, when Mackay stole a £30 cheque from Father Crean, the matter ended in court with an order to repay the money, which of course Mackay never did. It would introduce friction into the relationship and lead to disaster a year later. The first murder to be clearly attributed to Mackay was of 84-year-old Isabella Griffith, who was strangled and stabbed

By JOHN PENROSE

FURY erupted last night over the scandal of bloodlust killer Patrick Mackay. Mackay was jailed for life at the Old Bailey for the manslaughter of three elderly people.

The case raises disturbing questions about how he remained at large to rob and kill.

For 23-year-old Mackay had a history of violence going back to his boyhood.

When he was fifteen a doctor warned that he had the marks of a "cold psychopathic killer."

He was in and out of mental wards as a teenager, and was twice released from one top security hospital—Moss Side at Maghull, near Liverpool.

Clear

The warning signs were clear. Yet Mackay stayed free . . finally to stand accused of an astonishing catalogue of crimes:

At one stage he was suspected of being Britain's biggest mass killer—and detectives were studying files on ten unsolved murders.

Mackay was eliminated from case after case and was finally charged with five killings.

He pleaded guilty yesterday to the manslaughter of two old women and a 63-year-old Roman Catholic priest.

He had denied murder and his guilty pleas to manslaughter were on the ground of diminished responsibility.

The murder charges were left on the court file.

Passing sentence, Mr. Justice Milmo told Mackay: " The medical evidence makes it clear that you are not insane . . . because you knew what you were doing and that it was wrong."

Storm

Mackay preyed on defenceless pensioners. He told police that he had "bashed a lot of old ladies."

He said a "sort of curtain" came down on incidents too terrible to remember.

The case has raised a fresh storm over

LET LOOSE TO SLAUGHTER

Patrick Mackay

treatment of violent criminals and the system used to release them from special hospitals.

And MPs last night demanded a Home Office inquiry.

One MP, Mrs. Jill Knight, said members of the review bodies which freed Mackay should share the guilt.

Mrs. Knight, Tory member for Edgbaston, declared: "This is the classic example of why the general public are caught in a rising tide of fury at the inability

of the authorities to afford them normal protection in their daily lives.

"The cult of 'be kind to the criminal and shower blessings on the violent' has been responsible for countless deaths or injuries in the last decade."

Advise

Dr. Rhodes Boyson, Conservative MP for North Brent, commented: "This is a major scandal and there

must be an immediate inquiry. Dear old ladies in my constituency and elsewhere will be terrified to leave their homes for months on end now."

He added: "This sort of thing happens because the Government has been influenced by the trendy mish-mash of psychologists."

Lord Butler, who headed the recent Committee on Abnormal Offenders, referred to proposals for an independent body to advise about the transfer or

release of inmates from psychiatric hospitals.

Lord Butler said: " It was my committee's main recommendation, and this dreadful new case should jockey the Home Secretary along."

Mackay—a man obsessed with Nazi insignia and the history of dictatorship — had made eleven court appearances in eleven years and had been convicted of theft, burglary, assault and robbery with violence.

Rely

He was held in two London psychiatric units on police orders within days of the killings.

But at no time did the doctors who examined him suspect they had a mass killer on their hands.

For a spokesman for the hospitals admitted last night that they had to rely on Mackay's own word about his background.

And he did not tell them of his troubled past — including the two periods he spent at Moss Side hospital.

Find

The psychiatric units are at Tooting Bec Hospital and the South Western Hospital.

The spokesman explained : "We can only make whatever inquiries we can pursue from the patient.

"I am not aware of any centrally - kept registers to which doctors have access to find out if the patient has been in hospital before.

"Very little was known about this man.

He wandered quite a bit, and on the last occasion gave us the name of his G.P.

"But it was a bit of a blind alley."

The spokesman said that even if Mackay's previous history had been known it may "not necessarily have affected the treatment he received."

The spokesman added: " We were not aware he had been classified as a psychopathic killer. He was not considered a danger to other persons during his stays and he would have been judged in the light of that."

Call

A Health Department spokesman said the Moss Side hospital had no record of a telephone call from South Western asking for Mackay's medical details.

● It is a major scandal There must be a probe ●

Bloodlust of the Beast in Black—Pages 2 and 3

OPPOSITE LEFT:
Victims Isabella Griffiths and Adele Price.

LEFT: *Mirror* article.

bath whereupon he stabbed and hit him repeatedly with an axe. Despite the ferocity of the attack it took the priest an hour to die, as Mackay looked on, fascinated. This time the police quickly identified the perpetrator and Mackay was arrested. At one time he claimed to have murdered 11 people but later retracted most of the confessions.

in February 1974. It took two weeks before the body was found by the police, and until a stab wound was discovered it was believed that death had been by natural causes! Mackay spent more time in prison later that year before murdering Adele Price by strangulation in early 1975.

Five days later he killed Father Crean in his most violent and sadistic attack. He deliberately travelled down to Kent for the killing. He chased the priest down, causing him to stumble into a

He was eventually charged with three murders. His guilt was not in question; the only issue to be decided was his mental state and degree of culpability. The prosecution accepted a plea of guilty to manslaughter due to diminished responsibility. There was huge coverage in the press about the madman and his hopeless treatment. Mackay was sentenced to life imprisonment and will never be released; but many more psychopaths were still at large.

DONALD NEILSON

THE MURDER OF FOUR PEOPLE:

SYDNEY GRAYLAND 1974

DONALD LAWSON 1974

DEREK ASTIN 1974

LESLEY WHITTLE 1975

TRIAL STARTED 14TH JUNE 1976

SENTENCED TO LIFE IMPRISONMENT FOUR TIMES FOR THE MURDERS

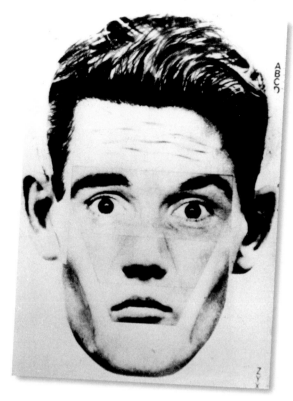

Donald Neilson, also known as the Black Panther, was one of the most feared criminals of the 20th century. His career in crime showed a progression from burglary, to post office raids, up to murder and kidnap. His crimes were planned with military precision and executed with a brutal ruthlessness. Unlike most serial killers the brutality wasn't an end in itself but a means towards financial gain. It is ironic that his career was ended by a stroke of bad luck and the extraordinary courage of a few individuals.

Donald Nappey changed his surname to Neilson in 1960 after the birth of his daughter. His early career was spent in the army, a career he'd enjoyed and which fitted in with his character. When his wife persuaded him to leave he took a series of jobs in civilian life, which failed to provide the financial reward he thought he deserved. To fill the gap he took to burglary, carrying out 400 jobs without being caught. When these still failed to provide adequate remuneration he progressed to raids on post offices throughout Lancashire and Yorkshire.

By 1974 the raids had become more bold and led to the fatal shootings of three sub-postmasters. Neilson's greed and confidence had now developed sufficiently for him to contemplate a much more ambitious crime.

PATH TO BATHPOOL PARK

TO KIDSGROVE

2nd ENTRANCE TO SHAFT

TENT OVER SHAFT WHERE LESLEY'S BODY WAS FOUND

POLICE VAN

RAILWAY LINE TO STOKE

On the television he learned of a 17-year-old heiress from Shropshire, Lesley Whittle. In a meticulously planned operation on 14th January 1975 he kidnapped Lesley from her bedroom as her mother slept in another part of the house. He left behind a ransom demand for £50,000 and a box of Turkish Delight. The note told the family not to involve the police, on pain of Lesley's death, and to be at a phone box the next day to take a call which would tell them what further steps to take. Despite the threat Mrs Whittle and Lesley's brother Ronald called in the police, who took over the

OPPOSITE
LEFT: Artist's impression of Neilson and (below) Lesley Whittle.

ABOVE: Bathpool Park.

LEFT: The Whittle family house.

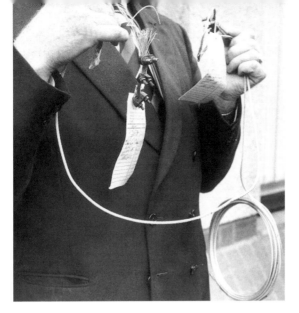

RIGHT: The noose from which Lesley Whittle was hanged.

BELOW: The police removing Lesley's body from the park.

negotiations. The call came a couple of days later with complicated instructions that led Lesley's brother Ronald to Bathpool Park in Kidsgrove. In the dark he was unable to follow the instructions and the drop-off of the money failed.

Nothing more was heard from Neilson. On 10th February the police lifted the media blackout and held a press conference on 2nd March. Now that the full story was out the police could initiate a full search of Bathpool Park and appeal for information about the aborted drop-off. One man reported finding a plastic label with the words "DROP SUITCASE INTO HOLE".

Some boys reported finding a torch wedged into the grill covering a ventilation shaft for the disused Harecastle Tunnel with another plastic label attached. On 6th March a full search of the park was initiated including the three shafts. In the largest shaft there were three landings connected by a ladder. On the third landing 54ft below the surface they found a sleeping bag, a foam mattress and silver survival blanket. Suspended from this level by a steel cable was Lesley's body. On the floor were found Lesley's slippers, some trainers, a cassette tape, microphone and a notebook with one partial fingerprint. Although the police spent the next four months trying to find a match there was none and the case was going cold. The solution came from a combination of good fortune with amazing courage.

On the night of 11th December two policemen in Mansfield saw a man behaving suspiciously and questioned him. Giving his name as John Moxon, the man drew a gun and forced the police into their car, telling them to drive to the nearby village of Blidworth. While driving there Neilson asked them if they had any rope,

LEFT: The equipment used by Neilson.

BELOW: Senior police team Dep. Com. Ernest Bond, Ass. Com. John Wilson and Dep. Ass. Peter Walton.

and while one of the policemen pretended to look he noticed that the gun was not pointed at them. He lunged at Neilson, forcing the gun into the air. His colleague simultaneously slammed on the brakes. The gun went off, grazing an officer's hand and blasting into the roof. The car had come to a stop outside the local chip shop and two of the customers rushed to help and did such a good job that the police ended up having to restrain them. A rather battered Neilson was arrested and found to be in possession of the paraphernalia of the most wanted man in Britain, the Black Panther.

His fingerprints were a match with the one from the shaft – the police had the murderer of Lesley Whittle. Eventually he divulged his real name and address, leading to a search of his house, where they discovered an arsenal of weapons. Neilson was charged with four counts of murder as well as kidnap.

Security guard George Smith is Neilson's forgotten victim. He died of wounds inflicted by Neilson when Smith found him putting out clues in Bathpool Park. Because his death occurred over a year after the injury Neilson could not be charged with murder. On all the main counts Neilson was found guilty and sentenced to life imprisonment with a whole of life tariff recommended. He is now suffering from a terminal illness, motor neuron disease, but it is not considered likely that he will be released.

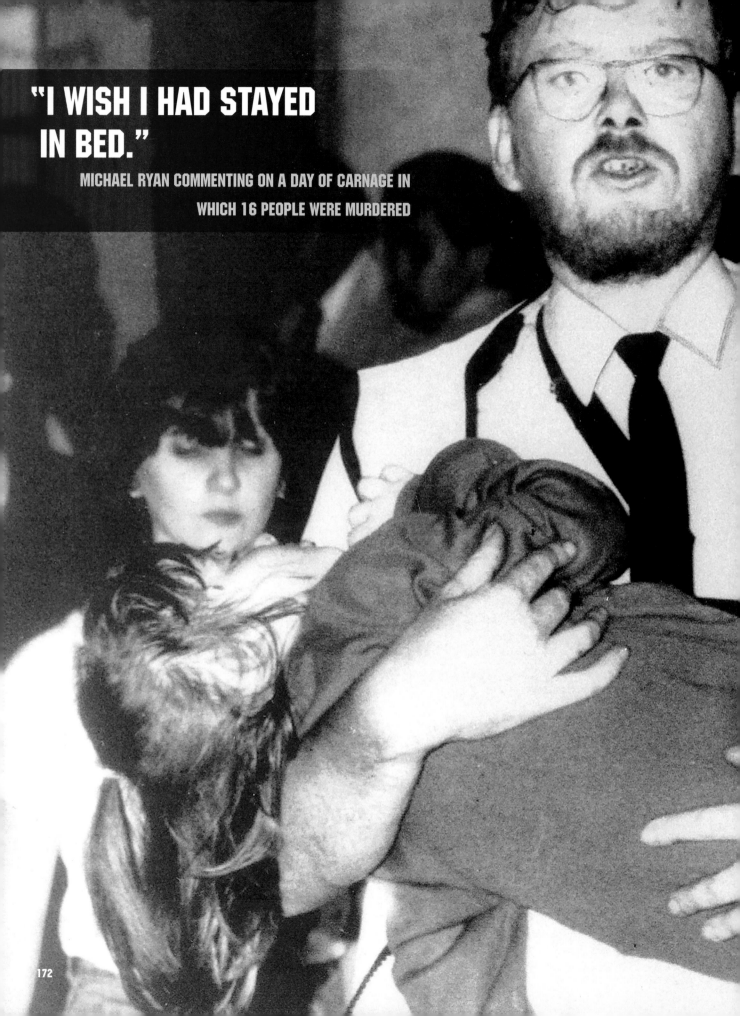

"I WISH I HAD STAYED IN BED."

MICHAEL RYAN COMMENTING ON A DAY OF CARNAGE IN WHICH 16 PEOPLE WERE MURDERED

1980-1989

1981 PETER SUTCLIFFE: The brutal murder of 13 women in the north of England.

1983 DENNIS NILSEN: The murder of 15 young men.

1983 THE BRINKS-MAT BULLION RAID: The most lucrative robbery of the century.

1985 JEREMY BAMBER: The murder of his step family to gain the inheritance.

1987 MICHAEL RYAN: The murder of 16 people in a quiet country town.

LEFT: A policeman carries a child to safety. Her mother had just been killed.

PETER SUTCLIFFE

THE MURDER OF 13 WOMEN: WILMA MCCANN 30TH OCTOBER 1975, EMILY JACKSON 20TH JANUARY 1976, IRENE RICHARDSON 5TH FEBRUARY 1977, PATRICIA ATKINSON 23RD APRIL 1977, JAYNE MACDONALD 26TH JUNE 1977, JEAN JORDAN 1ST OCTOBER 1977, YVONNE PEARSON 21ST JANUARY 1978, HELEN RYTKA 31ST JANUARY 1978, VERA MILLWARD 16TH MAY 1978, JOSEPHINE WHITAKER 4TH APRIL 1979, BARBARA LEACH 2ND SEPTEMBER 1979, MARGUERITE WALLS 20TH AUGUST 1980, JACQUELINE HILL 17TH NOVEMBER 1980

ARREST 2ND JANUARY 1981

CHARGED 5TH JANUARY 1981

TRIAL OPENED 5TH MAY 1981

SENTENCED TO LIFE IMPRISONMENT WITH A 30-YEAR TARIFF BEFORE PAROLE IS CONSIDERED

Peter Sutcliffe is the best-known British mass murderer of the century and earned the name "the Yorkshire Ripper" for the violence and frequency of his attacks on women. The case caused huge problems for the police because many attacks were on prostitutes who lived on the margins of society.

Sutcliffe, born in 1946, was a quiet child who showed little interest in other children, sport or even, in his teenage years, girls. He had no girlfriend until he was 20, when he met Czech immigrant Sonia Szurma. After eight years of living together they married in 1974. Throughout this period Sutcliffe had taken a number of jobs but had failed to keep any of them. The most significant in the light of future events was a period working at a cemetery where his less than reverential attitude towards the residents was noted by fellow employees. His few friends, including Trevor Birdsall, were aware that he frequented prostitutes and had a violent and contradictory attitude towards them. In 1975 he took the opportunity given by a redundancy package to re-train as an HGV driver.

The first known attack occurred on 5th July 1975 on 36-year-old Anna Rogulskyj, who was assaulted with a hammer and slashed across

the stomach. The assault only halted when a neighbour heard the commotion and came outside to investigate, but was reassured by Sutcliffe that everything was alright. Miraculously, Rogulskyj survived the assault. The next victim was Olive Smelt, who again survived but with severe injuries. Incredibly, after the assault Sutcliffe returned to the car, which was being driven by his friend Trevor Birdsall who did not suspect anything until many years later. The next attack on 30th October 1975 on 28-year-old Wilma McCann proved fatal. She was hit twice with a hammer and stabbed 15 times.

The police launched a massive investigation but came up with little information other than some semen stains on her pants. Little did the police suspect that the murders would continue for the next five years and involve them in the biggest investigation in the Yorkshire police's history. Each murder would provide the police with clues about the killer. The next victim, Emily Jackson, had a boot mark left on her body. When Irene Richardson was murdered tyre tracks were left in the mud, leaving the police with an enormous list of suspect vehicles to investigate. Another size seven boot print was found on the body of Patricia Atkinson. Sixteen-year-old Jayne MacDonald was the youngest and next victim. This was to start the bizarre references in the press to "innocent women" – as if all the women hadn't been innocent. However, the murder did have the effect of making all women in the Yorkshire area feel vulnerable and led to a flood of new information. Assistant Chief Constable Maurice Oldfield was now put in charge of the investigation and a more open flow

LEFT: The incident room.

MIDDLE: Photofit.

ABOVE: Maurice Oldfield.

of information to the public was allowed.

The most substantial lead was provided by the body of Jean Jordan. Before the murder Sutcliffe had paid her with a new £5 note which she'd put into a secret compartment of her handbag. After the murder he'd hidden her body

and left the scene, but realizing that the note could be traced had returned a few days later to retrieve the evidence. Unable to find the note he took out his frustration on the body, at first attempting to decapitate her and then battering her head so that she was unrecognizable. Unlike Sutcliffe, the police found the £5 note in the handbag, which was 100 yards from the body, and launched a massive effort to trace the bank it had been distributed from. The police narrowed the field down to 8,000 employees whom they then proceeded to question. Among them was Sutcliffe, although the police did not regard him as a strong suspect. His wife, Sonia, had not contradicted any of his statements. This would be the first of many times that he would be questioned.

The murders continued over the next 18

months with the police finding the mutilated bodies of Yvonne Pearson, Helen Rytka, Vera Millward and Josephine Whitaker. The police had what they believed to be a powerful new lead when they received a series of letters from the Sunderland area. The letters were followed by a cassette tape which taunted them with the failures of their investigation. A voice expert from Leeds University focused the location of the Geordie accent down to the Castletown area of Sunderland. The police had a massive response when the tape was broadcast. In retrospect it is now clear that the tape and letters were a hoax. The hoaxer failed to predict the victims of the Ripper and was unaware of some of the victims whose bodies had not been discovered. None of the women who survived had mentioned a Geordie accent.

A vast effort went into following up the Wearside leads, which inevitably led to alternative lines of enquiry being downgraded. In 2005 the hoaxer, John Humble, was discovered and sentenced to a well-deserved eight years in prison. The next victim, in September 1979, was Leeds University student Barbara Leach. Her murder was followed by another massive police effort which, although it focused on the Wearside connection, still led to Sutcliffe being interviewed twice more. The strain was starting to tell on the police, with Maurice Oldfield suffering three heart attacks and having to stand down from the

OPPOSITE LEFT TOP: Police examining the crime scene.

OPPOSITE LEFT BOTTOM: Maurice Oldfield at a map.

ABOVE LEFT: Olivia Reivers (left).

ABOVE RIGHT: Sutcliffe's house after the arrest.

LEFT: Jim Hobson who took over the investigation when Maurice Oldfield became unwell.

investigation. He was eventually replaced by Jim Hobson.

In April 1980 Sutcliffe was stopped for drink driving in Manningham, a red-light district of Leeds. Losing his licence would have a drastic effect on Sutcliffe. Not only would he lose his job but his nocturnal ventures would be impossible. He now started on his last bout of four attacks, two of which, on Marguerite Walls and Jacqueline Hill, would prove to be his undoing. Sutcliffe moved his attacks away from the poorer and red-light districts of Leeds to the wealthier areas, such as the university and other towns in the area. The last attack on Jacqueline Hill in the wealthy Headingly suburb of Leeds created a huge new wave of leads for

the police. One was an anonymous letter from Trevor Birdsall in which he wrote: "I have good reason to now [sic] the man you are looking for in the Ripper case. This man as [sic] dealings with prostitutes and always had a thing about them … His name and address is Peter Sutcliffe, 6 Garden Lane, Heaton, Bradford. Works for Clarke's Transport, Shipley." He even called in at the police station to repeat his allegations. Despite Sutcliffe being one of only 300 possible culprits the information disappeared into the vast archive of material.

Sutcliffe was finally caught in the new year on 2nd January 1981. Sutcliffe was stopped with prostitute Olivia Reivers by police in the Broomhill district of Sheffield. When they

ABOVE LEFT:
Sutcliffe leaving court.

ABOVE RIGHT:
Cartoon of the weapons used by Sutcliffe.

checked the car they found that it had false number plates and Sutcliffe was arrested. He asked to go to the toilet and went behind an oil tank out of the view of the police and disposed of a knife and hammer. Because the false number plate had come from the Dewsbury district Sutcliffe was transferred from Sheffield. As a matter of course the new head of the Ripper investigation had instructed that the investigation be informed of anybody arrested in relation to prostitutes. Sutcliffe had also hidden another knife in a toilet cistern at the police station. As the police investigated Sutcliffe they realized that they might have their man. The officer who had first arrested Sutcliffe, on learning of a possible Ripper link decided on his own initiative to go back to the scene and investigate the area and found the knife and hammer.

The police searched Sutcliffe's house and found a number of tools, including hammers, and took Sonia Sutcliffe into custody. When Sutcliffe was eventually made to strip at the police station he was found to be wearing a V neck pullover under his trousers with the V neck over the groin area. Sutcliffe gave up his denials and began a long statement telling the police that God had told him to murder women, and also telling of an experience when working at the cemetery as a young man when the grave of a Polish man had spoken to him. The psychiatrists diagnosed him as a paranoid schizophrenic and the prosecution had accepted a plea of manslaughter due to diminished responsibility. However, the trial judge Mr Justice Boreham decided that the case must go to trial and that the jury should decide whether he was sane or not. British juries are most reluctant to declare murderers insane and therefore not responsible for their actions The jury refused to accept the plea of diminished responsibility due to insanity and found Sutcliffe guilty of murder on 13 counts. In sentencing Sutcliffe the judge commented that he regarded him as "beyond redemption" and that he should serve at least 30 years before being considered for parole. Despite being found to be sane at the trial and sent to Parkhurst Prison he was soon diagnosed as suffering from schizophrenia and eventually moved to Broadmoor.

ABOVE LEFT: A *Mirror* headline from 2001 in which Sutcliffe claims that he is cured of his schizophrenia and is safe to release.

ABOVE RIGHT: The police team: Gerty, Harvey, Emmant, Hobson, Kind, Sloan.

DENNIS NILSEN

MURDER OF 15 YOUNG MEN. MANY ARE ANONYMOUS BUT THOSE WHO ARE KNOWN ARE:

STEPHEN HOLMES 30TH DECEMBER 1978, KENNETH OCKENDON 3RD DECEMBER 1979, MARTYN DUFFY MAY 1980, BILLY SUTHERLAND MAY 1980, MALCOLM BARLOW 18TH SEPTEMBER 1981, JOHN HOWLETT DECEMBER 1981, GRAHAM ALLEN (DATE OF DEATH NOT KNOWN), STEPHEN SINCLAIR 26TH JANUARY 1983, ARRESTED FEBRUARY 1983

TRIAL BEGAN OCTOBER 1983

SENTENCED TO LIFE IMPRISONMENT WITH A MINIMUM OF 25 YEARS. HE NOW HAS A WHOLE OF LIFE TARIFF

Dennis Nilsen is one of the most interesting and prolific British murderers of the 20th century. He preyed on young men drifting through London. Almost half of his victims have no names and their disappearance has passed unnoticed. The increase in the number of serial killers in Britain in the last third of the 20th century reflects the increasingly fractured nature of British society where the traditional extended family has collapsed and young people can disappear with no one noticing.

Dennis Nilsen was born into an unstable family in Fraserborugh. His father was an alcoholic and the parents divorced when Dennis was four and he was sent to live with his grandparents. His grandfather died when Dennis was six and he was taken to view the corpse. Nilsen believes that this event traumatized him and led to his

OPPOSITE LEFT:
The death room
and inset, Nilsen
in the police.

**OPPOSITE LEFT
BOTTOM:** Nilsen
trained as a
cook in the
army.

LEFT: 195
Melrose Place.

BELOW: One of
the neck ties
used to strangle
the victims.

fascination with corpses. He returned to live with his mother and her new husband who lectured him about the impurities of the flesh. In 1961 Nilsen enlisted in the British Army and served for 11 years, learning the skills of butchery that would be very useful in his later life as he disposed of the bodies of his victims.

On his return to civilian life in 1972 Nilsen joined the police but found that the lifestyle did not suit him. Eventually he became a civil servant and worked in a job centre in Soho. During this time Nilsen knew he was gay but had trouble finding meaningful relationships or satisfying sex. In 1975 he moved into a flat with David Gallichan at 195 Melrose Avenue, Cricklewood. The flat share didn't work out and so Gallichan moved out, leaving Nilsen with his flat, a big garden and a growing sense of loneliness. Eighteen months later came the first murder. The victim's name is unknown but we do know that he was picked up in a gay bar and returned with Nilsen to his flat where they had sex. Fearing that his new friend would leave, Nilsen took a necktie and strangled the man so that he became unconscious; he then drowned

him by putting his head in a bucket of water. Nilsen looked at the body, found it beautiful and slept with it. He stored the body under the floorboards for the next seven and a half months before dismembering it and burning it

on a bonfire in the garden.

The pattern was to be repeated another 11 times in the Cricklewood flat. Some young men, such as Douglas Stewart, would escape when Nilsen claimed that he snapped out of the killing frenzy. Nilsen hoped that the pattern could be changed by moving to a new flat in Muswell Hill.Instead, the urge to murder returned, but now with the practical difficulty of how to dispose of the bodies, with no garden for a bonfire. The first victim of the new flat was John Howlett, whom Nilsen referred to as John the Guardsman. Nilsen claims that he wanted John to leave the flat and avoid strangulation but that John insisted on staying and therefore had to die. Nilson hid the body in the closet while he pondered the problem of disposal. He decided on cutting the body into small pieces and flushing them down the toilet. The bones went out with the rubbish and the head was boiled down. Some parts were salted and stored in a tea chest.

There was another anonymous victim in Muswell Hill before Stephen Sinclair was murdered at the end of January 1983. Two weeks later the neighbours, tired of the malfunctioning plumbing system, complained. The first plumber failed

ABOVE: Douglas Stewart, a survivor.

MIDDLE: Vivienne McStay and Monique Van Rutte, the unfortunates who lived in the flat below Nilsen.

RIGHT: 23 Cranley Gardens, Muswell Hill.

to find the problem and called in a sewage specialist who removed a manhole cover outside the flats. There he found piles of half-rotten flesh which could not be identified but looked suspiciously human. Nilson and the other tenants looked on but were mystified. That night Nilson sneaked down to the manhole and removed the flesh; but he was spotted. The next day the workmen found the flesh gone and informed their managers of their suspicions. When Nilson returned from work in the evening he found the police waiting and was told of the discovery of human remains, to which he is reported to have responded: "Really, how awful". To this the police replied: "Don't mess about, where's the rest of the body?" Nilson explained that it was in some plastic bags in his flat and that they might like to know about another 14 or 15 bodies. Nilson's statement took 30 hours to give and led the police to his previous flat and the garden. He was charged with six murders and two attempted murders and sentenced to 25 years' imprisonment. A home secretary later increased the sentence to a whole of life tariff.

ABOVE: Nilsen handcuffed.

LEFT: Nilsen off to jail after sentencing.

THE BRINKS-MAT BULLION RAID

26TH NOVEMBER 1983

THE STEALING OF OVER £26 MILLION OF GOLD BULLION, DIAMONDS AND PLATINUM

BRIAN ROBINSON AND MICHAEL MCAVOY SENTENCED TO 25 YEARS EACH. SECURITY GUARD INSIDE MAN TONY BLACK RECEIVED SIX YEARS

TRIAL OPENED OCTOBER 1984

The Brinks-Mat bullion robbery was at the time by far the largest heist in British criminal history. The robbers had been expecting £3 million in cash when they broke into the Brinks-Mat depot at Heathrow on 26th November 1983. What they found instead was a huge cache of gold bullion weighing three tons. But this amount of bullion was a major problem. The robbers had no experience of turning the gold into cash. To do this they would have to turn for help to some of the most powerful underworld figures in the country, and the path of the gold would leave a trail of bodies and ruined lives.

Golden targets

By SYLVIA JONES

'Other bullion depots at risk'

HUGE stocks of gold bullion at depots throughout the country could be targets for raiders, a security expert claimed last night.

The claim followed the £25 million gold haul from a Heathrow Airport warehouse.

The security expert said that other depots in Birmingham, Bristol, Leeds and Warrington were all vulnerable to attack from gangs like the one which beat the high-security premises of Brinks Mat.

Detectives are refusing to disclose how the six raiders got in and out of the warehouse on a trading estate complex just outside the airport's security area.

But it is believed they were lying in wait for the guards arriving for work at 6.30 a.m.,

and then forced staff to reveal security codes for the strong room.

Six Brinks Mat staff were handcuffed and one pistol-whipped over the head. Another was doused in petrol and threatened with being set alight.

The security experts said that the high technology criminals can be beaten with:

● Round-the-clock guards at the bullion warehouses.

● Remote surveillance and video screens to pick up movement around the buildings.

● Infra-red spotlights and control over all people entering

the trading estates where the warehouses are located.

The expert added: "What is also disturbing is that Brinks Mat is one of the biggest cash-in-transit companies in the world—and they are better than a lot of other companies."

Special watch was being kept last night on a handful of top crooks thought to be capable of pulling off the raid.

● THE value of the haul leapt yesterday by £1,100,000 when the price of gold jumped sharply in London. Some dealers suggested the robbery had triggered the rise.

Although this was a massive raid it scales into insignificance when compared with the great financial frauds of the last 30 years such as Poly Peck or the activities of Nick Leeson. The proceeds of these frauds are believed to be greater than the value of all the burglaries in any one year.

At 6.40am on 26th November 1983, six men burst into the Heathrow depot of security company Brinks-Mat. In a meticulously planned and brutally executed operation the robbers stole 6,800 bars of gold bullion, two bags of diamonds and a quantity of platinum. To get the combinations for the locks the gang had doused the guards with petrol and held a match to them. Despite the planning the police

Perry. Perry is believed to have contacted experts in handling gold, Kenneth Noye and John Palmer. The scale of the movements of money necessary to process the gold was so great that it alerted the police. On one day £3 million was taken out of a Bristol bank

Savage threats of £26m bullion gang

By GEORGE GLENTON

RAIDERS threatened a security guard to force him to open a safe ...and made him so frightened he forgot the combination, a court heard yesterday.

The men—alleged to have stolen £26 million in gold, gems and cheques—poured petrol over a guard and said they would set him alight.

They also threatened to shoot him in the head and cut off his penis, the Old Bailey was told yesterday.

But every threat just made him more frightened and too scared to remember the safe's numbers.

One of the raiders said: "It looks like we have a hero here. It's a shame we are going to do him in," the court heard.

They even stabbed the security man, Robin Riseley, in the hand before he remembered.

As the gang left the Brinks-Mat warehouse near Heathrow Airport, Mr Riseley was punched in the stomach and told: "It is a good job it's Christmas."

The raid—Britain's biggest—succeeded because the gang had help from a security man who worked in the Hounslow warehouse, the jury was told.

He is Anthony Black, who confessed to giving them information and a key.

Jailed

He has been jailed for six years and will give evidence against three London men who have denied plotting and taking part in the raid.

They are Michael McAvoy, 32, Anthony White, 40, and Brian Robinson, 40.

● At the end of yesterday's hearing Judge Tudor Price, QC, told the jury that throughout the trial police officers will escort them to court and listen in on their phones.

had little difficulty unravelling the crime. They had deduced that it was an inside job and that one of the guards was related to well-known villain Michael Robinson. By offering Black a reduced sentence and protection the police persuaded him to help with the prosecution. McAvoy had not made much of an effort to disguise his recently gained fortune when he moved from his council house to a mansion and named his two Rottweilers Brinks and Matt. Black was sentenced to six years and Robinson and McAvoy to 25 years. A fourth man, Brian White, was acquitted, but within a short time was buying properties and in Spain police found £100,000 of jewellery. In 1997 he was jailed for 11 years for drug smuggling.

But this was only the start of the story because the vast majority of the gold was still undiscovered and yet to be processed. Before his arrest McAvoy had put his share of the bullion into the hands of fellow villain Brian

account. Kenneth Noye killed an undercover police officer who had been staking out his garden. Although he was acquitted of murder he was later sent to prison for 14 years for his part in handling the Brinks-Mat bullion. John Palmer and his family were in Tenerife when police raided his mansion near Bath. He stayed there as long as possible before returning, facing trial and being acquitted. He has since been jailed for his part in a timeshare fraud. It is believed that nine people have died in the underworld feuding over the missing Brinks-Mat millions. The most recent was George Francis in 2003. With £10 million of the bullion still missing he's unlikely to be the last. It is believed that any gold jewellery bought in the last 20 years will probably have some of the Brinks-Matt gold in it.

JEREMY BAMBER

MURDER OF HIS ADOPTIVE FAMILY MADE UP OF NEVILLE AND JUNE BAMBER, THEIR DAUGHTER SHEILA "BAMBI" CAFFELL AND HER TWIN SONS ON 7TH AUGUST 1985

TRIAL STARTED 14TH OCTOBER 1986

SENTENCED TO LIFE IMPRISONMENT WITH A RECOMMENDATION OF A MINIMUM TARIFF OF 25 YEARS

On 7th August 1985 five members of a wealthy Essex farming family were shot dead in their house. The police investigation of the murder of the Bamber family was a catalogue of errors that almost allowed the perpetrator to escape justice. In the end it was a combination of overconfidence and boasting to his girlfriend that caused the downfall of Jeremy Bamber.

He wouldn't share with sister, says neighbour
BAMBER 'WANTED ALL THE FAMILY FORTUNE'

THE BAMBI MURDERS

By PETER KANE and BOB GRAHAM

FARMER Jeremy Bamber vowed he would never share the family fortune with his adopted sister, the Bambi murder trial heard yesterday.

He revealed his true feelings about Sheila Caffell to a neighbour, the jury were told.

Bamber, 26, is alleged to have told Dorothy Foakes that he did not get on with Sheila. Mrs Foakes told Chelmsford Crown Court in Essex: "He said he would not share his money with her."

Bamber is accused of murdering the model, who was known as Bambi, and the other four members of his family in August last year.

Shortly after they were found dead with a total of 25 bullets in their bodies, Bamber spoke to a police doctor.

Row
He told the doctor of a family row at their farmhouse the night before the killings.

Bamber said the family had been discussing the possibility of having Sheila's twins fostered.

"He said the discussion arose because the family were concerned that his sister had been guilty of non-accidental injury to the children," said Dr Iain Craig.

"I asked him if he had reported his concern to the police and social services and he said 'No'."

Earlier the jury heard that Jeremy Bamber had a bizarre chat with armed police as all his family lay dead.

He revealed to them that his secret dream was to buy a luxury sports car — and said he wanted an alsatian similar to the one used by a doghandler at the scene.

Weapons
He spoke calmly of his desires as police laid siege to the farmhouse where he told them "Bambi" had gone berserk with a gun.

During one conversation Jeremy Bamber told police his sister was "a nutter," the court heard.

He warned them that a small arsenal of weapons was stored in the house — Whitehouse Farm, Tolleshunt D'Arcy, Maldon, Essex.

Bamber denies murdering his father Nevill and mother June, both 61, sister Sheila, 27, and her six-year-old twin sons Nicholas and Daniel.

The trial continues.

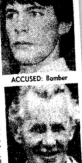

ACCUSED: Bamber

VICTIM: Nevill

Both Jeremy and his sister Sheila, nicknamed Bambi, had been adopted by wealthy Essex farmers Neville and June Bamber. The children had in different ways rebelled against a strict religious upbringing. Sheila had numerous arguments with her mother and an abortion had raised tensions even higher. Despite the arguments her parents had subsidized their

daughter's move to London and attempt at establishing a modelling career. She later married Colin Cuffell and gave birth to twin sons. After the marriage collapsed she became depressed and developed schizophrenia. She'd also become addicted to cocaine and at the time of her murder the media reported that she owed drug pushers over £40,000.

The problems caused her to move back in with her parents in the Essex farmhouse.

Jeremy Bamber lived with his girlfriend, Julie Mugford, a few miles from the farm in a rent-free cottage provided by his parents. He hated the lifestyle of the farm and held his family in contempt. He had no interest in farming yet he was tied to it by the prospect of the family inheritance. He was not impressed with his father's offer of £170 a week for working on the farm. This was not appropriate for someone aspiring to a playboy lifestyle.

At 3.26am on 7th August 1985 the police received a call from Jeremy Bamber saying that he'd just had a call from his father saying: "Your sister has gone crazy and has got the gun." The police rushed to the house, overtaking Jeremy Bamber who was driving to the crisis at a sedate 30mph. After a four-hour "siege" they entered the house and found a scene of carnage with Neville Bamber's badly beaten, bullet-riddled body in the kitchen, his wife's body in the bedroom, the six-year-old twins both shot in the head twice and Sheila's body

OPPOSITE
LEFT TOP: The Bamber family at Sheila's wedding, and inset, *Mirror* article.

ABOVE: White House Farm, and inset, Sheila, June, Nicholas and Daniel.

LEFT: The .22 rifle and silencer.

RIGHT: Police going to court with the murder weopon.

BELOW: Police fingerprinting Jeremy Bamber's car.

in another bedroom. She had been shot twice in the neck and was found clutching a rifle and Bible. The police convinced themselves that Sheila had shot the family before turning the gun on herself. They comforted the distraught Jeremy Bamber with a cup of tea and a whisky. They were so convinced that Sheila had committed the murders that they allowed vital

evidence such as the carpets and bedding to be destroyed. The coroner even allowed the bodies of Neville, June and Sheila to be cremated.

At the funeral Jeremy Bamber appeared distraught, leaning on the shoulder of his girlfriend, but by the evening he was out partying with friends. He seemed indifferent to how his apparently callous behaviour might be viewed. He made comments to his girlfriend Julie Mugford about his skills as an actor and that he'd hired a hit man to kill his family, which she then reported to the police. The police, along with the press, were starting to have doubts about their initial response. The only keepsakes that Jeremy had wanted from the house were his sister's modelling photographs, which he attempted to sell to the *Sun*. Meanwhile he had gone to the continent with friends for a holiday.

The police now realized that a silencer must have been used in the murders. Twenty-five shots had been fired which would have alerted

the other members of the family to the danger. But if a silencer had been used it would have made the rifle too long for Sheila to have committed suicide. In the strangest twist in the whole bizarre case the bloodstained silencer, along with a grey hair, was found hidden in the farmhouse by a cousin of the Bambers, David Boutflour. Before the police had a chance to examine the hair it had been lost. Despite all the mistakes, by 25th September the police felt that there was enough evidence to arrest Jeremy Bamber. On re-examining the gun and Bible on Sheila's body the police had found Jeremy Bamber's fingerprints. However, the case was largely built around the testimony of Bamber's girlfriend, Julie Mugford. Yet although the evidence was circumstantial there was a lot of it. Julie described his hatred of the family and the farm, and his desire to hire a hit man. The motive was the £500,000 inheritance. The jury found Bamber guilty by a ten to two majority verdict. The judge gave Bamber five life sentences with a recommendation that he should serve at least 25 years. He commented: "I find it difficult to foresee whether it will ever be safe to release someone who can shoot two

little boys as they lie asleep in their beds."

Bamber has always protested his innocence but remains in prison where he is likely to stay for the rest of his life. Appeals against the conviction have been rejected twice.

MIRROR COMMENT

THE evil Jeremy Bamber would have been jailed months ago for the murder of five members of his family but for the bumbling Essex police.

They decided within moments of finding the bodies that the killer was his sister, Bambi, who had then shot herself. They made no other inquiries.

This was compounded by breathtaking incompetence when police:

● Handled the murder weapon with bare hands

● Failed to find a bloodstained gun silencer and, when a relative discovered it, lost a hair — a vital clue — from it.

● Told the coroner it was murder and suicide and allowed three bodies to be cremated — thus losing vital forensic evidence.

When the Daily Mirror produced evidence to show that Bambi was NOT the killer, the police dismissed it as "speculative imagination" and protested to the Editor.

But the Mirror was RIGHT. The police were WRONG.

Today, Essex police should reflect on the horrifying possibilities of their self-satisfied and inadequate investigation.

Jeremy Bamber could be sipping champagne in the South of France with his family fortune in his back pocket.

ABOVE: Bamber arriving at court and being taken off to prison.

LEFT: *Mirror* editorial.

MICHAEL RYAN

MURDER OF 16 PEOPLE ON 19TH AUGUST 1987: SUSAN GODFREY, SHEILA MASON, ROLAND MASON, PC ROGER BRERETON, KENNETH CLEMENTS, GEORGE WHITE, DOROTHY RYAN, ABDUL KHAN, FRANCIS BUTLER, MARCUS BERNARD, DOUGLAS WAINWRIGHT, ERIC VARDY, SANDRA HILL, VICTOR GIBBS, MYRTLE GIBBS, IAN PLAYLE

THE MURDERER, MICHAEL RYAN, COMMITTED SUICIDE ON THE DAY OF THE MASSACRE

The Hungerford massacre when 16 people were gunned down with automatic weapons in a small Wiltshire town would change Britain for ever. All Michael Ryan's weapons had been legally held and the police had no reason not to grant him a gun licence. The murders would lead to a major tightening of gun control and an end to the private ownership of automatic weapons. It is surprising that it took a massacre for people to notice that it was strange for anybody to want to "collect" such weapons when their use was illegal outside of gun clubs. To most people in Britain such a desire demonstrated that the owner's mental stability was questionable.

HUNGERFORD

Michael Ryan was 27 when he committed the Hungerford massacre. Two years earlier his elderly father had died, leaving him living with his mother. He had recently lost his job, which had accentuated the reputation he'd had from schooldays as a difficult loner who was bullied. His mother doted on him and indulged his every whim. Ryan's hobby was his gun collection, which included a Beretta semi-automatic pistol, an AK47 and an M1 rifle. The guns were all legally held and used at the local gun club

where he was regarded as a good shot.

There seems to be no reason why Michael Ryan chose 19th August 1987 as the day to inflict carnage on his community. There is little evidence of planning. The first victim was a mother of two, Susan Godfrey, who was picnicking with her children in the nearby Savernake Forest when she was taken by Ryan at gunpoint into the forest and shot. Ryan returned to his car, leaving the children in their mother's car to be found by others.

He drove back to Hungerford, stopping at a filling station for petrol where he shot at the cashier but

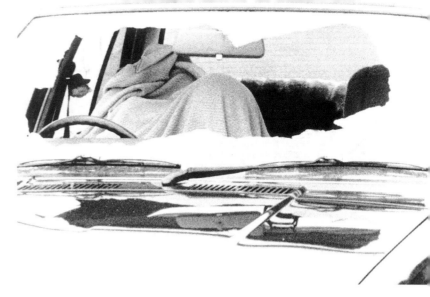

missed. He then went into the kiosk to shoot her, but the rifle failed to fire and she survived. By now the police were starting to receive reports of the shootings. Ryan returned to his home, shot his dog and set light to the building. The fire spread to three other properties. When he came out fully armed and got into his car it failed to start. In a tantrum he put five shots into the car boot before walking off to shoot dead his neighbours, Sheila and Roland Mason and

injure another, Marjorie Jackson. He warned some children off the street and was berated by an elderly deaf resident for making too much noise and told by her: "Stop it you stupid bugger". He just grinned and walked off. The next victim, Kenneth Clements, was walking along a footpath with his family when he was killed by a single shot. The rest of the family dived for cover and survived. PC Roger Brereton

OPPOSITE: Ryan's burntout house.

ABOVE LEFT: PC Roger Brereton.

ABOVE RIGHT: The car with the shrouded body.

LEFT: Police guide people away.

drove his car into a hail of bullets, four of which hit and killed him.

Abdul Khan was shot while mowing his lawn and died later of his wounds. More people were injured before George White became the next person to die when he responded to a friend's request to drive him home to see his wife. The car crashed into that of PC Brereton. Onto the scene drove Michael Ryan's mother, Dorothy. On seeing her son she asked: "Michael, why are you doing this?" She was shot four times and died. Francis Butler was walking his dog when he became the next fatality, followed by taxi driver Marcus Barnard who was on his way to see his wife and new son in the maternity ward of the hospital. Douglas Wainwright who, ironically, was the father of the policeman who had issued Ryan with his gun licence, was shot dead next, followed by carpenter Eric Vardy. Twenty-two-year-old Sandra Hill had the music turned up loud in her car and was oblivious to the chaos around her when she was killed by a single shot.

Ryan moved into Priory Road and shot his way into number 60 where he shot dead the occupants Victor and Myrtle Gibbs. Ian Playle was the last person to die when he was shot

LEFT: Ryan's house on fire.

BELOW: John O' Gaunt School on the third floor of which Ryan commited suicide.

There was of course considerable debate about the cause of the massacre. Ryan did have a miserable time at school and was badly bullied. He was traumatized by his father's death and the loss of his job, which had led to further isolation. However, it was clear that it was the ownership of an arsenal of automatic weapons that propelled what should have been a domestic tragedy into a national disaster. A few weeks later another four people were killed in Bristol by a gunman. The British people had seen enough and banned the private ownership of semi-automatic rifles and shotguns with a magazine capacity of more than two shots. Ten years later the massacre at Dunblane would see the end of automatic pistols.

in his car in Priory Road with his family in attendance. Ryan now moved to what was to be his final destination, the scene of his childhood humiliations, the John O'Gaunt secondary school. Here he took up residence on the third floor as the police closed in. The police attempted to negotiate a surrender and Ryan seemed to return to a degree of sanity. At 6.45pm he commented: "It's funny. I killed all those people but I haven't got the guts to blow my own brains out." At 6.52 he did just that. Ryan had killed 16 people and wounded 15 more, many very seriously.

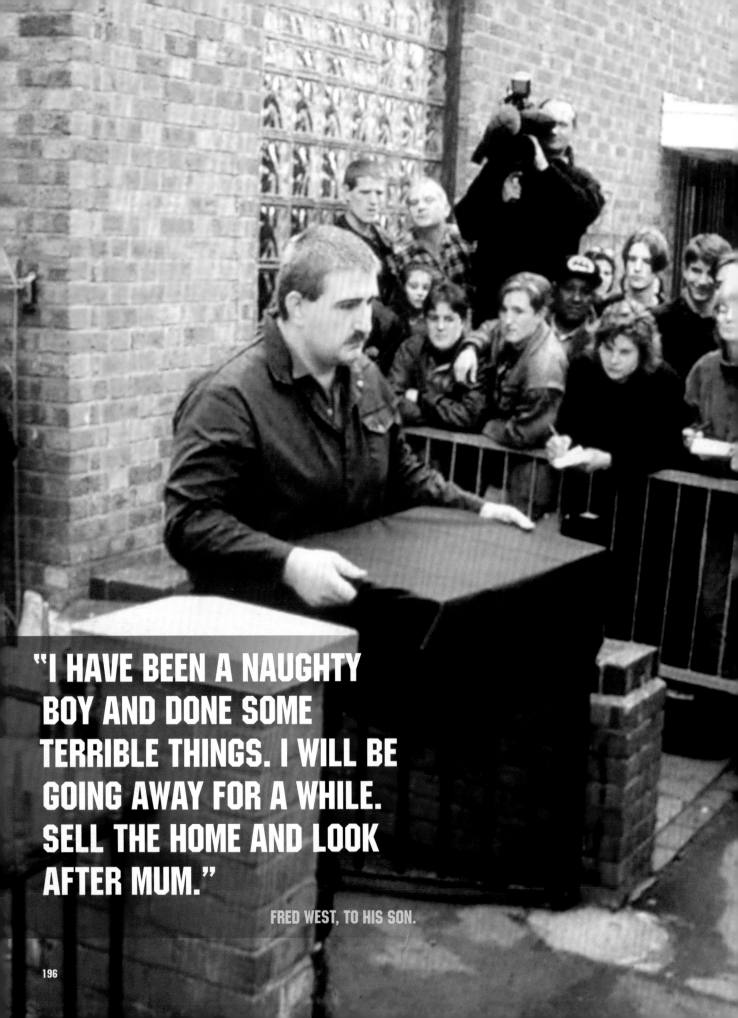

"I HAVE BEEN A NAUGHTY BOY AND DONE SOME TERRIBLE THINGS. I WILL BE GOING AWAY FOR A WHILE. SELL THE HOME AND LOOK AFTER MUM."

FRED WEST, TO HIS SON.

1990-1999

1992 MICHAEL SAMS: The murder of Julie Dart and the kidnap of Stephanie Slater.

1993 ROBERT THOMPSON AND JON VENABLES: The murder of toddler James Bulger by two junior school children.

1994 FRED AND ROSE WEST: The murder of at least 12 women.

1996 THOMAS HAMILTON: The murder of 16 infants and their teacher in Dunblane, Scotland.

1998 HAROLD SHIPMAN: Convicted of killing 15 women but the real total is far higher.

MICHAEL SAMS

MURDER OF JULIE DART ON 9TH JULY 1991 AND THE KIDNAP OF STEPHANIE SLATER ON 22ND JANUARY 1992

TRIAL OPENED JUNE 1993

SENTENCED TO LIFE IMPRISONMENT

Michael Sams was paid a ransom of £175,000 for the release of Birmingham estate agent Stephanie Slater. It is clear that he had studied Donald Neilson's kidnap of Lesley Whittle. Both cases involved meticulous and detailed planning. Sams seemed to have bettered Neilson by organizing the handover of the ransom in a far more effective manner. He thought that he had committed the perfect crime. However, three weeks after Stephanie's release the voice of the kidnapper was broadcast on *Crimewatch* and recognized by his ex-wife who informed the police and triggered his arrest. The investigation had revealed links to the earlier murder of Leeds teenager Julie Dart, and this was added to the charges.

On 22nd January 1992 Birmingham estate agent Stephanie Slater left Shipways Estate Agency to meet potential client Bob Southwall at 153 Turnberry Road, Great Barr. The client seemed disinterested and Stephanie left him alone to roam the upstairs of the house when suddenly he pounced on her, armed with a chisel. She was bundled into his car outside and driven away. She was kept bound and in terror in a green wheelie bin in a lock-up. She knew that her best strategy was to befriend the kidnapper so that he would find it difficult to kill her. This she did with great skill and it was this that probably saved her life.

The next day the estate agent manager Kevin Watts received a ransom demand for £175,000, which the owners agreed to pay. On 29th January, with the back-up of a large force of police, Watts was left a series of instructions to follow, which led him down a narrow, winding, three-mile long lane in South Yorkshire to an isolated bridge where he left the money on a tray. As he left he heard a scraping sound as the ransom was hooked off the bridge to the kidnapper below. In the dense fog the kidnapper escaped the police cordon. Two hours later Stephanie Slater was released a short distance from her parents' house, to which she walked.

OPPOSITE: Turnberry Avenue where Stephanie was abducted.

BELOW: A reconstruction of Stephanie Slater's prison, and inset, an artist's impression of the kidnapper.

The police were now free to go public and launch a massive operation spurred on by the knowledge of the similarities between the kidnap and the murder the previous year of Leeds teenager Julie Dart. They released an artist's impression of the kidnapper and speculated that he was a railway enthusiast, releasing an image of a blue railway badge that he wore.

On Thursday 20th February the police achieved the vital breakthrough when they broadcast a tape of the voice of the kidnapper on *Crimewatch,* which was recognized by the kidnapper's ex-wife, Susan Oake. Twelve hours later the police swooped on the Newark workshop where they arrested 51-year-old Michael Sams and charged him with kidnap. On 26th February the charge of the murder of Julie Dart was added to his crimes.

The police found most of the ransom money buried next to the London to Edinburgh train line, only two fields away from where they had found Julie Dart's body. Throughout the trial in June and July 1993 Sams denied the murder of Julie Dart but admitted to the kidnap of Stephanie Slater. He kept insisting that his mate had murdered and sexually assaulted the

ABOVE: Bridge where the drop was made.

ABOVE RIGHT: Sams leaving court.

21 REASONS WHY MICHAEL SAMS IS A MURDERER

– by Julie case prosecutor

KIDNAPPER Michael Sams left 21 clues which prove he murdered Julie Dart, a jury heard yesterday.

The one-legged toolmaker has admitted snatching estate agent Stephanie Slater and blames his unnamed "friend" for killing part-time prostitute Julie.

But the "friend" exists only in Sams' mind, prosecutor Richard Wakerley told Nottingham Crown Court on Day 20 of the murder trial.

"To think that there is more than one man involved is an affront to common sense," he told the jury. He listed similarities he said showed that Stephanie's kidnapper was the

By ROD CHAYTOR

same man who murdered 18-year-old Julie, whose body was found dumped near Sams' workshop at Grantham, Lincs.

1 The killer wrote to police saying a an officer was 'lucky to be happily married'. Sams' third marriage was on the rocks.

2 The killer had business cards - just like Michael Sams.

3 The killer said his insurance policies were paid up. So were Sams'.

4 The killer was knowledgeable about railways - a "railways buff". So was Sams.

5 A WPC who heard the killer's voice said it was like Sams.

6 The killer was a bad speller like Sams.

7 He thought a Leeds police station was called Millgate not Millgarth. So did Sams.

8 Documents written by the killer were found on Sams' computer discs.

9 The killer has a key to Sams' workshop.

10 The killer used materials of the same kind found at the workshop.

11 The killer used a wheely bin to dump the body, as Sams threatened with Stephanie.

12 Julie's killer spoke of keeping her body in a greenhouse. Sams had a greenhouse.

13 The killer tried to damage a train as a blackmail warning. Sams also spoke of proving his intent.

14 The killer was prepared to be cruel to a young woman as Sams was with Stephanie.

15 The killer used buff-coloured envelopes stuck with double-sided tape - just as Sams did.

16 The killer and Sams guarded victims with infra-red alarms.

17 The killer instructed couriers to open their car boot for 30 seconds - as Sams did.

18 Fibres from Sams' clothes were found stuck beneath Sellotape on the killer's letters.

19 A typewriter bought in Sams' name was used to write a Julie ransom letter.

20 The killer posted letters in areas Sams was visiting.

21 The killer wrote to police of his 'regret' that Julie Dart had to be killed. Sams wrote a similar letter.

The trial continues.

KIDNAPPED: Stephanie Slater   MURDERED: Julie Dart, 18

girl. Sams insisted that he had not raped Stephanie, something which she later contradicted. He seemed more concerned with his reputation than the verdict of the jury, who found him guilty of both the kidnap and the murder. He was sentenced to life imprisonment.

A few days after the end of the trial he confessed to the murder of Julie Dart, perhaps aware that his denial in the face of overwhelming evidence was making him look ridiculous, which he could not tolerate. Very soon after his conviction Sams started to write a book about his case, ostensibly to earn money for his wife but in reality to attempt to justify his behaviour. His sentence was later increased by a further eight years after he attacked a female prison warder.

ABOVE AND LEFT: *Mirror* newspaper articles.

DAILY Mirror

NEWSPAPER FOR THE NINETIES   Saturday, February 22, 1992   25p

FREE TODAY ★ALL the week's TV ★ALL the movies★

TV WEEKLY

ALL YOUR BBC, LONDON AND TVS PROGRAMMES

Kids FREE today Disney Mirror

Ex-wife rings police after hearing voice on TV

SHOPPED

One-legged man held over Steph kidnap

A ONE-LEGGED man arrested after a tip-off from his family was being questioned last night about the Stephanie Slater kidnap.

Mike Sams was held after a distinctive voice was broadcast to millions of TV viewers on the BBC Crimewatch programme. And 12 hours later armed detectives swooped on Sams' tool repair shop in a run-down area of Newark, Notts.

By BILL DANIELS and ROD CHAYTOR

Sams, 50, who has an artificial leg, was driven to Birmingham last night to be quizzed about the kidnapping of 25-year-old Stephanie a month ago.

Hundreds of people jeered and pointed at the car, with Sams hidden under a blanket in the back seat.

Mike left Newark's police station "There were shouts of 'Hang the bastard'.

Police said a charge was expected in the near future.

Estate agent Stephanie from Great Barr, Birmingham, was snatched

FREED: Stephanie after her nightmare

● Turn to Page 2

UNDER WRAPS: Sams, covered by a blanket, is led away by police at Newark last night

ROBERT THOMPSON AND JON VENABLES

THE MURDER OF JAMES BULGER ON 12TH FEBRUARY 1993

TRIAL BEGAN NOVEMBER 1993

AFTER MANY CHANGES TO THE LENGTH OF THE SENTENCE THEY WERE EVENTUALLY GIVEN EIGHT YEARS'. THEY WERE RELEASED IN 2001 ON A "LIFE LICENCE"

The murder of James Bulger with its CCTV images of a two-year-old boy being led away by other children caused in Britain one of the great moral crises of the 20th century. Commentators predicted the imminent collapse of society from a generation of feral children about to overwhelm us. The truth was rather different, with the vast majority of crimes against children being committed by adults. Cases of rape and murder by children are mercifully very rare and show no sign of being any higher now than they were 30 years ago.

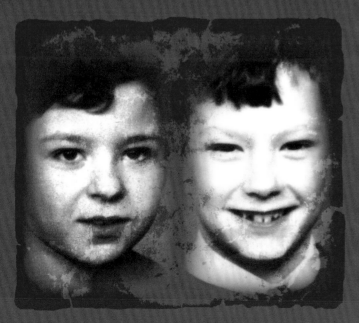

Robert Thompson and Jon Venables came from single-parent families with only struggling mothers to help them. Thompson's mother was an alcoholic and had seven boys to bring up. Robert was one of the youngest and the older children were regularly violent towards the younger members. Jon Venables' mother had severe psychiatric problems. Her other children were educationally subnormal and attended special schools. Jon's behaviour was noted as being attention-seeking and abnormal but no action was taken to address it. As the boys were tried in an adult court none of this evidence was admissible. The court only had to address whether the boys understood what they had done.

James Bulger was kidnapped by Thompson and Venables from the Strand Shopping Centre

in Bootle, near Liverpool. The boys were caught on video camera leading him outside. In a recent TV documentary the police alleged that the boys had made a number of attempts earlier that day to kidnap a child. The abduction was therefore premeditated and not a spur of the moment decision. James Bulger was led on a circuitous two and a half mile route towards the boys' homes, stopping on the way at a canal where he seems to have been beaten. Thirty-eight people saw the boys on their journey and two intervened to ask whether James was alright but had their fears calmed by Venables and Thompson. Eventually he was led to a railway line where blue paint and stones were thrown at him. He was killed by being hit by an iron bar and his body then laid across the tracks to be hit by a train, in the hope that his death would seem an accident. His death has startling similarities to the film *Child Play 3* which had been seen by the boys three weeks before the murder. In the film a child is splashed with paint and lured to a railway line. Two days later James Bulger's severed body was found.

OPPOSITE LEFT: Denise Bulger.

ABOVE: Drawing of James being led away.

The pathologist found that James was dead before he was hit by the train. There followed a two-day search for the youths on the CCTV footage. Thompson went to the murder site and laid flowers. Venables and Thompson were recognized on an enhanced CCTV image by a local woman who knew them from their bad behaviour. The boys initially denied involvement but the forensic evidence was clear and the boys soon started blaming each other. It is said that Thompson showed no remorse for his actions. The charging of the two boys caused shock. The public and the police had been led to believe that the culprits were at least teenagers. At 10 years old they were the youngest people to be charged with murder in the 20th century.

They were tried in an adult court where the only aim was to establish whether they were guilty. Outside, a crowd of 500 expressed the general feeling of hatred towards the pair. The European Court of Justice would later describe

ABOVE: Police checking for evidence.

RIGHT: Crowds outside court.

the trial as unfair. The jurors could see that these children were severely damaged but that they knew what they had done was wrong and were therefore culpable. They were sentenced to be detained at Her Majesty's Pleasure with a recommendation of a minimum of eight years'. This was later increased to ten and then reduced back to eight. In 2001 the home secretary, David Blunkett, not known for his liberal views, agreed to the boys' release on licence after eight years in a young offenders' institution. Their behaviour there had been good and they were regarded as reformed characters. They have been established with new identities, which the media are prevented by injunctions from divulging. There are regular rumours about their activities and relationships but so far the young men seem to be succeeding in establishing new lives.

> *"Come on, join our gang, we are going to kill someone."*
>
> **Robert Thompson in a playground chant two weeks before the murder**

FRED AND ROSE WEST

THE MURDER AND SEXUAL ASSAULT OF AT LEAST 12 WOMEN:

ANNA MCFALL 1967, CHARMAINE WEST 1971 RENA WEST 1972, 1972–1978: LYNDA GOUGH, LUCY PARTINGTON, JUANITA MOTT, THERESA SIEGENTHALER, ALISON CHAMBERS, SHIRLEY ROBINSON, CAROL ANN COOPER, SHIRLEY HUBBARD, HEATHER WEST 1986

FRED WEST IS CHARGED WITH 12 COUNTS OF MURDER ON 13TH DECEMBER 1994

FRED WEST HANGS HIMSELF ON 1ST JANUARY 1995

ROSE WEST GOES ON TRIAL ON 3RD OCTOBER 1995 ON 10 COUNTS OF MURDER

ROSE WEST IS SENTENCED ON 22ND NOVEMBER 1995 TO A MINIMUM OF 25 YEARS, LATER EXTENDED TO A WHOLE OF LIFE TARIFF

The conviction in November 1995 of Rose West brought to a close 25 years of depravity which constitute for many the worst series of crimes in British history. Rose with her husband Fred perpetrated numerous rapes, acts of incest and at least 12 murders. At the time of the trial the media speculated that there might have been 60 murders. Criminal psychologists believe that the total might be at least 30. There are long periods where no murders are committed, which is rare in the careers of serial killers. Fred West always boasted that they "didn't know the half of it". When Fred West committed suicide in January 1995 he took these secrets with him to the grave.

BAD TH

PICTURE FROM FAMILY ALBUM: Fred West poses among relat

described. Steve, who works for the same building firm as his father, added: "It was there! I s*** myself."

After his arrest, West admitted murdering the first three victims found five feet under his patio at Cromwell Street.

Search

Police told him that unless he confessed to the rest they would pull down his house in the search.

He then led them to the other nine.

A police source said: "West had killed so many people over so many years that he couldn't remember where they all were.

"He walked around his basement saying he had put one there, and one over there.

"Then he would change his mind. You could tell he had simply lost count."

The Mirror gave information about Steve's comments to the murder hunt team last night.

LAST PICTURE: West jokes with guards o

GS, SON

...ing. His wife Rosemary is on the left and their murdered daughter Heather on the far right

I escaped from the sex monster

EXCLUSIVE
By HOWARD SOUNES

A PRETTY divorcee told last night how she cheated death at the hands of Fred West after he brutally raped her.

The sex-crazed monster punched Caroline Raine senseless and took her back to 25 Cromwell Street.

There he trussed her to a bed and subjected her to a terrifying 12-hour ordeal before she escaped.

Former beauty queen Caroline said of his death: "I hope the bastard rots in hell."

Caroline, 39, was just 17 when West kidnapped her in his van as she went to meet her boyfriend.

She woke to find herself bound hand and foot on a double bed in the cellar that was to become the

grave of many of West's victims.

His monkey-like face leered down from above.

The evil beast gagged her with masking tape and cotton wool, then raped and sexually abused her.

Caroline recalled: "I was petrified. He said he would keep me in the cellar and he and his

friends would use me for sex.

"He said when they'd finished with me they'd kill me and bury me under the paving stones of Gloucester."

With a sinister grin, West said there were a "few women there already."

Caroline was convinced she was going to die.

Only when West was satisfied by is vile attack did she get her chance to trick him into undoing her bonds.

Caroline's heart missed a beat as he drew out a knife and used it to brutally cut the tape from her face. She conned him into

thinking that she would not run away.

Then, when he dropped his guard, she slipped out of the house and fled.

West was arrested and later convicted of indecent assault and causing bodily harm.

Amazingly, he was fined just £50 and walked free from the court.

The chairman of the bench said: "We do not think that sending you to prison will do you any good."

Caroline said: "It made me feel like I wasn't worth anything. It had been a difficult decision to go to the police in the first place."

60 VICTIMS – PAGES 4 AND 5

Both Fred and Rose were born to unskilled and poorly educated parents. In Rose's case physical and probably sexual abuse was commonplace. Rose's father was schizophrenic and her mother suffered from severe depression. She had been receiving ECT when pregnant with Rose and the family always regarded her as being "not normal". Fred's father gave him the advice: "Do what you like, just don't get caught." Fred said that his father's attitude to incest was: "I made you so I'm entitled to have you." Fred, unlike Rose, had quite a good relationship with his father. Fred's personality is said to have changed after a motorcycle accident when he was 17 left him in a coma for a week. His family said that afterwards he became far more aggressive. Two years later he was knocked unconscious in a fall from a fire escape. From the age of 17 Fred had been regularly involved with theft and in 1961 was convicted of a sexual assault on a minor who was a friend of the family. Fred's attitude was: "Well doesn't everybody do it?" By the age of 20 he was a convicted child molester and thief.

During this period he met Scottish teenager Rena Costello, who became his lover. She moved back to Scotland for a time during which she fell pregnant by an Asian bus driver. When she returned to Gloucester Fred and

LEFT: Rose and Fred West all smiles at a wedding.

Rena married but soon moved back to Scotland where Rena gave birth to Charmaine and then a couple of years later to Fred's own daughter, Anna Marie. During this period they met Anna McFall. All three moved back to Gloucester, where Fred was involved in a fatal accident while driving an ice cream van, which killed a child. Although cleared of responsibility he feared retribution from the family of the child.

During the mid-Sixties there were eight sexual assaults in the Gloucester area but despite his previous conviction West wasn't questioned. The West marriage was tempestuous and Rena moved back to Glasgow. By the time she returned in 1967 she found that Anna McFall had become Fred's lover and was pregnant with his child. Anna, however, made the mistake of pressuring Fred to divorce Rena and thereby became his first murder victim. Anna was buried in a field near the caravan park where they were living. Her fingers and toes were removed in what would be the trademark of Fred's murders. Rena moved back in after Anna's disappearance. It was during this period that 15-year-old Mary Bastholm disappeared from a bus stop in Gloucester.

Fred confided in prison to his son that he had killed her but said that he would never divulge the location of the body. It was in November 1968 that Fred met 16-year-old Rosemary Letts, who quickly moved in with him. In 1970 Fred was sent to prison for theft and Rose was left pregnant and looking after Rena's children, Charmaine and Anna-Marie. She was soon looking after a baby as well when she gave birth to Heather. It was during this period before Fred's release that Rose murdered Rena's

daughter Charmaine, leaving Fred to dispose of the body when he got out of prison. He took his customary souvenirs of fingers and toes. When Rena appeared looking for Charmaine she, too, was disposed of and buried in the field near Anna McFall.

In January 1972 Fred and Rose married and moved to 25 Cromwell Street, which had sufficient room to take lodgers and a basement which they fitted out as a torture chamber. One of the first victims was Fred's daughter, eight-year-old Anna-Marie, who was held down by Rose as Fred brutally raped her. She was threatened with dire consequences if she talked about what had happened. The Wests employed 17-year-old Caroline Owens to be a nanny. Because she was very attractive both the Wests tried to seduce her and eventually resorted to raping her in the dungeon, along with issuing

threats of murder to ensure compliance. When she escaped she reported the attack to the police, who prosecuted the couple. In one of the most tragic and mystifying episodes of the tragedy the magistrate, despite Fred's record, believed that no violence had been involved and only fined the couple. The magistrate commented: "We do not think sending you to prison will do you any good."

This seemed to give Fred and Rose the confidence to engage in an orgy of sexual violence and murder over the next five years. Lynda Gough, Lucy Partington, Juanita Mott, Theresa Siegenthaler, Alison Chambers, Shirley Robinson, Carole Ann Cooper and Shirley Hubbard were all sexually assaulted, murdered, and dismembered before having their fingers and toes removed. We know of no murders between 1978 and 1986 when Rose's daughter

ABOVE: 25 Cromwell Street, and inset, the West's four-poster bed.

DAILY MIRROR, Monday, January 2, 1995 PAGE 5

12 murders .. but West's true toll is staggering

THE first of the 12 known murder victims was 16-year-old Anne McFall – born in Glasgow where West lived with his first wife. She met West there and moved to the Gloucester area in 1966, living at caravan sites at Brockworth and Sandhurst.

She was last seen in April, 1967, when heavily pregnant. She was a nursery nurse who looked after West's children. Her remains – the last to be uncovered – were found in the Fingerpost field at Kempley, Glos, last June after a 36-day dig by police.

WEST'S first wife Catherine is thought to have been the next to die. She met him while working as a waitress at the New Inn in Ledbury, Glos. They married there in 1962 and their daughter Charmaine was born two months later. In Coaldridge, Lanarkshire, Catherine's home town.

Their second daughter Anne Marie was born in Glasgow in 1964. Police diggers excavated Catherine's remains last April in the Letterbox field at Kempley, within sight of West's childhood home.

THE third victim, daughter Charmaine, is believed to have died early in 1971 when she was just eight.

Her remains were uncovered when police searchers broke through a concrete kitchen floor at West's first Gloucester home at 25 Midland Road, on May 4, last year.

The property is only a few hundred yards from 25 Cromwell Street on the opposite side of Gloucester's Central Park, where the other nine victims were found in either the house or garden.

YOUNG Co-op girl Lynda Carole Gough was one of the nine Cromwell Street victims. West was jointly accused with his second wife Rosemary of committing these murders between 1973 and June 1987.

Lynda, nearing her 20th birthday, went missing in April 1973. She had only recently moved out of parents' home to live in a flat in Gloucester.

Her remains were uncovered by searchers below the ground-floor bathroom at 25 Cromwell Street.

THE remains of Carole Ann Cooper were recovered from the basement of 25 Cromwell Street.

The 15-year-old, who was born in Luton, Beds, had been living at a children's home in Bilton Road, Worcester.

She was last seen on November 10, 1973, getting on a local bus to the Warndon area of Worcester after an outing with friends.

Carole was planning to visit her grandmother. But she was never seen alive again.

STUDENT Lucy Katherine Partington, 21, was in the third year of an English degree at Exeter University when she vanished in 1973.

She had been visiting friends at Pittville, Cheltenham, and left around 10.10pm for the bus journey to her family home at The Mill, Gretton, near Winchcombe.

But Lucy did not catch the bus and was never seen again. Her remains were also found in the Wests' basement in Cromwell Street.

ANOTHER student, Therese Siegenthaler, 21, disappeared in April 1974. She was living in a flat in Caterham Road, Lewisham, south-east London, while studying sociology at the Woolwich College of Further Education.

Therese apparently set out for a weekend break in Ireland, intending to travel via North Wales.

But Therese – born in 1953, Switzerland – never reached her destination. Police also recovered her remains from the Cromwell Street basement.

THE eighth of the 13 – Shirley Hubbard, aged 15 – was a shop girl fresh out of school.

She been working just one month at Debenhams store in Worcester. On November 7, 1974, Shirley left work at 5.30pm to travel home to Ouslerlie Road, Droitwich, on February 24.

The basement at 25 Cromwell Street also yielded the remains of tragic Shirley as police and forensic experts conducted their long search.

HAZEL-EYED Juanita Mott, 18, vanished in April 1975 after telling pals: "I'm just nipping out."

The part-time botler left her home in Newent to travel by bus to Gloucester 10 miles away.

She was due to return the next day for a friend's wedding, but Juanita was never seen again.

The remains of Juanita, who was born in Gloucester, were found in the basement of 25 Cromwell Street.

TEENAGER Shirley Ann Robinson, who was born in Melton Mowbray, Leicestershire, became a lodger at the Wests' home at 25 Cromwell Street.

Her remains and those of her unborn child were the third and last of those discovered in the narrow rear garden of the house in Gloucester. Six other victims were uncovered elsewhere in the house.

Eighteen-year-old Shirley was heavily pregnant at the time of her disappearance in 1978.

ALISON June Chambers, 16, was the 11th of the 13 known victims. She was born in Hanover, Germany, where her father was serving in the Army.

She settled with her mother in Swansea, South Wales. In 1979 she moved to Gloucester to work under the youth training scheme with a firm of solicitors.

In September 1979, she was thought to be living in Gloucester. Her remains were the second to be uncovered in the Cromwell Street garden.

THE remains of 16-year-old Heather West – the first child of Fred West and second wife Rosemary – were found in the garden of 25 Cromwell Street.

Startled-eyed officers digging beneath the patio discovered Heather's skull on February 24.

Heather – one of the Wests' six children – had last been seen by social security benefits staff on May 29, 1987. Her disappearance had not been reported at the time.

● ANIMAL INSIDE WEST – PAGE 6   ● LAST DAYS OF PRISONER THEY CALLED DIGGER – PAGE 7

ABOVE: Ladder down to the cellar and inset, child's room in cellar.

ABOVE RIGHT: *Mirror* page with some of the victims.

Heather was murdered by the couple and buried in the garden. Heather had been resisting her parents' assaults and had mentioned the attacks to friends. The Wests explained her disappearance with the story that she'd left home.

For the next six years 25 Cromwell Street continued with its everyday life of sexual torture, incest, prostitution and abuse. There are no known murders during this period but by 1992, however, their sexual misdemeanours were starting to catch up with them. A young girl complained to the police of rape and her case was taken up by Detective Constable Hazel Savage. She remembered the allegations against Fred West from the 1960s. In August 1992, 25 Cromwell Street was searched by the police who found large amounts of pornography, evidence of child abuse and torture. Fred was charged with the rape and sodomy of a minor, and Rose with assisting him. The younger children were taken into council care and Rose attempted suicide. They got a short-lived reprieve when the complainants failed to testify and the case collapsed. The police and Hazel Savage were now at last investigating the activities at Cromwell Street.

The children were questioned in depth and began to divulge some of the family secrets including the rumour that Heather was buried beneath the patio. When on 24th February 1994 the police arrived to begin the massive job of digging up the patio and garden, Rose phoned Fred with the news: "You'd better get home. They're going to dig up the back garden looking

for Heather." At first Fred feigned nonchalance but with the discovery of the first bones he started slowly to divulge the grisly tale. It is assumed that Fred and Rose had preplanned what to say in this situation. Fred took all the blame on himself and Rose depicted herself as the victim. However, Fred's stories were shown to be full of lies as he tried to avoid implicating Rose.

With Fred's help and many false leads nine bodies were found at Cromwell Street, one at Midland Road and two at the caravan site at Much Marcle. Fred hinted at others but did not reveal any details. On 13th December 1994 Fred West was charged with 12 murders. Less than three weeks later he committed suicide in prison, leaving Rose to stand trial alone. Although the police case was largely circumstantial Rose was convicted on account of her own testimony and that of her daughter, Anna-Marie. Rose showed herself to be a liar and a bully, and her husband's stories absolving her of knowledge and responsibility for the murders untrue. She was sentenced to a minimum term of 25 years', which has now been extended to a whole of life tariff.

ABOVE: The pub-style bar in the West's lounge.

MIDDLE: Police carrying out a body part.

LEFT: A view from the kitchen out to the patio where Heather was buried.

THOMAS HAMILTON

THE MURDER OF 16 CHILDREN AND ONE ADULT IN A MASSACRE AT DUNBLANE PRIMARY SCHOOL 13TH MARCH 1996:
GWEN MAYOR (SCHOOLTEACHER), VICTORIA CLYDESDALE, EMMA CROZIER, MELISSA CURRIE, CHARLOTTE DUNN, KEVIN HASSELL, ROSS IRVINE, DAVID KERR, MHAIRI MACBEATH, BRETT MCKINNON, ABIGAIL MCLENNAN, EMILY MORTON, SOPHIE LOCKWOOD NORTH, JOHN PETRIE, JOANNA ROSS, HANNAH SCOTT, MEGAN TURNER

Of all the crimes covered in this book that of Thomas Hamilton is the most shrouded in controversy and conspiracy theories. The arguments are about how it was that such a clearly unstable man with so many queries about his personality could be allowed to run a series of boys' clubs and hold a gun licence. Despite a major inquiry no adequate explanation has been given. Due to the massacre Britain now has some of the toughest gun control laws in the world. Combined with much tougher child protection legislation and checks on people who work with children, there is reason to hope that such an appalling event can be prevented from ever happening again.

By the time Thomas Hamilton was born his parents had divorced. He was brought up in Glasgow by his grandparents, and Thomas was told that his mother was his sister. The family moved to Stirling when he was 12. His two interests at school were the Boys Brigade and the air rifle club, and these continued into his adult years. He started collecting guns in his twenties and joined the Scouts rising to be the Assistant Scout Leader of the Stirling Troop. His period in the Scouts caused complaints from parents who felt that he took inappropriate risks with their children.

It seems that he contrived on at least one occasion for the children to stay the night in the mini-coach when their accommodation fell through. Much to his disgust he was forced to resign and was taken off the list of those felt appropriate to be a Scout leader. Hamilton reacted with fury believing that he'd done nothing wrong and that there was a conspiracy against him.

By the Eighties Hamilton had moved his activities to setting up a series of boys' clubs targeting seven to eleven year olds, teaching them gymnastics, swimming and football skills. It would seem that Hamilton's only qualification was a relatively low coaching standard in gymnastics which should have meant that he could not coach on his own. The clubs at first were highly successful until the boys and their parents tired of his strange approach and behaviour. The swimming costumes and gymnastics kit were very skimpy. There were rather too many photographs of the boys that focused on their groin areas, and the frequent vigorous application

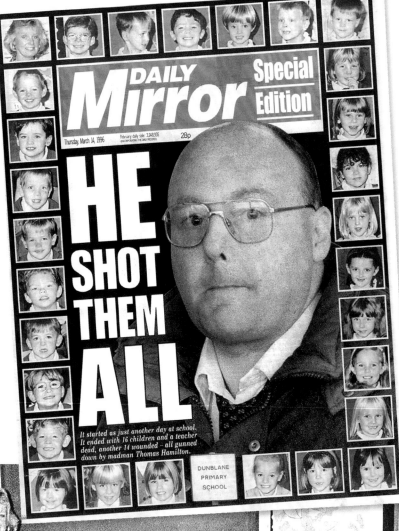

DAILY Mirror Special Edition

Thursday, March 14, 1996   February daily sale: 3,248,305   28p

HE SHOT THEM ALL

It started as just another day at school. It ended with 16 children and a teacher dead, another 14 wounded – all gunned down by madman Thomas Hamilton.

DUNBLANE PRIMARY SCHOOL

LEFT: *Mirror* front cover.

BELOW: The class attacked by Hamilton and their teacher.

responsible for child protection sought to have Hamilton's gun licence revoked. Hamilton reacted to the complaints with displays of righteous indignation, claiming that he was being victimized; he even sent a letter to the Queen. When one club dwindled away he simply set up another.

It is not known what tipped Hamilton over from being a strange, paranoid loner with a predilection for young boys to being a killer. It is clear that he had been planning the massacre for at least six

of ointment. There were many complaints, including some from high-profile figures such as George Robertson. It is also said that the officer

months. He had bought extra ammunition and stepped up his target practice at the gun club. A pupil from the school testified that Hamilton regularly questioned him about the geography of the school for two years before the fateful day. At 9.30am he strode into Dunblane primary school after having cut the telephone wires. He walked into the gymnasium, shot and injured two of the teachers, Mary Blake and Eileen Harrild, before opening fire on the five-and six-year-old children.

The remaining teacher, Gwen Major, heroically threw herself in front of her charges and was shot dead. All but one of the children were hit before Hamilton momentarily stepped out of the gym to fire rounds at the rest of the school. He then stepped back into the gym, fired at the children again before putting the gun in his mouth and pulling the trigger. Hamilton died instantly, leaving 16 children and one teacher dead and a further 17 injured. It was 15 minutes before the emergency services were on the scene and in that time the staff of the school led by the headmaster, Ron Taylor, worked with great calmness to treat the injured and reassure the traumatized children. The massacre scarred the community of Dunblane, who successfully campaigned for much tighter gun control through a massive petition. There are numerous conspiracy theories implicating secret societies and paedophile rings, but it would be surprising if they have much credibility. Hamilton was too much of a loner and anti-social to be part of such a major conspiracy involving so many people. Like Michael Ryan, Thomas Hamilton was a dangerous madman, whose madness the authorities, for whatever reason, failed to recognize and was allowed to own automatic weapons. Without the automatic weapons these two tragedies would have been on a far smaller scale.

HAROLD SHIPMAN

BELIEVED TO HAVE MURDERED AT LEAST 215 PEOPLE. CONVICTED OF KILLING 15 WOMEN WHO DIED BETWEEN 1995 AND 1998.

THEIR NAMES WERE: MARIE WEST, IRENE TURNER, LIZZIE ADAMS, JEAN LILLEY, IVY LOMAS, , MURIEL GRIMSHAW, MARIE QUINN, KATHLEEN WAGSTAFF, BIANKA POMFRET, NORAH NUTTALL, PAMELA HILLIER, MAUREEN WARD, WINIFRED MELLOR, JOAN MELIA, AND KATHLEEN GRUNDY

TRIAL OPENED 5TH OCTOBER 1999

SENTENCED TO 15 CONCURRENT LIFE SENTENCES FOR THE 15 MURDERS

Harold Shipman is the only British doctor to be convicted of murder. He is also the most prolific murderer in British history with at least 215 victims. Shipman was only caught when he forged a patient's will in his own interest. The forgery was so incompetent that it has led to speculation about whether Shipman wanted to be caught.

Harold Shipman was regarded as a plodder at school with a very high opinion of himself. He was his mother's favourite and they formed a close relationship that was torn apart only in 1963 by her slow death from lung cancer. She was in severe pain for a long time, finding relief only when the family doctor administered morphine on his visits. This experience at the age of 17 was to scar her son's life, and many psychiatrists believe that the murders were an attempt to recreate the circumstances of his mother's death. We must assume that the experience spurred a desire to get into medical school, which he did after resitting his exams. At Leeds University his superior attitude meant that he was regarded as a loner.

he revealed an aggressive and competitive personality. He met his future wife, Primrose, at university when he was 19 and she 16. They married soon after when she was five months pregnant.

By 1974 he was a GP in Todmorden in Yorkshire. Although hard working he had an arrogant manner and made the junior staff feel stupid. However, his career path altered dramatically when he started experiencing blackouts. At first they were attributed to epilepsy, but the other partners in the practice soon found evidence that their new doctor was using a morphine-type drug, pethidine, and had been forging and faking prescriptions. He was forced out of the practice and in 1975 spent time in drug rehabilitation. Two years later he was fined £600 for drug offences and prescription fraud. Despite these problems, within a couple of years he was back practising as a GP at the Donnybrook Medical Centre in Hyde. He was open to his fellow doctors in the practice about his past problems and challenged them to monitor him closely.

The only activities to counter this perception were a prowess at athletics and football, where

Over the next 20 years Shipman gave the

impression of being a conscientious doctor much loved by his patients, and it took many years for suspicions of any wrongdoing to materialize. Undertaker Alan Massey noticed a high death rate among Shipman's patients and that a high percentage died sitting up and fully clothed. He confronted Shipman about these issues but was reassured by the doctor's confident replies. His daughter, fellow funeral director Debbie Brambroffe, was not so easily appeased and spoke with Doctor Susan Booth who had countersigned a large number of Shipman's cremation certificates. She spoke to colleague Doctor Linda Reynolds, who passed on her concerns to the coroner, John Pollard. He, in turn, spoke to the police.

The police discretely investigated the relationship between Shipman's treatment of his patients and the medical records of their conditions and found that they correlated. There seemed to be no motive for murder and no cause for concern. They failed to investigate Shipman's record or contact the relevant professional body, either of which might have raised concerns. It could be argued that the police should have delved deeper, but this would be to disregard the deep culture of deference towards the medical profession in Britain. The police found it very difficult to comprehend that a member of a caring profession could commit murder. It would take the intervention of the medical profession's great rival, the legal profession, before Shipman's activities would be revealed. Kathleen Grundy, a wealthy widow and former mayor of Hyde, was found dead, fully dressed and

LEFT:
Exhumation of a
Shipman victim.

BELOW: Joel
Lane, where Mrs
Grundy and ten
other victims
lived.

CRIMES OF THE CENTURY HAROLD SHIPMAN

sitting on the sofa in her house. She had been
visited by Doctor Shipman earlier that day.
Her daughter, Angela Woodruff, a solicitor, was
devastated because her mother was believed
by the family to be in good health. The doctor
told her that because he had seen the deceased
so soon before her death a post-mortem was
unnecessary. This was accepted and Kathleen
Grundy was buried.

A few weeks later Angela Woodruff received
a call from a solicitor claiming to have the will
of her mother, the late Mrs Grundy. This was
a surprise to her because she knew that her
solicitor's practice held her mother's will. It was
even more of a surprise when it was revealed
that the will left £386,000 to her doctor, Harold
Shipman. The police quickly deduced that the
will was a very poor fake and investigated the
circumstances of Mrs Grundy's death. They
raided Shipman's house and surgery and took
away, among other things, a typewriter.

The body of Mrs Grundy was exhumed and
the post-mortem showed very high levels of
morphine. This is a very strange drug to use for
murder as it stays in the blood for many years
after death. Shipman must have known this and
either felt compelled to use it or was confident
of not being caught. The typewriter was shown
to have been used to type the will. Shipman
would claim that he'd lent the typewriter to
Mrs Grundy. The police now broadened their
inquiries, looking for other suspicious deaths
among Shipman's patients. They looked for
patients who had died soon after his visits
or at home. There were hundreds who fitted
these criteria; the police started to realize the
potential scale of the crime and investigation.
They selected 15 suspicious deaths over the
previous three years for the prosecution.

After the death of a patient, Shipman often
falsified the medical records to justify his
treatment and the ensuing fatality. In Mrs

Grundy's case he depicted her as a morphine addict. Understandably, the vision of an addict grandmother proved difficult for anybody to believe and it would bring ridicule at the trial. Shipman didn't understand computers and failed to realize that every time he changed a medical record the time of the change was recorded on the hard drive. All the post-death changes to medical records were discovered by the police when they investigated the computers.

Shipman often pretended to make phone calls to the ambulance service when he found one of his patients ill and then made a show of cancelling it when the patient died. The ambulance call logs showed these deceptions.

Shipman was often patronizing and obscure to the relatives of the dead. He would often make a friend or relative ask whether the person was dead and demean them for their question. He clearly enjoyed this belittling of people at a moment of vulnerability. He maintained his arrogance to the end, saying to District Nurse Marion Gilchrist: "The only thing I did wrong was not having her cremated... I wouldn't be having all this trouble." Throughout the trial Shipman maintained his innocence but the police case was formidable, with the evidence of each case accumulating in the minds of the jury. In contrast to the case of fellow doctor Bodkin Adams, the police had the forensic evidence

Application Number ... G005044

CAUTION—It is an offence to falsify a certificate or to make or knowingly use a false certificate or a copy of a false certificate intending it to be accepted as genuine to the prejudice of any person, or to possess a certificate knowing it to be false without lawful authority.

QD 027073

CERTIFIED COPY ⚜ OF AN ENTRY

DEATH	Entry No. 281

Registration district Tameside

Administrative area

Sub-district Tameside

Metropolitan District of Tameside

1. Date and place of death Twenty-ninth May, 1997. The Surgery, 21 Market Street, Hyde.

2. Name and surname

Ivy LOMAS

3. Sex Female

4. Maiden surname of woman who has married PITT

5. Date and place of birth 31 August 1933. Hyde.

6. Occupation and usual address Widow of Ronald Lomas. Engineer 32 Thornley Street, Hyde, Greater Manchester

7. (a) Name and surname of informant Certificate on inquest adjourned received from John S Pollard Coroner for county of Greater Manchester South District. (b) Qualification Inquest held 11th January 1997 (c) Usual address _____

8. Cause of death

1 (a) Morphine toxicity.

9. I certify that the particulars given by me above are true to the best of my knowledge and belief .... Signature of informant

10. Date of registration Twenty-first January 1999 On the authority of the Registrar General

11. Signature of registrar C. L. McCann. Registrar.

CERTIFIED to be a true copy of an entry in the certified copy of a register of Dea District above mentioned. Given at the GENERAL REGISTER OFFICE, under of the said Office on 12th October 1999

This certificate is issued in pursuance of the Births and Deaths Registration Act 1953. Section 34 provides that any cert an entry purporting to be sealed or stamped with the seal of the General Register Office shall be received as evidence of death to which it relates without any further or other proof of the entry, and no certified copy purporting to have been said Office shall be of any force or effect unless it is sealed or stamped as aforesaid.

Form A504A Dd 0053 1,500 2/98 Mcr(202666)

Shipman was struck off the medical register. In January 2004 he committed suicide. It is believed that he wanted to ensure that his wife would get the full NHS pension which she would not have received if he'd lived to 60. Police inquiries after the trial calculated the likely total number of victims between 1975 and 1998 as 215. There is a lot of evidence that the killings started with his first postings and that another 35 murders can be added to that total.

from the bodies and a clearly falsified will.

The jury found Shipman guilty on all counts, and he was sentenced to 15 life terms. We will never be certain of his motivation, but the comments of the prosecuting counsel seem to sum up as well as any: "He was exercising the ultimate power of controlling life and death and repeated the act so often he must have found the drama of taking life to his taste." In 2002

OPPOSITE LEFT: Primrose leaving Strangeways prison after a visit.

LEFT: The death certificate of Ivy Lomas one of Harold Shipman's many victims.

BELOW: *Mirror* front cover.

SUNDAY Mirror
www.sundaymirror.co.uk
January 28, 2001 60p
VINNIE'S HOME EXCLUSIVE: CENTRE PAGES
CAROL'S NEW MAN EXCLUSIVE : SEE PAGE 11
WORLD EXCLUSIVE
Dr Harold Shipman is the world's biggest serial killer, with the blood of 345 victims on his hands. But while he danced with the Devil it was party time for him and his wife.
THE MOST AMAZING PICTURES EVER OF BRITAIN'S INFAMOUS MURDERER Pages 2,3,4&5